David Lewis is a Denver-based journalist who has written for publications from *Town & Country* to *Institutional Investor.* A former columnist and reporter for Denver's *Rocky Mountain News,* Lewis has also worked for *Oil & Gas Investor, InternetWeek,* and *ColoradoBiz.* He is the co-author of *Amazing Places to Go in North America* with Eric Peterson.

Eric Peterson, a Denver-based freelance writer and Colorado native, has contributed to numerous guidebooks about the western United States. He is author or coauthor of the books *Amazing Places to Go in North America, Roadside Americana, The Great American Road Trip,* and *Ramble: A Field Guide to the U.S.A.* His recent credits include *Frommer's Colorado, Frommer's Texas,* and *Frommer's Yellowstone & Grand Teton National Parks.*

Jennifer Pocock is a freelance Green writer for HowStuffWorks.com and Big Green Monster. Additionally, she has worked with the Sierra Club, Common Ground Athens, and Amnesty International, and she has served on the Environmental Executive Committee at the University of Georgia. She currently volunteers with the Hike Inn at Amicalola Falls.

Additional material by: **John Boslough, John Gattuso,** and **John A. Murray**

Factual verification by: **Kathryn L. Holcomb**

Copyright © 2009 Publications International, Ltd. All rights reserved. This book may not be reproduced or quoted in whole or in part by any means whatsoever without written permission from:

Louis Weber, CEO
Publications International, Ltd.
7373 North Cicero Avenue
Lincolnwood, Illinois 60712

Permission is never granted for commercial purposes.

ISBN-13: 978-1-4127-9809-9
ISBN-10: 1-4127-9809-4

Manufactured in China.

8 7 6 5 4 3 2 1

Library of Congress Control Number: 2009926207

Pictured on the front cover: Death Valley National Park (top left); Everglades National Park (top right); Grand Teton National Park (bottom)
Pictured on the back cover: Katmai National Park and Preserve

Photo Credits:

Front cover: **PhotoDisc** (bottom); **Shutterstock** (top left); **Stock Solution** (top right)

Back cover: **Frans Lanting/© Corbis**

age fotostock Tom Till, 41 (bottom); **Alamy Images:** Peter Arnold, Inc., 57 (bottom); Brett Baunton, 106; Don Breneman, 281 (bottom); Danita Delimont, 109; Kevin Ebi, 58 (right); John Elk III, 272 (top); Clint Farlinger, 282; FL Stock, 39; Dennis Hallinan, 250; Hombil Images, 285; Chris Howes/Wild Places Photography, 75; Kerrick James, 190; Jon Arnold Images Ltd, 128 (top); Paul Kuhn, 112; Mark Lewis, 246; Jason Lindsey, 268; Jonathan Little, 182; Buddy Mays, contents, 171; Steven Milne, contents, 304; North Wind Picture Archives, 298 (top); Mervyn Rees, 180; RF Company, 185; Robert Harding Picture Library Ltd, 92; John Schwieder, 94 (top), 199; Tom Till, 213; Tom Uhlman, 247; Greg Vaughn, 182; Jim West, 266; Wendy White, 206; **Stephen Alvarez:** 210; **AP Images:** 168, 176; **Art Resource:** National Museum of American Art, Washington, D.C., 8; **Brand X Pictures:** 141, 295; **Jan Butchofsky-Houser:** Houserstock, 64–65; © **Corbis:** 212, 222, 270 (bottom); Theo Allofs, 178; Theo Allofs/zefa, 46, 254 (bottom); Tony Arruza, 96, 150 (top); Atlantide Phototravel, 245; William A. Bake, 103 (top); Tom Bean, 108, 121, 124, 195, 214–15, 278, 291 (top); Peter Beck, 95; Joel Bennett, 187; Bettmann, 10, 103 (bottom), 114; Tom Bol/Aurora Photos, 132 (top); Matt Brown, 229; Andrew Brown/Ecoscene, 244; William Campbell, 298 (bottom); Gary W. Carter, 150 (bottom); Ralph Clevenger, 93, 258 (top); Lloyd Cluff, 116; Sheldan Collins, 30 (bottom); W. Perry Conway, 100, 143; Diane Cook & Len Jenshel, 164, 307; Richard A. Cooke, 217 (bottom); Philip James Corwin, 242; Richard Cummins, 181; Fridmar Damm, 183; Macduff Everton, 144; Stephen Frink, contents, 38; Lee Frost/Robert Harding World Imagery, 26; Raymond Gehman, 267 (bottom); Farrell Grehan, 97; Gunter Marx Photography, 9; Jon Hicks, 163; George H. H. Huey, 16, 17, 27, 51, 160; Hulton-Deutsch Collection, 208; Steven Kaziowski/Science Faction, 194; Layne Kennedy, 29 (bottom), 175, 177, 271, 279; Bob Krist, 98; Lake County Museum, 166, 296 (right); Frans Lanting, 189, 286, 290; Lester Lefkowitz, 240; Danny Lehman, 94 (bottom); Charles & Josette Lenars, 217 (top); George D. Lepp, 56; G. Brad Lewis/Science Faction, 312; W. Wayne Lockwood, M.D., 232; Gerd Ludwig, 153; William Manning, 149; Don Mason, 11; Charles Mauzy, 313; Buddy Mays, 148, 154, 170; Joe McDonald, contents 252; Tim McGuire, 305; Momatiuk–Eastcott, endsheets, 133; David Muench, contents, 32–33, 54 (bottom), 72, 73, 105, 145, 151, 152, 155, 157, 158, 161, 172, 191, 211, 234, 237 (top), 251, 264, 291 (bottom); Marc Muench, 25 (top), 125; Pat O'Hara, 30 (top), 123, 262; Owaki–Kulla, 19, 48, 231; Greg Probst, 218; Louie Psihoyos, 235; Neil Rabinowitz, 118; Jose Fuste Raga, 302; James Randklev, 110–11, 253, 254 (top); Hans Reinhard/zefa, 300; John M. Roberts, title page, 130, 227; Bill Ross, 303; Galen Rowell, 107, 192; Anders Ryman, 23; Phil Schermeister, 173; G. E. Kidder Smith, 86; Scott T. Smith, 36 (top), 248; Paul Souders, 77, 120; George Steinmetz, 296 (left); Jim Sugar, 162; Rudy Sulgan, 87; Swim Ink 2, LLC, 122 (top), 221 (left); Tim Thompson, 197; Tony Waltham/Robert Harding World Imagery, 89; Craig Tuttle, 223; Underwood & Underwood, 6; Kennan Ward, 68 (top); Ron Watts, 135, 207, 257; Stuart Westmorland, 224; Gordon Whitten, 237 (bottom); Staffan Widstrand, 196; Peter M. Wilson, 35; Winfred Wisniewski/Frank Lane Picture Agency, 186; Jim Zuckerman, 113, 127; **Kent & Donna Dannen:** 193, 270 (top); **Dick Dietrich:** Dietrich Leis Stock Photography, 238–39; **DigitalVision:** 50, 310; **Georgette Douwma:** 275; **Fred Hirschmann Photography:** 201; **Getty Images:** 99 (right), 297; Laurance B. Aiuppy/FPG, 115; National Geographic, 216; Time Life Pictures, 131; **The Granger Collection:** 258 (bottom); **iStockphoto:** 3, 219, 306–7; **Andre Jenny:** The Image Works, 233; **Laurence Parent Photography:** 166–67, 265; **Media Bakery:** 220, 236, 243, 294; **Megasquib:** Dreamstime, 156; **John Murray:** 198; **National Park Service:** 12, 18, 20, 21, 22, 24, 25 (bottom), 28, 32, 34, 36 (bottom), 42, 43, 44, 45, 49, 52, 53, 54 (top), 55, 57 (top), 58 (left), 68 (bottom), 70, 78, 79, 81, 82, 83, 84, 88, 101, 117, 119, 122 (bottom), 126, 128 (bottom), 129, 132 (bottom), 134, 138, 142, 146, 147, 184, 188, 200, 202, 203, 204, 209, 225, 228, 230, 238, 241, 267 (top), 269, 272 (bottom), 273, 283, 284, 287, 288, 292–93, 309, 314, 315; Peter Jones, 60, 61, 62; Amy Leist, 71; Derek Lohuis, 66; Ray Mathis, 47; Kent Miller, 91; Russell Virgilio, 205; **PhotoDisc:** 14, 299, 308; **Shutterstock:** 41 (top), 74, 76, 85, 102, 301, 311; **Stock Solution:** 13; **SuperStock:** 7, 90–91, 179; age fotostock, 29 (top), 104; **Thinkstock Images:** 159, 165; **LarryUlrich.com:** 59, 140; Craig Blacklock, 174–75, 281 (top); John Dittli, 139, 263; G. Brad Lewis, 221 (right); Larry Ulrich, 15, 69, 256, 259, 260, 261, 274, 276, 277; **Visions of America:** Joe Sohm, contents, 66–67; **Willard Clay Photography:** 136–37; **George Wuerthner:** 99 (left)

We need wilderness preserved—as much of it as is still left, and as many kinds—because it was the challenge against which our character as a people was formed.

—Wallace Stegner

Contents

166

252

302

America's National Parks: Sanctuary and Preservation

"...from sea to shining sea."

Who doesn't know these words? They're from "America the Beautiful," a song that *is* America, a song that distills the essence of the nation's unmatched natural beauty. Anyone who has explored the United States by visiting its national parks has a sense of the diversity of that beauty as it's found in the 50 states—as well as in the Virgin Islands, American Samoa, and other U.S. possessions. When people visit a national park, they walk in the footsteps of Teddy Roosevelt and John Muir; Mormon pioneers and Herbert Hoover; fur trappers and gold-crazed '49ers; dinosaurs and Native Americans; Spanish explorers and the pirate Black Caesar.

Visitors also see the archaeological record and living traces of landforms and animals as diverse as baked deserts and pristine coral reefs; bison and manatees; soaring mountain peaks and otherworldly caverns; great blue herons and kangaroo rats; natural rock staircases and limestone hoodoos. The list could go on for pages, forever.

These national parks are as extraordinary as the land and people that make up America. With each passing year, as Americans better understand the impact they have on the environment, they become more aware of the inestimable value of this important national resource.

New Thinking about Nature

The establishment of Yellowstone as the first national park in March 1872 marked the beginning of a new attitude toward wilderness. Until that time, most Americans had

thought of the nation's virgin forests, vast expanses of prairie, pristine waterways, incredibly rich mineral deposits, and other natural assets as sources of personal wealth to be used in whichever ways any individual who owned them wanted. But the astounding natural wonders of Yellowstone were catalysts that helped change the prevailing American attitude about wilderness from a desire to exploit into a wish to protect.

The passion that led to national park status for Yellowstone had been bubbling for decades. In Pennsylvania in 1824, a 28-year-old attorney named George Catlin was deeply affected when an American Indian delegation traveled through the state. In a curious twist, Catlin's mother had once been a captive of Indians, so the young lawyer was predisposed to a keen interest in Native American culture. Shortly after observing the delegation, Catlin began to explore

Left: *President Theodore Roosevelt was a great booster of protecting American wilderness. Here he saddles up for a ride in Yellowstone National Park.* Opposite: *Towering Mount Shuksan is one of the loveliest views in Washington State's North Cascades National Park, particularly when it is reflected in Highwood Lake.*

Left: *George Catlin painted* Big Bend on the Upper Missouri, 1900 Miles above St. Louis *in 1832. He wrote at that time,* "Scarcely anything in nature can be found, I am sure, more exceedingly picturesque than the view from this place." Opposite: *Mammoth Hot Springs is one of the most famous geological features at Yellowstone National Park.*

for future ages, a national park containing the finest of nature's beauty," Catlin wrote. "I would ask no other monument to my memory, nor any other enrollment of my name amongst the famous dead, than the reputation of having been the founder of such an institution."

Happily, the attorney-turned-artist was not shouting into the wind. In 1832, while Catlin was observing, painting, and writing, Congress and President Andrew Jackson designated Hot Springs, Arkansas, as America's first-ever federally protected reservation. (Although Hot Springs was named a national park in 1921, many years after the establishment of other national parks, local boosters insist to this day that the area is the first U.S. national park.) President Jackson's interest in the natural wonders of Hot Springs was a potent precedent that suggested not only that the federal government can involve itself in wilderness protection, but also that it *should*.

the headwaters of the Missouri River and moved on from there, marshaling his gifts as a painter to chronicle Pawnee, Cheyenne, Crow, Assiniboine, and other Native Americans against the backdrop of America's natural wonders. Aware, of course, that America was expanding westward, as well as further developing already-settled areas, Catlin hurried to complete his wilderness documentation. He worked with phenomenal speed and dedication. During one three-month period he traveled 1,500 miles and completed more than 100 oil paintings.

After Catlin returned from the far west frontier with his paintings and a clutch of detailed journals bound in elk skin, he wrote a book entitled *Letters and Notes on the Manners, Customs, and Conditions of the North American Indians.* Published in 1841, it was a pioneering work of natural history in which the artist/naturalist proposed creating "a nation's Park" at the headwaters of the Missouri River.

"What a beautiful and thrilling specimen for America to preserve and hold up to the view of her refined citizens and the world, and

The Wonders of Yellowstone

In the late 1860s, rumors began circulating in Washington, D.C., about an unearthly land of bizarre topography, bubbling hot springs, geysers erupting a hundred feet in the air, and other phenomenal thermal spectacles in the Yellowstone region of the Rocky Mountains. Three men from Montana were dispatched to the area in 1869 to prove the rumors true or put them to rest, but their reports left the public as skeptical as ever.

The following year, a survey team under the leadership of Henry Washburn, the surveyor general of Montana, conducted a more thorough and systematic exploration of Yellowstone, ultimately concluding that even some of the most fantastic rumors about the place were true. Keeping careful records as they moved through the region, the 19 explorers named the thermal wonders, often picking epithets derived from the netherworld.

By law, the explorers were entitled to stake individual claims on the territory and its natural wonders. But one evening, at the junction of the Firehole, Gibbon, and Madison rivers, the men sat around what has proved to be one of history's most significant campfires. They had been talking about the

way in which they were planning to divide Yellowstone among themselves, when one member of the expedition, a young attorney named Cornelius Hedges, eloquently proposed another alternative: Instead of seeking private gain, they should persuade the federal government to preserve the Yellowstone region in its entirety.

All but one member of the party agreed. When the men returned home, they lobbied vigorously for government protection of the area. They were highly persuasive, and in March 1872, Congress passed legislation creating the world's first national park "as a pleasuring ground for the benefit and enjoyment of the people."

Of course, Cornelius Hedges doesn't deserve all the credit. He merely articulated a notion that had been circulating for years, although he and his companions were the first to see it to fruition. Nature activists like the aforementioned George Catlin, who feared that the western frontier would be overrun with settlers and the detritus that was inevitably left in their wake, looked at the great spaces of America's West and Great Plains and saw what Catlin envisioned as a "magnificent park . . . containing man and beast, in all the wild[ness] and freshness of their nature's beauty."

Busy building a nation, however, most Americans weren't ready to hear what Catlin and the others had to say. There were exceptions, those who found a deeper value in nature. In the eastern United States, writers and thinkers the likes of Ralph Waldo Emerson, Henry David Thoreau, and Walt Whitman looked to the natural world for spiritual renewal and a sense of the divine.

Thoreau suggested that every town set aside small parks so that residents would never be far from the healing power of living things. "In wildness is the preservation of the world," he wrote, suggesting that to experience nature is a deep human need.

John Muir and the Sierra Club

In the West, John Muir, a self-taught naturalist and cofounder of the Sierra Club, championed the cause of wilderness with great passion. Wandering the great mountain ranges of the West, particularly his beloved Sierra Nevada, Muir developed a vision of wilderness as an ecological and spiritual necessity.

He sought union with the natural world as a living entity, climbing to the peak of a 100-foot fir in order to experience firsthand the rage of a windstorm, riding an avalanche above Yosemite Valley and calling it "the most spiritual and exhilarating of all the modes of motion," and hiking the Sierra for weeks with little more than bread and tea to sustain him. "Climb the mountains and get their good tidings," he advised his fellow Sierrans. "Nature's peace will flow into you as sunshine flows into trees. The winds will blow their own freshness into you and the storms their energy, while cares will drop off like autumn leaves."

A persuasive writer, Muir quickly became the voice of the conservation movement. He wielded his pen against loggers, sheepherders, and other "temple destroyers" who threatened his beloved Yosemite, and he campaigned for the creation of parks dedicated to mountains and forests elsewhere in the West. "God has cared for these trees,

John Muir (right) *basks in the glory of nature with fellow conservationist John Burroughs, a prominant nature essayist in the 19th and early 20th centuries.*

saved them from drought, disease, avalanches and floods, but he cannot save them from fools. Only Uncle Sam can do that."

Slowly, grudgingly, Uncle Sam acted. In 1890, after much campaigning and cajoling, Congress authorized Sequoia, General Grant (later incorporated into Kings Canyon), and Yosemite national parks in California. Several years later, Mount Rainier in Washington was added to the list.

Then, in 1901, Muir and his fellow conservationists found a powerful ally in President Theodore Roosevelt. An avid outdoorsman and a firm believer in the goals of the conservation movement, Roosevelt added more than 130 million acres to the national forests, launched a system of wildlife ref-

uges, and created 18 national parks and monuments, including Petrified Forest, Mesa Verde, and Devils Tower.

"Leave it as it is," Roosevelt said of the Grand Canyon, which he saved from developers by designating it a national monument. "You cannot improve on it. Keep it for your children, your children's children, and for all who come after you as the one great sight which every American should see."

Refining the Park System

As Muir quickly learned, however, creating parks and protecting them were two very different things. In 1901, the thirsty city of San Francisco filed a request to dam the Tuolumne River in Yosemite National Park

The establishment of Yosemite National Park was one of John Muir's crowning achievements. The breathtaking beauty of the landscape is clear as this man rappels down from Glacier Point.

and drown the Hetch Hetchy Valley. Muir led a campaign against the project, but Congress was not persuaded. The dam was approved in 1913 and completed several years later.

The so-called "Rape of Hetch Hetchy" was a major defeat for conservationists, but it galvanized supporters of the national parks. One of them, Stephen T. Mather, a wealthy Chicago entrepreneur, was invited by Secretary of the Interior Franklin Lane to take charge of park policy.

Mather advocated a centralized park administration, and in August 1916, America's 35 national parks and monuments were placed under the supervision of the newly created National Park Service. Mather was appointed director and, together with his young assistant, Horace M. Albright, set about shaping the mission of the National Park Service "to conserve the scenery and the natural and historic objects and the wild life therein and to provide for the enjoyment of the same in such manner and by such means as will leave them unimpaired for the enjoyment of future generations."

Mather and Albright immediately began to push for expansion, especially in the field of historic sites. By the 1930s, a dozen natural areas and more than 40 historic sites were added to the National Park Service, including large eastern reserves such as the Great Smoky Mountains, Shenandoah, and the Everglades.

There was an important shift in philosophy at this time, too. Parks weren't being set aside merely for scenic beauty, but for their ecological value as well. More than natural curiosities, they were seen as "vignettes of primitive America," pristine samples of New World ecology preserved in a wild condition.

Nature Collides with Progress

The proliferation of automobiles during the 1930s made national parks much more

The Colorado River in Grand Canyon National Park, seen here from the Nankoweap Trail down from the North Rim of the canyon, continues to sculpt the landscape of northern Arizona.

accessible to Americans, but most visitors were content to merely drive by the major sights for a quick look, preferring to be entertained by animal acts, drive-through sequoia trees, sound-and-light shows, and other amusements only marginally related to their wilderness setting. Such attractions not only trivialized the experience of nature—and encouraged visitors to unknowingly cheat themselves of what the parks really had to offer—but changed the very dynamics of nature: Careless tourists, hikers, and campers strayed from designated roads and paths, tramping through animal habitats, crushing delicate flora underfoot, and disturbing migration and nesting patterns. Discarded food attracted bears and other animals, bringing them into unnatural contact with humans that endangered people and gave them a distorted view of animal behavior, and that placed the animals at risk, as well.

By the 1950s, many Americans had gotten into the habit of making one national park the destination for an entire vacation. The parks were routinely overfilled with family cars and trailers that brought with them all the comforts of home, including coolers stuffed with food, charcoal cookers, and mountains of throwaway packaging material.

Numberless postcards and snapshots created from the 1930s well into the 1960s capture such anomalies as bears who stand on their hind legs, begging at the open windows of station wagons; raccoons burrowing into unsecured coolers; and birds and other small creatures picking at discarded salami sandwiches and potato chips. This was not natural or healthy animal behavior, and Americans didn't seem to notice.

Portable and transistor radios and, later, portable televisions, were additional scourges, piercing the parks' quiet, day and night, with thumping music and inane chatter. Poorly maintained automobiles and burping motorcycles contributed to the racket. Then there was the constant wall of sound sent up by the visitors themselves—shouts, laughter, bawling, the occasional shriek—that contributed to the questionable feat of turning America's national parks into America's urban and suburban backyards—only with more things to look at.

Beginning in the 1970s, the park service started to make difficult but necessary choices intended to return the parks to their original mandate. Use of the parks began to be limited to activities that are more in tune with the natural aspects of the parklands. As a result, natural cycles have been reestablishing themselves; food chains have been rebuilding. Animals that had almost completely disappeared, including bison, wolves, and white trumpeter swans, have been successfully reintroduced.

There is much that still needs to be accomplished, but it is comforting to know that the legacy of Catlin, Thoreau, Muir, and other early conservationists still guides the mission of the National Park Service. Visitors can see it—indeed, *feel* it—every time they travel to a national park.

The sun sets over Florida's Everglades National Park, where seawater meets freshwater and marshland, seeking to strike an environmental balance.

Overcrowding

A park visit is an experience that people don't forget, and they return with friends and family so that they can once again enjoy, and share, this precious gift. These are truly extraordinary places, the crown jewels of American wilderness, where the grandest landscapes and most diverse wildlife are protected by rangers, naturalists, and other members of the National Park Service.

With budgets growing ever tighter, the job isn't getting any easier. It's not that Americans don't care about the parks. Attendance is healthy (averaging about 275 million

Carved by glacial ice thousands of years ago, the mountains and sheer-walled canyons of Wyoming's Grand Teton National Park still harbor snowfields and several small glaciers.

visitors annually, on the heels of a record 287 million in 1999), but has generally been on the decline since 1988, after 50 years of uninterrupted growth. A 2006 study funded by the Nature Conservancy attributed the falloff to higher fuel prices, as well as an increased array of recreational options, particularly video games, DVD rentals, and the explosive growth of the Internet.

The centennial of the National Park Service will come in 2016, and to get the public excited about it, President George W. Bush announced a "centennial initiative" late in 2006. Visitor numbers blipped upward again in 2007, which prompted National Park Service director Mary A. Bomar to remind the nation that "national parks still draw more visits than Major League Baseball, the National Football League, professional bas-

ketball, soccer, and NASCAR combined." The positive aspect of this is obvious, but so is overcrowding, which remains a challenge that isn't likely to be resolved anytime soon.

"We may love a place and still be dangerous to it," environmentalist and author Wallace Stegner warned. "The best thing we have learned from nearly 500 years of contact with the American Wilderness is restraint, the willingness to hold our hand, to visit such places for our souls' good, but leave no tracks."

International Impact— and the Human Heart

These uniquely beautiful places must be protected, because the national parks give us something that isn't easily found elsewhere— an idea of ourselves in relation to nature, a

sense of how vast and wondrous and varied the earth can be.

America's national park system has inspired the formation of wonderful national parks around the world, from Italy to Indonesia, and from Brazil to Botswana. These parks symbolize the collective commitment of humankind to preserve the beauty and diversity of nature for generations to come.

"The wilderness is the creation in its pure state, its processes unqualified by the doings of people," wrote Wendell Berry. We need exposure to that, and that's exactly what the parks provide, places to remind ourselves that nature exists on its own terms, according to its own rules and rhythms. There's something comforting in that thought, something that touches our deepest feelings of awe and reverence for the magnificence of creation. In an unfinished book, writer and naturalist Rachel Carson called this feeling simply "the sense of wonder," an almost childlike recognition that nature occupies a world "beyond the boundaries of human existence."

"Those who contemplate the beauty of the earth find reserves of strength that will endure as long as life lasts," she wrote. "There is symbolic as well as actual beauty in the migration of the birds, the ebb and flow of the tides, the folded bud ready for spring. There is something infinitely healing in the repeated refrains of nature—the assurance that dawn comes after night, and spring after the winter."

Perhaps this is the most telling statement about why we love the national parks. More than islands of nature, they are sanctuaries of the human heart. They are the summer sun rising over the sea cliffs of Acadia and

the misty waterfalls of the Smokies; the shadowless heat of Big Bend country and the quiet twilight woods of Isle Royale; the sulfur vents along the Yellowstone River and the sudden swell of the Tetons from the valley of the Snake River. They are places to go when you are lost and need to be found, broken and in need of repair, out of tune and ready to be brought back into harmony. They are the most perfect antidote ever devised for urban civilization. Their open spaces and friendly, helpful staff are a natural balm, a soothing medicine, a dependable remedy.

Beautiful aspens frame Wheeler Peak, which itself dominates Great Basin National Park in Nevada.

During the Middle Ages, the faithful in England, at least once in life, made the pilgrimage to Canterbury, where they beheld the most beautiful cathedral in the land. In America, in our time, we have the privilege of a pilgrimage to these national parks.

Now more than ever, the parks deserve our support, our care, and, above all, our protection. Their future is in our hands.

Acadia National Park

Ancient glaciers, long-ago mountain uplift, and the unceasing actions of the sea created the jagged, broken coasts and majestic cliffs of Maine's Acadia National Park. This is a park whose spruce and fir forests and stands of maple, beech, and oak fill with the songs of hundreds of species of breeding birds, and whose tide pools crawl with anemones, mussels, and sea stars.

Acadia National Park, the earliest national park east of the Mississippi, has plenty for the casual visitor, the determined trekker, or the serious scientist or historian—from bicycling, boating, tide-pooling, and fishing to climbing, hiking, swimming, horseback riding, leaf peeping, and bird-watching. Everything anyone ever imagined about the Maine wilds, the park includes 30,300 acres on Mount Desert Island as well as parcels of more than 2,000 acres on Isle au Haut and the Schoodic Peninsula. Acadia was created by President Woodrow Wilson as Sieur de Monts National Monument in 1916, and in 1919 it was designated Lafayette National Park. A decade later, the park's name was changed to Acadia.

In Times Past

About 6,000 years ago, visitors to this area left deep heaps of shells, which, if nothing

Coast of Maine
Established January 19, 1929
74 square miles
Things to See: *Cadillac Mountain; Mount Desert; Islesford Historical Museum; Wild Gardens of Acadia*
Things to Do: *Hiking; Fishing; Climbing; Bird-watching; Swimming; Boating; Horseback riding; Bicycling; Leaf peeping*
What's Nearby? *Maine Coastal Islands National Wildlife Refuge; Saint Croix Island International Historic Site; Moosehorn National Wildlife Refuge*

else, indicates that they appreciated the fine shellfish found throughout the area. They weren't the only ones: In a 1614 survey, Captain John Smith wrote of the abundant clams and lobsters to be had.

The first recorded histories of the region tell of the Abanaki culture, which hunted and fished, built cone-shape, bark-covered shelters, and traveled in birch bark canoes famed among other peoples for their design. The Abanaki also used dugouts and canoes made from moose hide. Most people flee the ferocious cold of the Maine coast in winter, but members of the Wabanaki Confederacy and other native people moved to the coast in winter to fish salmon runs and avoid the even fouler inland weather.

No one seems to know for sure how Acadia came to be named. Some say it came from the area's native Abanakis. Others credit Giovanni da Verrazano, another larger-than-life figure who may or may not have set foot

More than one-fifth of Acadia National Park is considered wetlands. Here is pictured Bass Harbor Marsh, on Mount Desert Island's northeast corner, called "the quiet side" by locals.

As the sun rises over Mount Desert Island in Acadia National Park, the swelling surf of the Atlantic Ocean pounds against the rocks crumbling before a jumble of broken cliffs, as it has for millennia.

Down East but who first used the name "L'Acardie." Verrazano was an Italian explorer who, in the service of the French crown, explored the east coast of North America from Nova Scotia to North Carolina in 1524. This name, however, which is "Arcadia" in English and means a "pastoral paradise," later came to name the "Acadians" of Canada and, later still, the "Cajuns" of Louisiana.

Samuel de Champlain was a French explorer, cartographer, sailor, soldier, and diplomat who in 1604 first chronicled Mount Desert Island and its glorious environs. Sailing down its coast, Champlain saw the island's barren mountaintops, sheared off by the ancient glaciers that created Cadillac Mountain, a granite-topped peak of 1,532 feet and the highest along the East Coast. "The mountain summits are all bare and rocky," he wrote. "I name it 'Isles des Monts Desert.'" Mount Desert Island today contains the majority share of Acadia National Park as well as the towns of Bar Harbor, Southwest Harbor, Mount Desert, and Tremont.

Champlain claimed the land for France, but French dominion was brief. Jesuits in 1613 established a mission on Isles des Monts Desert and had started building a fort there when their settlement was crushed by the forces of an English vessel commanded by Captain Samuel Argall.

The Lay of the Land

Glaciation tells much of the story of Acadia. Look at a topographical map of the island from above, and you will see that Mount

fractures in the granite mountain peaks and then receded, scouring the island valleys. One notable trough gouged by the glacier, now the Somes Sound fjord, was carved deep enough to fill with saltwater.

Today, the tides, winds, and waves continue to shape the shoreline, while protected coves nurture salt marshes rich with life.

Summers here are ideal, with temperatures from 45 to 85 degrees Fahrenheit and wildflowers such as purple loosestrife (pictured), *goldthread, wild lily-of-the-valley, and starflower.*

Desert Island looks as if it was ripped by a giant bear claw, with deep ravines and Long Pond, Echo Lake, Jordan Pond, Eagle Lake, and the seven-mile-long Somes Sound, said to be the only true fjord on the East Coast, all canted in parallel lines north to south.

The park's geological history began more than 500 million years ago. Mud, sand, and volcanic ash were deposited in an early ocean. Over time the pressure of these buried sediments turned them to rock that was heated and squeezed into Ellsworth Schist, the area's oldest rock. It is a metamorphic rock with thin, twisted bands of feldspar, green chlorite, and white and gray quartz. Uplift and volcanic eruptions followed, pro-

ducing the largest granite body on the island, Cadillac Mountain Granite. Giant granite ridges weathered and fractured, forming huge square blocks of rocks and cliffs that broke apart, sending rubble to the sea.

In more recent geological times—the last two to three million years—as many as 30 ice sheets covered most of New England over time, each succeeding glacier advancing and receding, scraping away earlier glaciations. The last glacier grew out of Canada between 3,000 and 9,000 feet thick—it came to cover large parts of New York and New England. When the edge of the last glacier reached the Maine coast and Mount Desert's highlands, the ice swelled into

Modern Times

Mount Desert Island natives know that for Verrazano to have called this a peaceful, pastoral place, he must have sailed by in summer. Acadia and all of Down East are tormented by wicked weather throughout the winter and often the spring and summer, too. Tourists swarm Acadia in Maine's blissful summertime, so it is vital to plan ahead.

It's long been a tradition for visitors to crowd Acadia. For centuries the Abanakis fished the island's sylvan shores; then, in the 1800s, farming, fishing, and lumbering provided a local economy.

That all began to change when artists showed up in the mid-1850s. Great Hudson River School painters such as Thomas Cole and Frederic Church started to display their Mount Desert landscapes. Eventually this led to more "rusticators," at first bohemians, and later the rich and famous. But by 1880, Bar Harbor had 30 hotels, and one ambitious businessperson built an inn and a cog railway on Cadillac Mountain. Alarmed by the commercialization, a group of wealthy islanders began piecing together the national park in 1919. Acadia remains Maine's only national park.

Today, visitors to this sometimes crowded island paradise enjoy the outdoors through dozens of trails, beaches, coves, and mountain cliffs. For sheer enjoyment, panoramas are plentiful. One such view is Thunder Hole, a coastal rock pounded by huge waves. There's Acadia Mountain Trail, with views of Somes Sound, Echo Lake, and the Cranberry Isles. Another is Sand Beach, a pristine beach between the rugged coastal rocks and the mountains made of tiny crushed shells. Eagle Lake, 425 acres, is the island's largest (and fishing is permitted). Another fine sight is Bass Harbor Head Lighthouse, the only lighthouse on Mount Desert Island. Easy hikes on either side offer gratifying ocean views.

Deep evergreen forests and metamorphic rock smoothed by ancient glaciers and speckled with lichens and mosses characterize Maine's only national park.

Park to the Stars

The creation of national parks in the East was notoriously difficult. Back in the days of Teddy Roosevelt, the West was still, for the most part, wide open and almost unfathomably large. The most scenic land had merely to be plucked out and set aside, developed with roads for access to the most beautiful spots, and managed.

In the eastern United States, however, much of the land was already private, owned by logging companies or investors. Private owners didn't want to give up their pristine locations, and the loggers were even more stubborn. Proposing that they set aside stands of large, old-growth trees that could otherwise make them a nice profit would generally earn a hearty laugh in return. In addition, many politicians of the time largely agreed—taking over potentially profitable land just for the sake of scenery was ridiculous. How, then, were parks supposed to thrive when it seemed everyone was against them? Two words: star power.

Many rich and powerful people of the late 1800s—especially those living in New York City—were discovering the appeal of getting away from the hubbub of everyday life and communing with nature. Today's Acadia National Park was originally a retreat for the wealthiest New York elite. The Vanderbilts, Morgans, Fords, Carnegies, and Astors were all frequenters of the area in the summers during the 1880s and '90s, building grand estates on today's park grounds. Acadia was similar to today's Hamptons.

It was a Harvard president named Charles W. Eliot, however, who started the bid for parkdom in 1898 after the death of his son, who dearly loved the lands. Eliot encouraged others who longed to see the lands preserved to organize a group of trustees who worked tirelessly to petition for a bill creating the park and to raise money and land donations for parklands. One trustee, George B. Dorr, organized the donation of 5,000 acres. This became the national monument that was signed into existence by Woodrow Wilson in 1919.

After the park's creation, the Rockefellers took a hand in developing the area. John D. Rockefeller Jr. had a long history of devotion to the conservation movement. His estate's 45-mile spiderweb of carriage roads today help make Acadia a hiking and mountain biking mecca, highlighting the most stunning views of the park. Rockefeller gave 10,000 acres to Acadia National Park, including some of its most spectacular coastline.

National Park of American Samoa

Samoa is a dazzling chain of jewel-like islands twinkling across a lonely expanse of the South Pacific. Four of its easternmost islands and two coral reefs comprise the National Park of American Samoa. Formed by volcanic activity originating on the ocean floor, the islands are a tropical paradise of mountains, rain forests, deep harbors, and stunning white beaches.

This is certainly America's most far-flung and exotic tropical paradise of a national park. Closer to Auckland, New Zealand, than to Oakland, California, and 2,300 miles southwest of Hawaii, the park and its coral reefs and rainforest, its beaches and mountains, span 9,000 acres. More than 2,500 acres of the park lies under water.

American Samoa's five volcanic islands are Tutuila, Ta'u, Ofu, Olosega, and Aunu'u; the atolls are Rose and Swains islands. It is the only U.S. territory south of the equator. The national park is part of American Samoa, whose population is roughly 65,000, with most Samoans living on Tutuila fishing and canning fish.

The park was authorized by Congress in 1988 and officially became a national park in 1993, when it agreed with Samoa's village councils to lease their lands (and waters) for a 50-year term. The park draws scarcely more than 1,000 visitors each year. Its secluded beaches, Samoan villages, exquisite animal and plant life, and vistas of land and sea make it an island paradise.

Borrowing Land

Because Samoan law prohibits the sale of communal land, none of the National Park of America Samoa is actually owned by the U.S. government. Rather, the park's lands are leased from native villages and from the American Samoa government. Plans for this park began through talks with traditional high chiefs negotiating for village landowners. Former Governor A. P. Lutali once explained, "We are not only preserving the forest, the animals, the shoreline and reefs, but we can have an interactive park that assists in the preservation of Samoan life and culture."

The national park preserves tropical rain forests, coral reefs, and an endangered 4,000-year-old culture. Tutuila, the park's largest island, is crowned with two great volcanic peaks

American Samoa
Established October 31, 1988
21 square miles

Things to See: *Lata Mountain; Mount Alava Trail; Tufu Point*

Things to Do: *Snorkeling and swimming; Hiking and beachwalking; Sightseeing*

What's Nearby? *Aunu'u Island National Natural Landmark; Fagatele Bay National Marine Sanctuary*

The underwater life of the National Park of American Samoa is one of its most popular features. Here, a sea anemone called Heteractis Aurora *displays its myriad beauties.*

rising above steaming rain forests. A large natural harbor nearly cuts the island in two. At the island's head lies Pago Pago, sometimes called Pango Pango, a South Seas island village that is American Samoa's capital and only port of call.

The northern and most accessible section of the park rises above Pago Pago's harbor in great volcanic ridges covered with dozens upon dozens of species of tropical trees and vegetation. The Samoan islands were created when the tectonic plate under

The National Park of American Samoa includes some of the most attractive beaches in the world, such as this one on Ofu Island.

the ocean moved over an area where hot molten rock came through the earth's crust and thrust itself upward. The rising heat, pressure, and rock eventually formed a line of volcanoes, some of which ascend above the ocean's surface.

The park encompasses coastal villages, tropical lagoons, and a dramatic scenic highway with fine views of a Pacific coral reef. Among the unusual wildlife found here are 35 species of brightly colored birds, as well as the endangered flying fox, which is actually a bat that has the wingspan of an eagle.

The largest section of the park, about 5,000 acres, lies on Ta'u, the easternmost island and a 30-minute flight from Pago Pago. This section includes Lata Mountain, which seems to rise nearly straight up from the Pacific and, at 3,170 feet, is the highest volcano in the islands. The Ta'u section of the park also includes 300 offshore acres.

The park's smallest section is on Ofu, an island just west of Ta'u. It encompasses only 260 acres of land and water, but it has one of the finest beaches in the South Pacific. Most people would agree that this stretch of white sand and stately palms defines what a tropical paradise should look like. Lying just offshore and protecting a lovely blue lagoon, a healthy coral reef teems with a vast array of sea life.

Living on the Islands

For about 3,000 years, members of Polynesia's oldest culture have lived on these islands. Samoa means "sacred earth," the name reflecting the belief of the people that the islands are a special place to be cherished and protected. This is also the basis

for the park, which provides some protection to the ancient culture there. Permanent leasing arrangements are still being worked out, and visitors must obtain permission to enter this new and unusual park. The act of Congress establishing the National Park of American Samoa allows some subsistence fishing and farming.

Visitors to the park have an opportunity to see firsthand some of the best preserved coral reefs in the Pacific Ocean. A 1906 survey, "The Fishes of Samoa," described the islands as having "the richest fish fauna in the world."

The park's 2,550 acres of coral reefs are among the most pristine remaining on the

planet, and they harbor an astonishing array of sea life, from monocle breams to mackerel sharks, and from morays and Moorish idols to swordfish and stingrays. Even humpback whales stop by, giants that weigh in at roughly 40 metric tons and grow up to 50 feet long. Most humpbacks migrate in September and October, although they can arrive in Samoa as early as July or leave as late as December. They travel 3,200 miles from the waters of frigid Antarctica to the south up to the island warmth of Australia, Tonga, and Samoa (they have been spotted as far away as Tahiti) to mate and give birth. These mammoths stop feeding when they arrive in warm waters; no one knows why.

The coastline of Tutuila Island features dramatic clusters of volcanic rock and the clear blue waters of the Pacific Ocean.

Samoan life and culture are woven into the fabric of the park. Almost all Samoans are of Polynesian ancestry, and they are noted for their respect for tradition and social customs. The Samoan way, called *fa'asamoa,* observes hierarchies and customs from long before Europeans came to the area. Notable is the Samoan *matai* system, which encompasses both an organization and a philosophy. Villages are made up of groups of *aiga,* or extended families, which encompass as many relatives as possible. Each aiga is headed by a *matai,* the chief who represents the family before the village council, or *fono,* which includes the matais of all the aiga associated with the village. Powerful matais enforce the law and hold title to all the assets of the aigas they represent while they are in negotiations with other members of the fono. The formal Samoan language used by matais when discussing matters of importance relies heavily on proverbs that might hearken back to long-ago island history or myth.

Park visitors need to plan well in advance to see the National Park of American Samoa. The nearest airport is Pago Pago International Airport on Tutuila, which has been known to host only two round-trip flights from Honolulu per week. American Samoa's neighboring nation, Western Samoa, has an international airport at Upolo, which serves flights from Australia, New Zealand, and Fiji that connect to flights by twin-otter floatplane to Tutuila Island. Small planes serve the park areas of Ofu and Ta'u, but, the Park Service warns, "air travel to the outer islands continues to be erratic."

An Entirely New Cultural Experience

Not only does the National Park of American Samoa offer a tropical getaway with stunning landscapes and endless activities on land and water, it also affords a glimpse into new people, languages, and ways of life. The Samoan people are the oldest of the Polynesian groups, emigrating from Southeastern Asia more than 4,000 years ago. They are a proud, traditional society with a deep cultural heritage. Their ownership of this land lends an authenticity to the park that is rarely found in the other national parks, and the Samoans are happy to share their living heritage with visitors to their islands.

For guests in the park, the Samoan way of life is difficult to avoid, since all but a few thousand of the small islands' inhabitants belong to traditional Samoan groups. Visitors often accidentally find themselves brushing elbows with inhabitants. Because of this, it's important to be aware of the Samoan way of life and how to treat the land and its people with respect. The code of conduct, *fa'asamoa,* includes rules such as asking permission to use beaches or take pictures if you find yourself near villages, being careful not to disturb evening prayer times, and not eating or drinking while walking through villages. These rules are a general courtesy for visitors to the islands. The Samoans are open and understanding, always happy to share their lives and lands with guests.

Visitors can get the most of this beautiful park and its culture by participating in a Samoan Home Stay program. Through this program, native Samoan families open their homes to those who may wish to stay for an extended length of time and learn more about the local customs and activities. Participants in the home stay program can expect not only to witness, but to participate in, traditional activities such as fishing and basketweaving. They may learn how to prepare traditional meals and participate deeply in the *fa'asamoa* practices.

Arches National Park

Chiseled by the powerful, perpetual forces of wind and water, this surprising natural rock garden contains the planet's most remarkable collection of abstract sculpture. Arches National Park sits on a great plateau in southeastern Utah, encompassing a stark landscape of broken red sandstone. The park contains more than 2,000 natural stone arches. But these spectacular sandstone portals, braced against the desert sky and revealing lovely desert terrain through their openings, are only part of the stunning landscape here.

A geological fantasyland, the park is filled with giant balanced rocks that look as though they are about to teeter and fall. There are pedestals and spires that resemble a child's drip castles enlarged to enormous scale. Glistening slickrock domes are inlaid with swirls of stone cut by red sandy washes and dotted with wildflowers in spring. These formations sparkle and shimmer beneath an enormous blue sky.

Millions of Years in the Making

High above the Colorado River, the park has been shaped by eon after eon of weathering by rain, snow, ice, and wind. Most of the formations in the park are composed of

Southeastern Utah
Established November 12, 1971
120 square miles

Things to See: *Delicate Arch; Fiery Furnace; Wolfe Ranch; Balanced Rock; Double Arch*

Things to Do: *Hiking; Backpacking; Camping; Climbing; Biking*

What's Nearby? *Colorado National Monument; Canyonlands National Park; Glen Canyon National Recreation Area; Black Canyon of the Gunnison National Park; Hovenweep National Monument*

Entrada sandstone, which geologists say was part of a low arid coastal plain adjacent to a great inland sea 150 to 200 million years ago. The waters of the sea gradually retreated, leaving behind a massive salt bed called the Paradox Formation.

Over time, the salt bed was buried by layers of sediment, which hardened into sandstone. Thousands of feet thick in places, the Paradox Formation was less stable than the sandstone, leaving the rocks prone to buckling and tilting, as well as to erosion, leaving the pinkish red Entrada layer exposed to the harsh elements of southeastern Utah's high desert. A number of below-ground faults further contributed to the instability that eventually led to the unique formations on the surface. The results of one such fault, the

Featured on many Utah license plates, the 52-foot-tall Delicate Arch is one of the most iconic sights in the Beehive State and one of about 2,000 arches in the park.

Moab Fault, are visible from the main visitor center: a 2,500-foot vertical displacement of the earth.

Water and wind conspired against the exposed sandstone, scouring narrow canyons and gullies of the stone and leaving thin walls called "fins" in between. The next phase in the process occurred as wind and frost brushed away at the soft interior area of some of these fins, eventually perforating them with a window. Water would expand into ice with the wild temperature swings of the region, further carving the rock away, and these openings gradually enlarged until the window became an arch. Many fins collapsed before they could become arches because their rock was too soft or their geometry too unstable. While most of the arches are Entrada sandstone, many—including Stevens Arch—are comprised of the tan-colored Navajo sandstone.

The park's most photographed attraction, Delicate Arch, is famous as the icon seen on Utah's license plates. It is isolated in its own amphitheater accessible by trail one and a half miles from the parking lot, framing a stunning view of endless sandstone formations. Landscape Arch, with a span of 306 feet, is the longest in the world and one of six dramatic arches along the popular Devils Garden Trail. The two-mile trail once featured seven arches, but that number declined in August 2008 when Wall Arch collapsed into rubble—a reminder that this landscape is constantly changing and impermanent.

Life Among the Arches

Arches National Park is perched atop the Colorado Plateau, a high desert region stretching from western Colorado across southern Utah and northern New Mexico to Arizona. This area is the most sparsely populated region of the contiguous 48 states, but it contains the nation's greatest wealth of national parks. It is a place teeming with scenic treasures almost beyond belief: mountains, gorges, rushing rivers, great canyons, escarpments, buttes,

Above: *The sandstone that defines the park is reflected in a seasonal desert pool, fed by torrential rains that typically come in the fall.* Below left: *Collectively nicknamed Park Avenue, these majestic sandstone formations are known as fins, the geological precursor to arches.*

spires, pinnacles, and endless stretches of desert landscape.

But the dearth of water and cold winters make for sparse and specialized forms of life. The soil itself is alive: Known as biological soil, a symbiotic crust of lichens, mosses, fungi, blue-green algae, and other organisms covers much of the park's surface. All of Arches' plants need the ability to survive long periods of drought in one form or another. Cacti and yucca are prominent examples of drought-resistant perennial plants found in the park, but others leave drought-resistant seeds in their wake that could take years to bloom. Pinyon-juniper woodlands are also common, as such trees can take root in rocky land inhospitable to most other plants.

Another critical feature in Arches' harsh terrain is the ephemeral pools, or "potholes,"

Rock Graffiti

It cannot be denied that there is something completely magnetic about the rocks of Arches National Park. Their wild, seemingly painted-on colors, their awe-inspiring size and delicate balance attract people from all over. When people see something like these rocks, they just want to touch them, to be a part of them—to live through the rocks as the rocks seemingly live forever. Throughout the millennia, many different people and cultures have passed through the park. Whether calling it home, like the Fremonts and the Pueblos, the Ute and the Paiute, or just visiting, all seem to leave their mark in one way or another—though some have done so more blatantly than others.

The early Fremont people were especially known for their use of petroglyphs and rock inscriptions, which are carvings of people and animals that record certain events in Fremont history. They often appear near ancient watering holes, where people would sit for hours, whittling down arrowheads or doing other tedious types of tasks while waiting for game to hunt.

Another piece of rock art that survives at the park today is that of Dennis Julien, a French American trapper who wandered across the United States. His is the first date known to appear in the park: June 9, 1844. What kind of archaeological marvel is this? Absolutely none—Julien carved his name and the date into the side of an arch as he passed through! He'd been doing this across the country for as long as he traveled.

Today, visitors are asked not to leave their marks. In fact, following in Julien's footsteps and carving the date on an arch or wall would result in a hefty fine for anyone caught. So many people come through the park every year that, should they all carve out a little place for themselves, the park would soon be nothing but mounds of rock dust. Visitors should allow the park to live on in their memories and their photographs, leaving it unspoiled for those who come after.

that fill with water during the rare rainstorm and provide habitat to a number of specially adapted plants and animals, including spadefoot toads, fairy shrimp, and snails. Some of these animals cannot survive without water—but their eggs can. Others go into dormant stages during drought.

Most of the mammals that live in Arches are nocturnal, including kangaroo rats, skunks, foxes, and bats. Other animals in the park are crepuscular, meaning they are active at dawn and dusk. Arches' crepuscular animals include jackrabbits, songbirds, coyotes, and mule deer. Of those awake during daylight hours, lizards are some of the most commonly seen denizens of this rugged land. The population includes the vibrantly hued collared lizard, which often appears to be doing pushups as part of its mating dance and various communiqués to other lizards. But they are not out dancing all year long: The reptiles hibernate during the park's cold winters.

The Influence of People

Arches also has a long and storied human history. While Native Americans never inhabited what is now the park on a full-time basis, many people hunted and sought rocks to make tools in the area starting about 10,000 years ago. Closer to 2,000 years ago, nomadic peoples began cultivating crops at more permanent dwellings on the Colorado Plateau but likely found the Arches area too arid for year-round habitation. The Ute people are thought to be the creators of several works of rock art in the park.

When Mormon pioneers first came to Utah in the mid-1800s, the Utes successfully fought their attempts to build a mission in what is today the city of Moab. It wasn't until the end of the century that people of European ancestry permanently settled the area and established farms, ranches, and mines. As Moab grew, more and more accounts of the wondrous arches and mind-boggling geology made it to the East Coast. Locals drummed up support for a new national park among railroad executives and politicians, and President Herbert Hoover established Arches National Monument. In 1971, Congress passed the legislation that made Arches a national park.

In the time since, annual visitation to the park has mushroomed from 200,000 to around one million as Moab has grown from a dusty desert town to an increasingly modern municipality of 5,000 residents. With more people have come several non-native plant species and increased erosion of Arches' soil. More development has, not surprisingly, also increased the number of lights, which impacts the night sky.

In spite of the growth, Arches remains a world away. This completely unique geological masterwork is the stuff postcards are made of—and always will be. It would take a lifetime for someone to trek to all 2,000 recorded arches on park land, a worthy pursuit if ever there was one.

Accessible via a short loop trail, Balanced Rock (left) *is one of the most photographed formations in Arches, a globe of red sandstone precariously teetering on its pedestal.*

Badlands National Park

South Dakota's rolling prairie is uncannily interrupted by the collection of otherworldly ridges, spires, turrets, buttes, battlements, and canyons called the Badlands. Badlands National Park takes in 242,756 acres of this territory where history and geology seem to collide, sometimes in strange and unexpected ways.

The stark, uninviting terrain of the Badlands has been called a masterpiece of natural sculpture, of wind and rain that carves uncanny shapes, revealing colored bands in stratified layers. Rain comes rarely, washing away an average of an inch of sediment annually in South Dakota's White River Badlands. Some observers say one thunderstorm can create perceptible changes in the Badlands landscape, and this process has been going on for about 75 million years.

Dinosaur Playland

It all started when the Rocky Mountains began rising in the west. The Rockies spilled an untold tonnage of sediment—ash, silt, clay, sand—toward the central continent. Toward the end-stages of this buildup, volcanoes deposited thousands of feet of ash. The dinosaurs loved it, which is why the Badlands continue to be one of the world's paleontological treasures.

Approximately 75 million years ago, a vast sea lay where the park is today. This sea covered the Great Plains of North America, and at the location of the modern-

Tortured shapes—mounds, towers, spires, bridges—show why the Badlands has been called a masterpiece of natural sculpture, caused by the rise of the Rocky Mountains and eons of volcanic activity.

Southwestern South Dakota
Established November 10, 1978
380 square miles

Things to See: *Big Pig Dig; Robert's Prairie Dog Town; the Wall; the Castle Trail*

Things to Do: *Hiking; Camping; Studying fossils*

What's Nearby? *Minuteman Missile National Historic Site; Wind Cave National Park; Jewel Cave National Monument; Black Hills National Forest; Mount Rushmore National Memorial; Crazy Horse Monument*

day Badlands, it left a layer of dark gray sedimentary rock. Paleontologists have long found this layer of Pierre shale to be a source of fossil treasures. There they have found fossils from giant sea lizards to flying pterosaurs, from Archelon giant sea turtles to loonlike Hesperonis birds, as well as crabs, clams, snails, and ancient, squidlike cephalopods.

Later, when the water retreated, it yielded a subtropical forest. Fossils of wildlife from this long-ago period have also been found, including three types of hippo, the deerlike *Leptomeryx,* the *Oreodont,* the saber-tooth *Hoplophoneus* cat, the three-toed *Meso-hippus,* the rhinolike *Subhyracodon,* and *Paleolagus,* the protorabbit.

Pig Wallow Site, better known as the Big Pig Dig, was established when two visitors from Iowa near the Conata Picnic Area discovered a large backbone protruding from the ground in 1993. After many years of study, scientists decided the bone came from a Subhyracodon, a hornless rhinoceros. Student paleontologists have worked summers at the excavation site since then, helping to excavate 17 other animal species and more than 14,000 bones.

These lucky Iowans were far from the first to make important discoveries in the Badlands. Native Americans, such as the Lakota, found fossilized seashells, large fossilized bones, and other treasures such as turtle shells.

Walls and Rivers

The massive environmental uplift that yielded the subtropical forest ultimately caused the erosion that created the Badlands and its key geological feature, the Wall. The Wall is a strip of gullies, ridges, and spires that range from one-half mile to three miles wide. Narrowly defined, the Wall is more than nine miles long—some say the Badlands' wall is closer to 100 miles long.

Today the White River flows south of the national park, but it once eroded a line of cliffs that itself eroded into the Wall. Over time, rain and water flows carved the scarp and created the Badlands, making and remaking it for the next five million years.

Above: *Badlands National Park is believed to be home to the largest bison herd in the United States.* Left: *This 35-million-year-old tortoise fossil is an example of the paleontological riches of Badlands National Park, which has produced fossils ranging from giant sea lizards to three kinds of hippopotamus.*

Right: *Epochs of erosion through stratified layers of soft rock and volcanic ash have produced the colorful banded landscape that makes up much of the Badlands.* Below: *The Eye of the Badlands was formed in sandstone after eons of weathering away softer sediments.*

For visitors of the park, the Wall provides terrific hiking, with three trails from Windows Overlook universally recommended: Door Trail, which ushers visitors though a "door" in the Wall into an instant encounter with the Badlands' moonscape; Notch Trail, which winds its way up to a "notch" in the Wall that serves as an overlook; and Windows Trail, which leads to a natural window in the Wall that has a view of the deep canyon carved into the tableland.

North of the Wall, the frosting of volcanic ash at Badlands National Park yields to the original land surface's underlying bed. Here, slender spires rise above sharp ridges and intricate slopes.

Territory in Conflict

The first people to enjoy the outrageous splendor of the Badlands were, of course,

Native Americans, notably the Lakota Sioux. The Lakota Sioux culture finds its greatest monument still under construction: the magnificent Crazy Horse Memorial near Custer, South Dakota, about 80 miles from the park. For 1,000 years, the Badlands served as hunting grounds for the Sioux and other tribes, such as their predecessors, the Arikara, who camped in secluded valleys and hunted bison and hare.

By the 19th century, the seven tribes of the Sioux Nation dominated the region, with Oglala Lakota Sioux predominant in the Badlands area. By the late century, when eastern settlers started arriving, the stage was set for conflict and tragedy. The U.S. government took Indian territory and forced the Sioux onto reservations. However, today more than 120,000 acres of Badlands National Park remains in Sioux territory.

It may be surprising that paleontology developed in the Badlands almost 70 years before settlement began in earnest in the early 20th century. The area continued to be a hard place to farm for a living right up until the 1930s, when the Dust Bowl drove away many who remained. Residents of the area today are a hale and hardy breed.

A Successful Partnership

The 133,300-acre Stronghold District, famed for its spectacular views, is managed together by the National Park Service and the Oglala Sioux Tribe, which perhaps befits a place where the history of the Lakota Nation and its ancient ancestors left their mark. Perhaps unexpectedly, World War II left its mark, as well. When that war commenced, the U.S. Air Force took possession of part of the land for a gunnery range of 341,726 acres, almost all of it Pine Ridge Reservation land; only 337 acres were commandeered from what was then Badlands National Monument. Today, you can visit for the views, but be careful of leftover ordnance.

The vast Badlands National Park is divided into the North Unit, which consists of parkland north of Highway 44; and the South Unit, parkland south of Highway 44. The less-visited South Unit, which has no tracks or trails, perhaps deserves more consideration from visitors.

More-visited sites in the park include the White River Visitor Center (staffed by members of the Oglala Sioux Tribe) and the hour-long Highway 240 Loop Road—with a side trip down Sage Creek Rim Road to Robert's Prairie Dog Town, where you can expect to see wildlife and panoramic views of the park not far from the Big Pig Dig. You can also stop by the Ben Reifel Visitor Center and see the park video and exhibits.

Hiking is a good way to get away from it all. Don't neglect the ten-mile Castle Trail,

the longest trail in the park, five miles to the Fossil Exhibit Trail and back. Most of the other trails are easier: the half-mile Cliff Shelf, which makes up for its brevity by climbing stairs through a juniper forest along the Badlands Wall; the strenuous Saddle Pass, a loop of just one-quarter mile up the Wall to a view of the White River Valley; the Castle and Medicine Root Loop trails, which take the hiker through mixed grass prairie; and the Fossil Exhibit Trail, a quarter-mile round-trip featuring exhibits and fossil replicas.

"Hell with the fires out," is what an early explorer is said to have called the Badlands. Visitors today can, perhaps, afford to disagree.

The Ghost Dance Religion and the Last Stand at Wounded Knee

The 1870s were difficult for the Sioux people. While life in the Badlands had never been easy, it had always been theirs. But with the invasion of a group of U.S. homesteaders, life became a lot worse. All across America, native peoples had been deprived of their lands and forced onto reservations. In 1876, that time had come to the Sioux.

Finally defeated, they were moved from the hunting grounds that had been a part of their lives and their ancestors' lives for the past 11,000 years. Pushed onto reservations, they were given poor plots of land that they attempted to turn into successful farming ventures. But the Sioux weren't the only ones who thought that present-day South Dakota had the makings of an agricultural paradise—white settlers, too, took up plots of land in the area, mostly on the Sioux's stolen hunting grounds. All failed. The lands may have been fertile hunting grounds, but the soil, sun, and lack of rain made for disastrous farming.

By 1890, the feelings of the Sioux were bitter. Many turned to a prophet by the name of Wovoca, who preached the rise again of the Sioux Nation, the disappearance of the white settlers, and the restoration of the hunting grounds. He envisioned great Ghost Dances, in which all participated, calling up the spirits. The members of the Ghost Dance religion wore Ghost Shirts, which Wovoca told them were impervious to white bullets. One of the final Ghost Dances ever recorded was in what is now the Badlands National Park, on Stronghold Table.

Originally a pacifist people, Ghost Dance Sioux were now starving and frightened. One chief, Big Foot, led his people away from Stronghold through Badlands Pass. His hope was to keep his angry men separated from encroaching army soldiers so that he could work out an agreement. Unfortunately this was never to be. Near Wounded Knee Creek, about 45 minutes south of the park area, the soldiers caught up with the American Indians and attempted to disarm them. Fighting erupted on each side, though it is said that neither were looking for a battle. In the end, shots were fired and the Sioux were hopelessly outnumbered and outgunned. By the time the conflict was finished, more than 200 Native Americans lay dead, as did 30 army soldiers. This massacre was the last of the skirmishes between the army and the Sioux.

Big Bend National Park

More than 800,000 acres in all, Big Bend National Park encompasses a seemingly endless expanse of forested mountains, impossibly sheer canyons, and rugged desert wilderness just across the Rio Grande from Mexico in West Texas. Here the river winds south then suddenly veers north in a great horseshoe curve before turning southward again, thus the moniker, *Big Bend.* Other nicknames for this dramatic and remote landscape are "America's Last Frontier" and the "Texas Outback."

One other label is *"Despoblados"*—the depopulated zone—which is what Spanish explorers dubbed the area west of the Pecos River when first exploring it four centuries ago. That name still holds true today. The Big Bend region is home to some of the least densely populated counties in the United States.

All of this wide-open wilderness was covered 135 million years ago by the blue waters of an inland sea that stretched all the way into what is today Arkansas. Underneath all that water was ancient strata that geological activity had squeezed upward in the millennia prior. The layer of limestone that covers much of the park's topography today is a remnant from this era and features fossilized shellfish and snails—proof that this desert was once underwater. The sea began to retreat about 100 million years ago, exposing fins, mountains, and canyons.

Southwestern Texas
Established June 12, 1944
1,250 square miles

Things to See: *Santa Elena Canyon; Castolon Historic District; Sotol Vista; Sam Nail Ranch; Window View Trail; Mule Ears Overlook; Homer Wilson Ranch; Tuff Canyon*

Things to Do: *Hiking; Camping; Rafting; Backpacking; Climbing; Bicycling; Birding*

What's Nearby? *Fort Davis National Historic Site; McDonald Observatory; Amistad National Recreation Area*

Left: *Robert Hill's 1899 party, pictured here, took three months to navigate the Rio Grande from Presidio, upriver from the modern-day park, to Langtry, the home of the legendary Judge Roy Bean.* Opposite: *Their flanks adorned by the changing fall colors, the Chisos Mountains are among the highest and most striking mountains in all of the Lone Star State.*

This historic photo of the Rio Grande cutting through Santa Elena Canyon, taken by Robert Hill in 1899, depicts a landscape that looks exactly the same as its 21st-century counterpart.

including 50-foot crocodilians and flying reptiles with wingspans of 35 feet—as well as more recent rhinoceroses, camels, and other mammals. The fossil record of Big Bend is especially diverse, although most specimens are from the Cretaceous or Tertiary periods.

Environmental Variation

There are three principal ecosystems in the park: the forests of the Chisos Mountains, the fertile riparian environment on both sides of the Rio Grande, and the harsh and rugged Chihuahuan Desert. Each of these unique environments offers distinct and diverse habitat for a wide range of plant and animal life. The altitude of the Chisos and the waters of the Rio Grande offer respite from the heat, but the surrounding desert wilderness is the most rugged and bleak—albeit starkly beautiful.

Looming as the centerpiece of this prototypical desert preserve, the Chisos Mountains, a spectacular self-contained massif, serve as a natural geographic anchor for the park. The centrally located mountains are a complicated geological wonderland of volcanic plugs, igneous crags, forested buttes, jagged outcrops, wild dry pastures, and bone-dry streams. The panoramic view from the south rim of the Chisos Mountains, looking out over thousands of square miles in northern Mexico, is one of the best in the national park system.

Literally the southern border of the park—as well as the country—the Rio Grande has sliced several deep chasms through more than 100 miles of red and orange rock. Santa Elena Canyon is so deep and nar-

Continued uplift, volcanism, and erosion further shaped the undulating landscape of Big Bend.

The park has proven to be a treasure trove for paleontologists. Researchers have unearthed the remains of extinct dinosaurs—

row in places that the sun barely penetrates it: Its walls range from 1,200 to 1,600 feet. Other canyons are Mariscal and Boquillas. Down along the river the thick subtropical vegetation forms a veritable jungle. The summer heat that regularly hits 120 degrees Fahrenheit is amplified by the narrow canyons and the humidity of the river. High temperatures in the 140s are not uncommon on the canyon floor.

Beyond the heat from the sun, there is also geothermal heat below, a remnant of once-active volcanoes in West Texas. Several hot springs still bubble up under the Rio

The scenery along the five-mile Lost Mine Trail includes rocky outcroppings, the panoramic desert valley below, and views that stretch south into Mexico.

Right: The last vestiges of the light of day are reflected off of this idyllic pool in Oak Creek Canyon, below the aptly named Window in the Chisos Mountains. Below: The foothills of the Chisos Mountains in Big Bend National Park form an ecological transition from the lower desert and riparian environments to the forested crags.

Grande in the park, the most famous being Langford Hot Springs. Once the site of a spa resort that has long since washed away, remnant foundations of long-gone structures today serve as pools for soakers.

An Area in Transition

But recent changes in the river's flow and less recent changes in volcanic activity merely underscore how dynamic this region has been over the millennia. As was mentioned above, great inland seas flowed through the region hundreds of millions of years ago, depositing thick layers of limestone and fossil-bearing shale. About 60 million years ago, mountains began thrusting up through the ground. At about the same time, a 40-mile-wide plain began sinking along fault lines. This left the awesome cliffs of Santa Elena Canyon to the west and the Sierra del Carmen Mountains to the east. Later volcanic activity formed the Chisos Mountains. Some of the magma that cooled and hardened underground was later exposed by erosion.

This remarkable topographic variety provides a habitat for a surprising diversity of life: more than 1,200 plant species, many found nowhere else on earth, and more than 400 species of birds, which are many more than can be found in any other national park. It is also possible, along the junglelike stretches, for visitors to see some of the most rare wild felines in the United States—the ocelot, the jaguarundi, and the jaguar. The cool Chisos Mountains, of which Emory Peak is the highest with a peak elevation of 7,825 feet, harbor forests of pine and oak that provide a habitat for deer, mountain lions, and other animals. At lower-lying elevations, there are 70 species of cactus found in Big Bend, more than any other national park.

Among the other notable beasts found in the Big Bend area, the collared peccary, commonly known as the javelina, is a wildlife watcher's favorite. These piglike hoofed herbivores live in herds with a range that extends south to South America and west to Arizona. There are also 3,600 species of invertebrates in Big Bend's ecosystems, including big hairy tarantulas as well as tarantula hawks—large wasps that prey on tarantulas, paralyzing them and dragging them away for their larvae to consume.

The Human Touch

People have lived in what is now Big Bend National Park for thousands of years. Mexican settlers farmed both banks of the Rio Grande in the early 1800s, and Americans from the East began homesteading two decades later. The idea of turning the area into parkland followed soon after that. Texas Canyons State Park was established by the state legislature in Austin in 1933. After another decade, the National Park Service came on the scene, and Big Bend National Park formally came into being in 1944.

But like many other parks, modern problems have encroached on this remote corner of the country. Air quality has declined, sometimes marring the superlative views from the South Rim of the Chisos Mountains. The Rio Grande itself is threatened by development; the stretch downriver from El Paso, Texas, often runs dry. Increased border security has cut off Mexican villages once frequented by park visitors who took human-powered ferries across the Rio Grande.

But there are many bright spots as well. Black bears have crossed the Rio Grande from Mexico's Maderas del Carmen Range and taken up residence in the Chisos, and the Maderas are increasingly better managed and protected. There is an increasingly stronger push for binational environmental protection and reform. And the vast and wild landscape of Big Bend remains one of the best places to watch brilliant sunsets and sunrises, over and over again.

Everett Townsend, "Father" of Big Bend

It's a story as big as Texas, with a personality and a will to match. The story of Big Bend's creation and the man behind it will live forever in the hearts of those who visit this park. It was only due to his Texas-sized tenacity that this park exists as it does today.

Everett Townsend, born into a ranching family in 1871, was the driving force, the heart and soul, behind the park from the moment he first laid eyes on the view from the South Rim of the Chisos Mountains. Because of his ailing father, Townsend lied about his age and faked his way into the E Company of the Texas Rangers, ultimately making his living protecting the U.S.-Mexico border. He rose in the ranks quickly, and in 1893, at age 22, he was appointed deputy U.S. marshal. By 23, his promotion to mounted customs inspections officer in Presidio County paved the way for his lifelong devotion to the creation of a national park on this site.

It was in this position, while he was hunting down some stolen mules in the Chisos Mountains, that Townsend happened upon the moment, and the view, that would change his life forever. As he saw the panorama stretching before him, he discovered his calling: to preserve these lands for every generation to come. The view from the South Rim caused him, as he said, "to see God as he had never seen him before."

Over the years, Townsend did many things, from managing his own ranch and serving three terms as sheriff of Brewster County to finally being elected as state representative in 1932. This appointment put him in the position to do what he had always wanted: save the parklands. Townsend was credited as a coauthor on the bill that first created the park—as a state park. From there, he worked tirelessly to make sure that the park fulfilled its potential. From the organization of the Civilian Conservation Corps encampment that would actually organize the park to the finding of usable water for the park—even to the drawing of the borders and the purchasing of lands for an official national park, Townsend had his hand in the entire process.

It was largely because of his work that the United States recognized Big Bend as a national park in 1944, when Townsend was 73 years old. A full 50 years of his life had gone into the creation of this reality, and it was because of his willingness to fight through legal battles and physical limitations that visitors can enjoy these lands as they do today. Townsend Point, the second-highest peak in the Chisos Mountains, was named for the man who dedicated his life to the park.

Biscayne National Park

Biscayne Bay, a breeding ground for 200 kinds of marine creatures, contains vast beds of fantastically shaped coral and colorful marine life. Shown here is coral and a school of grunts among a shipwreck.

Legend has it that Florida's Biscayne Bay was the 17th-century hideaway of the pirate Black Caesar, who launched his career as a brigand by pretending to float adrift in an open lifeboat and then attacking ships that came to help him and his crew.

These buccaneers are now long gone; today, Biscayne National Park, which comprises part of Biscayne Bay and much else, is patrolled by gentle manatees. With their doleful faces, these enormous mammals can grow as long as 13 feet and weigh a ton or more. Manatees are aquatic relatives of elephants. They have thick gray skin, coarse hairs, big toenails on their flippers, and lips that can rip and tear plants. Manatees use their front flippers to shove sea grasses and other underwater plants into their mouths. Population counts of the manatee are notoriously variable, and the remaining numbers of these great creatures is estimated to be between 1,000 and 3,000; in either case, far too few. All of them roam the waters of Florida.

Southern Florida
Established June 28, 1980
270 square miles

Things to See: *Convoy Point; Boca Chita Key; Elliott Key; Adams Key*

Things to Do: *Boating; Camping; Snorkeling, swimming, and diving; Canoeing and kayaking; Fishing*

What's Nearby? *Everglades National Park; Big Cypress National Preserve*

Under the Surface

Biscayne National Park also contains a remarkably varied spectrum of fish, fantastically shaped coral, and vast beds of waving turtle grass. The bay is only four to ten feet deep, making it a breeding ground for more than 200 kinds of marine creatures, including shrimp, spiny lobsters, sponges, and crabs. Looking into the shallow water, you might be able to see the colorful flash of a parrot fish swimming by, the bright glimmer of an angelfish, or the surprisingly graceful movements of an immense sea turtle.

The park encompasses Biscayne Bay between Key Biscayne and Key Largo, the northernmost islands of the Florida Keys. It is the only national park that is almost entirely underwater. Only 4 percent of its 172,971 acres is on dry land; the rest is an ocean wonderland. Remarkably, Biscayne National Park is a mere 20 minutes' drive from Homestead, Florida, and 50 minutes to an hour from either Key Largo, Key Biscayne, or Miami. Its largest island, Elliott Key, is formed from a fossilized coral reef called Key Largo Limestone—some say making it the first "true" northern Florida key. Farther north in the park the islands are coral and sand.

Like nearby Everglades National Park, Biscayne was created by Congress under intense pressure from environmentalists, sports enthusiasts, and other concerned citizens who wanted to save the bay from the threat of developers. In the 1960s, plans were made to build resorts and subdivisions on the northern keys and to put an oil refinery on the adjacent mainland. To prevent this from happening, Biscayne Bay was

The 65-foot lighthouse on Boca Chita was built of coral in the 1930s by a one-time owner of the island, before it became public property. Its views are unsurpassed.

made a national monument in 1968. The protected area was expanded to encompass more keys and reefs when it became a national park in 1980.

In Times Past

Joan Gill Blank notes in her book, *Key Biscayne: A History of Miami's Tropical Island and the Cape Florida Lighthouse,* that the bay has been known by many names over several centuries. In 1513, Juan Ponce de Leon called it *Chequescha.* In 1565, Pedro Menéndez de Avilés called it *Tequesta* after the Tequesta people, who, until they vanished in the mid-1700s, lived in what today are Miami-Dade and Broward counties and the Florida Keys. During their occupation of Florida, the British called the bay *Cape River, Dartmouth Sound,* and *Sandwich Gulph.* As for the Biscayne name, Blank also notes that a 17th-century map shows a *Cayo de Biscainhos,* named after Spain's Bay Biscay, the probable origin of Key Biscayne, which became Biscayne Bay by the late 19th century.

Scientists believe humans began visiting Biscayne Bay about 10,000 years ago when Paleo-Indians migrated down the Florida peninsula, as evidenced by finds from Biscayne Bay's Old Cutler Fossil Site. But after these ancient people faded away, the bay probably remained unoccupied until about 2,500 years ago, when the Tequesta arrived. The Tequesta gathered prickly pear, sea grapes, and coco plum; hunted deer and freshwater turtles; and fished for sea

The Legend of Black Caesar

Florida has a long and sordid history of piracy, extending far back into its past. The area that is now Biscayne National Park was once home to one of the most fearsome pirates to roam the high seas.

In the mid-to-late 1600s, Black Caesar was a mighty leader in Haiti. The legend goes that he and his followers were tricked on board a boat visiting his shores with promises of treasure. While the boat's crew entertained Black Caesar and his crew with music, dancing, and rare jewels, the boat quietly cast off, leaving them trapped on board. Subsequently, they were locked in the hold, destined for slavery in the Americas. His crew fought for freedom, trying to overtake the slavers—but it was a battle that the Haitians ultimately lost.

While on the sea, however, the slaver's ship ran into a hurricane near Biscayne Bay. With the help of a friend (some accounts say that he was a crew member who took pity on him), Black Caesar escaped in a long boat with a few supplies while most of the other men perished. When the storm cleared, the ship had been washed ashore and smashed by the reef and high winds. With his friend, the downed ship, and the longboat, Black Caesar devised a plan: Whenever a ship passed by, Caesar and his crew floated in the longboat near their wreckage, pretending to be victims of a shipwreck. When the new ships took them aboard, the brigands would attack, taking the treasure captive and, sometimes, the ship and crew, as well. The name of Black Caesar came to be feared among those who sailed near Florida's coast, and the base of his operations is still known as Black Caesar's Rock.

This buccaneer fell in with an even fiercer pirate: Blackbeard. In the early 1700s, Blackbeard's ship was caught with Black Caesar on the crew. The tale says that, in attempting to avoid capture, Caesar tried to blow up the ship's hold with black powder but was caught just before he lit the match. Black Caesar was hanged in 1718 in Williamsburg, Virginia.

egg chamber in which to hide her eggs. Once she has laid her eggs, she buries the chamber and the hole, returns to sea, and never sees the eggs or the hatchlings again. Florida's sea turtle populations are declining for a number of reasons, including light interference. Hatchlings rely on the reflection of the moon on the water to guide them to the sea, and lights on the coast can fatally confuse them.

Nature Prevails

Despite the bay's startling proximity to civilization, Biscayne National Park remains one of the East Coast's major undeveloped coastal areas. The surface areas of the park consist of about 50 barrier islands strung across the water like pearls on a strand and the magnificent mangrove shoreline. Mangroves help stabilize the shore, trapping their own fallen leaves in networks of tangled roots, providing protein-rich food for some of the park's smallest undersea creatures.

But the most prominent life-forms in Biscayne National Park are the extensive communities of underwater coral reefs. These are the only living reefs within the continental United States. Coral comes in many forms. As park visitors tour the bay in glass-bottom boats, the floor show includes giant brain coral and mountainous star coral.

Near the national park is Barnacle Historic State Park, a five-acre Florida state park located on Biscayne Bay in Miami's Coconut Grove neighborhood. That park contains the oldest house in its original location in Miami-Dade County, built in 1891 by Ralph Middleton Munroe. Commodore

mammals, sea turtles, manatee, porpoises, sharks, sailfish, and stingrays. Amid such abundance, the Tequesta developed pottery, dugout canoes, and bow hunting. They used marine shells as tools, decorations, and trade items. By 1763, diseases such as smallpox and measles had nearly decimated the Tequesta.

These first residents were far from the last to note the extraordinary bounty of the bay. "Fish are abundant," surveyor Andrew Ellicott wrote in 1799. "Turtles are also to be had in plenty; those we took were of three

kinds; the loggerhead, hawk-bill, and green." Sea turtles were so abundant in Biscayne Bay at one time that turtle hunters routinely caught as many as 20 per day, each weighing at least 300 pounds. Today, loggerhead sea turtles are the park's most common. Loggerheads can be spotted by their enormous heads. Most turtle nests in the park are loggerhead nests, too, each containing an average of 100 eggs.

A normal female turtle will nest four times per season at two-week intervals. She digs a large hole and then a deeper, narrower

Munroe wrote *The Commodore's Story: The Early Days on Biscayne Bay* and was the subject of 1980's "The Forgotten Frontier: Florida Through the Lens of Ralph Middleton Munroe," a collection of his photographs. Of the bay's incomparable coral reefs, the third-largest in the world, he wrote in 1877:

"No sea-lover could look unmoved on the blue rollers of the Gulf Stream and the crystal-clear waters of the reef, of every delicate shade of blue and green, and tinged with every color of the spectrum from the fantastically rich growths on the bottom, visible to the last detail through this incredibly translucent medium. It scarcely resembles northern seawater at all—a cold semi-opaque, grayish-green fluid, which hides the mysteries of the bottom. Drifting over the Florida Reef on a quiet day one may note all the details of its tropical luxuriance twenty feet below, and feels himself afloat on a sort

of liquid light, rather than water, so limpid and brilliant is it."

Or Does It?

The park shows some of its more visible human history in Stiltsville, which dates back to the 1930s, when "Crawfish" Eddie Walker built a shack

on top of stilts to keep it above the waterline in the bay. Accessible only by water, the area became the coolest spot in Miami, its nightclubs subject to frequent police raids. By the 1960s, however, it had been battered by hurricanes, and Stiltsville began to decline. In 1985, Florida deeded the area's bottomland to the federal government, and

it became part of Biscayne National Park. Perhaps true to its unsavory origins, Stiltsville's remaining seven buildings continued to be an issue between the park service and the building owners until a 2003 agreement established a nonprofit organization called the Stiltsville Trust to preserve the structures.

Above: *Sunset illumines Biscayne Bay's magnificent mangrove shoreline. These trees and shrubs help stabilize the shore while providing a protein-rich environment for smaller undersea creatures.* Left: *Convoy Point's Dante Fascell Visitor Center, just nine miles east of Homestead, Florida, offers this view of the Lone Mangrove Islands. The center is a magnet for area artists.*

Black Canyon of the Gunnison National Park

Starting at its headwaters high in the central Rocky Mountains of Colorado, the hypnotically blue Gunnison River flows for nearly 100 miles through the rolling sage- and aspen-covered scenery before entering one of the most spectacular gorges in North America—the Black Canyon of the Gunnison River.

This canyon is dramatic and impossibly steep, crafted by the river in grand fashion. At its deepest, the Black Canyon is 2,722 feet from river to rim. At its narrowest, it tightens to a mere 40 feet on the floor in the aptly named Narrows. Here, the melted snow from the distant peaks cut through dark-colored gneisses and schists, decorated by streaks of pink pegmatite. Some of these formations are among the oldest rocks on the planet, dating back more than 1.7 billion years.

A 50-mile-long gorge cut from the earth over the millennia, the Black Canyon of the Gunnison is a spectacular feature that extends far beyond the boundaries of the national park—in fact, only about 14 miles are part of the park, which was a national monument from 1933 until 1999, when President Bill Clinton signed legislation raising it to national park status. Accompanying the bill signing that created the country's 55th national park, Clinton issued a statement. "The Black Canyon . . . is a true natural treasure," it read in part. "No other canyon in North America combines the remarkable depth, narrowness, and sheerness of the

Western Colorado
Established October 21, 1999
50 square miles

Things to See: *Gunnison Point; Painted Wall; Chasm View; Dragon Point*

Things to Do: *Hiking; Rafting; Rock climbing; Kayaking; Camping; Horseback riding*

What's Nearby? *Curecanti National Recreation Area; Colorado National Monument; Mesa Verde National Park*

Only a few hikers a day undertake the challenging trek down into the Inner Canyon in Black Canyon of the Gunnison National Park, nearly 2,000 dizzying feet below the rims.

Black Canyon of the Gunnison." Clinton's words continue to ring as true as ever.

Spectacular Vistas

Visitors to the relatively new national park can take a look at the steep bluffs from viewpoints on the North Rim, which is accessible from Crawford, Colorado, or on the South Rim, which is reached through an entrance near the city of Montrose. The North Rim is more remote and sees very little traffic; most visitors take South Rim Drive. With ten overlooks on seven miles, the road offers panoramas every bit as remarkable as those at the considerably more crowded Grand Canyon in Arizona. Each of these overlooks offers a look at a different chapter in the geological history book that is the Black Canyon of the Gunnison. The Precambrian gneisses and schists were formed after a volcanic island chain smashed into what is now Wyoming when much of the modern-day western United States was submerged under a vast inland sea.

Fast-forward hundreds of millions of years: The entire area started buckling skyward about 70 million years ago as part of a phenomenon known as the Gunnison Uplift. This period was followed by an era of volcanism that covered the area in a thick layer of ash, lava, and other debris. As the uplift caused the Gunnison River to have an unusually steep course, the river—fueled by several periods of glaciation—washed the volcanic layer away over the last 25 million years or so as it created the geological masterwork that's on display today.

The river has been dammed upstream of the park to create three reservoirs, including

Painted Wall is perhaps the most iconic image of the Black Canyon of the Gunnison, a sheer multihued rock face that's twice the height of the Empire State Building.

Often the first overlook of the canyon seen by visitors, Gunnison Point offers an ideal perch to gander at the dramatic scenery, with the river cutting its way through the canyon floor.

and juniper forest, known as a pygmy forest, is interspersed with high desert and populated with coyotes, mountain lions, ravens, porcupine, and jays; and the oak flats, a dense thicket offering a haven to black bears, mule deer, and mountain bluebirds. The rims' ecosystems are quite dry, and, without access to the river below, resident animals rely on "potholes," depressions in the rock that catch and hold rainfall in between the rare storms. (The potholes also are thriving ecosystems of their own.)

Below the rim, a different ecological universe begins. The walls are dotted with pockets of Douglas fir and aspen, clinging to the most unlikely folds in the canyon's sheer walls. The Douglas fir enjoys a symbiotic relationship with a fungus that makes their roots absorb water more efficiently. Bighorn sheep are occasionally spotted expertly navigating the narrow ledges. The park is a bird-watcher's paradise—home to peregrine falcons, golden eagles, bald eagles, and red-tailed hawks, as well as common

Blue Mesa Reservoir. This has slowed the rate of erosion considerably, as the river is now a shadow of its former self, running at about 20 percent of its rate before the dams were built.

Outdoor Adventures

In terms of summer recreation, the Black Canyon is a favorite destination among kayakers and hikers, as well as backpackers, fishers, and expert climbers. Later in the year, "leaf-peepers" flock to the Rockies, and this park is no exception; it is particularly beautiful in the autumn when the Gambel oak turns a warm, rusty red and the aspen are as bright as gold. In wintertime, cross-country skiers and snowshoers take to the powder-covered trails.

Wildlife viewing is a popular activity year-round, for the park offers excellent habitat in four distinct ecological zones. Two of them are on the rims: The pinyon

upland species, such as ravens, black-billed magpies, and violet-green swallows. From the safety of one of the rims, the sight of birds crisscrossing the void above the river is exhilarating.

Delving into the Landscape

For quite some time, Native Americans and European explorers and settlers alike believed that a descent into the canyon was impossible—or that such a descent meant certain death on the way back out. The 1873–74 Hayden Expedition dismissed the Black Canyon as "inaccessible," and even Captain John Gunnison, for whom the river is named, decided to take the long way around. By the end of the 19th century, however, the canyon had been thoroughly surveyed and mapped.

Today, just a few hikers a day descend into the inner canyon. There are no marked trails down, only routes that can be difficult to follow. Most of the routes involve more than 1,000 vertical feet worth of switchbacks, and some are supplemented by lengths of chain to help hikers on their way up or down. All of the routes are strenuous and usually require two hours to descend to the canyon floor—and at least three or four hours to ascend back to the rim.

While the Black Canyon's sheer walls do not figure into the total land area, the park encompasses just a little more than 30,000 acres, making it among the smallest in the national park system. Although small in terms of acreage, Black Canyon of the Gunnison National Park offers the dizzying depth of one of nature's most remarkable creations in the Rocky Mountains.

Dangerous Beauty

Not one of the hundreds of parks in the National Park Service put the word *wild* in wilderness quite like Black Canyon of the Gunnison. While sheer, stomach-dropping cliffs, unbridled greenery, and racing rivers make for spectacular, incomparable beauty, so do they make for a potentially dangerous experience.

The *Black* in Black Canyon comes from the fact that, at the canyon's deepest points, sunlight only reaches the bottom for an hour a day. Varying heights and depths in the canyon mean extremes in temperature. The canyon has some of the coldest recorded temperatures at its latitude, dropping to −40 degrees Fahrenheit during the winter. The Ute Indians, who have lived in what are now the parklands since before recorded history, have remained along the rim. There is no evidence of any human culture living in the gorge.

Beginning at the bottom, the section of the Gunnison River that flows through Black Canyon is a particularly dangerous portion of the river. The rapids here drop an average of 95 feet per mile (which is a lot—the Colorado River drops only about 7.5 feet per mile as it runs through the Grand Canyon). Even expert paddlers are discouraged from kayaking through the park, as death can be a possibility. Also, along the riverside, unchecked poison ivy grows more than five feet high—about shoulder height for most people!

On the rocks themselves, the geology makes for a slippery, though interesting, hike. Soft sandstone and igneous rocks weather easily, forming natural potholes in the ground. While that may mean twisted ankles for some unfortunate hikers, these holes are an important part of the landscape for the animals that live there. Rainfall is scarce in the gorge, but these natural bowls collect what does fall. The animals depend on the water gathered here to get through the harsh summers.

Bryce Canyon National Park

A maelstrom of rock figures of every size, shape, and color, sculpted by the elements over millions of years, Bryce Canyon National Park is one of the most amazing landscapes nature has to offer. The resulting labyrinth of stone is high among the visually stimulating natural wonders on the planet for sightseers and hikers alike.

Bryce Canyon is not a true canyon; rather, it's the scalloped edge of a huge mesa called the Paunsaugunt Plateau in southwestern Utah. On a grand scale, the geological formation containing Bryce resembles a loaf of bread that has been chewed away on one side. Erosion has taken about a dozen big bites out of the pink cliffs that form the plateau's eastern rim.

This hypnotic and otherworldly landscape looks as if it has been gouged free of earth and then filled with hoodoos, orange and red rock pedestals of all descriptions. These endless rock towers take on all kinds of shapes—resembling castles, bridges, towers, presidents, prime ministers, Thor's

Southwestern Utah
Established September 15, 1928
56 square miles

Things to See: *Inspiration Point; Thor's Hammer; Riggs Spring Loop; Bryce Point; Wall Street Trail; Paunsaugunt Plateau; Sunrise Point; Paria View*

Things to Do: *Hiking; Horseback or muleback riding; Cross-country skiing in winter; Snowshoe hikes in winter*

What's Nearby? *Glen Canyon National Recreation Area; Cedar Breaks National Monument; Rainbow Bridge National Monument; Zion National Park; Grand Canyon National Park*

hammer, and even Queen Victoria—and sizes—ranging from human-size to more than 100 feet tall.

Powered by Erosion

The Bryce escarpment, with its thousands of geological gargoyles and castellated spires, is the product of the relentless strength of water and time. The canyon is one of the best places on the planet to observe the forces that shape the surface of the earth. A single summer cloudburst can carry off thousands of tons of gravel, sand, and silt to the Paria River and then on to the Colorado River and into the Grand Canyon. Bryce is changing at a fantastic rate: Its rim recedes one foot every 65 years.

About 60 million years ago, a vast body of water called Lake Flagstaff covered southwestern Utah. As the ages passed, sediments of gravel, sand, and mud beneath the

Bryce Canyon's population of multihued fins and hoodoos offer little purchase for plant life, save the hardy Douglas fir and a few other evergreens. The Douglas fir's seeds support a host of rodents and insects.

The Paiute people lived in the Bryce Canyon area starting in A.D. 1200. They utilized what is now the park for hunting and gathering, but they never established a permanent settlement inside its boundaries.

sea accumulated to a thickness of 2,000 feet or more. Eventually, cemented together by minerals and pressure, the sediments turned into solid rock, which is now called the Wasatch Formation. Beginning about 16 mil-

lion years ago, colossal movements of the earth's crust forced the formation upward. The resulting stress produced great breaks in the rock. One of the resulting chunks is the Paunsaugunt Plateau.

Once exposed, the plateau's rocks were subject to the ravages of southern Utah's extreme climatic swings. Water freezes on more than half of the nights of the year at this high elevation, which allows a phenom-

But many more arches have come and gone: Many have collapsed into hoodoos over the millennia. Additionally, Bryce Canyon features a number of angular walls and fins, often several hundred feet tall and just as long but only a few feet thick. As is the case with the park's other features, erosion has often cut arches and hoodoos from these formations over Bryce Canyon's long and turbulent geological history.

A Sedimentary Rainbow

Another unmistakable geological feature that runs through Bryce Canyon is the 200-mile-long Grand Staircase, a massive band of sedimentary rock that continues south through Zion National Park. It is exposed only in certain areas, revealing 600 million

The Navajo Loop Trail (pictured) offers hikers a scenic route down into the main amphitheater of the canyon from Sunset Point. The 1.3-mile hike winds past such formations as Two Bridges and Wall Street.

enon called "frost-wedging" to sculpt the rocks into the formations seen today—and continues to do so. The volume of water expands by nearly 10 percent when it freezes, so ice can exert several thousand pounds of pressure per square inch and, consequently, shear chunks of rock away. Rainwater is slightly acidic and smoothes away the sharp edges of the hoodoos. Most of the hoodoos are visibly capped with

magnesium-rich limestone called dolomite; this grey stone is particularly resistant to the forces of erosion that wear away the layers of some of the softer rock below.

But the hoodoos are just the beginning of a deep inventory of unusual geological formations that populate Bryce Canyon. There are also hundreds of arches whittled from wind and water within park boundaries, ranging in diameter from three to 60 feet.

years of sediments, each differently colored layer a different chapter of geological history. Of the park's 13 overlooks, Yovimpa Point is the best place to get a sense of the sheer size of the Grand Staircase. From this magical rock spur nearly two miles above sea level—atop the aptly named Pink Cliffs and just above the Grey Cliffs—more than 3,000 square miles of desert fall away to the south.

In winter, Bryce Canyon's thousands of hoodoos take on the appearance of figures made of red and orange wearing white mantles of snow. The park service plows the 15-mile-long scenic drive to Rainbow Point, making this winter wonderland accessible by car. In the snowy season, cross-country skiers and snowshoers take to the same trails that are popular with hikers and backpackers in summer.

The park is home to a number of animals on both the forested plateau and the treeless amphitheater, including elk, mule deer, pronghorn, peregrine falcons, and hummingbirds. Many of these species are migratory,

Paiute Coyote Stories

Nearly every culture has one: the trickster. People may know them in their office or their social group. These are individuals who have stories to tell and pranks to play. People laugh when they're around—that is, everyone except the person who has just been humiliated. Everyone almost always likes them, if only because it's unwise to be on their bad side. Part joker and part bully, these people sometimes pull off amazing feats only to crash and burn, giving rise to cautionary tales. In Greek myth, the trickster's name was Hermes. In Norse myth, it was Loki. More recently, in the Southern United States, he was known as Brer Rabbit. To the Paiute, he was Coyote.

Coyote played an integral part in many aspects of the culture. In one story, a young Coyote went abroad and took a woman for his wife. They had many children, who were the Native Americans. One day, Coyote wished to go back to the Rocky Mountains, and he wanted to take his children with him. His wife put his children into a basket, warning Coyote not to open the basket until he got to the mountains. On his journey, he heard beautiful singing coming from it, and to hear the music better, he opened the lid. Before he could close it, however, his children jumped out and spread across the world. This is said to be how the different cultures came to be in the West and why there are so many spread far and wide.

Another Coyote story tells of how Bryce Canyon itself came to be formed. Coyote was well-known for being a troublemaker, causing mischief, and being reckless with people. He was not only reckless, but he had a cruel sense of humor, as well. Once as a joke, he kidnapped the children of the Water Monsters. In revenge, the Water Monsters sent a flood onto the land like none had ever seen, driving the Paiute away to the Land Above. The Paiute were so angry with Coyote that they abandoned him altogether. The only beings who would listen to him now were the bugs, lizards, bats, and snakes—all of the creatures that the Paiute shunned.

Coyote built a village for these creatures out of the way of the rain and sun where they lived happily for a long time. Soon, however, the creatures became lazy. They stopped listening to Coyote and thought they knew better than he did. They would no longer even hunt for their own food! Fed up and angry, Coyote called a council. Each of the beings came to the council in human form and lined up across the canyon, row upon row upon row of creatures standing in silence. Coyote paced up and down and started to yell at them, chastising them for their laziness and disrespect, calling them ungrateful. The more he paced, the angrier he became and the more he yelled and waved his arms. These actions cast a powerful magic, which turned all of the ungrateful creatures to stone, where they remain to this day as pillars in Bryce Canyon.

crossing through the park on a seasonal basis. Mountain lions are often seen in the park in winter, when they have an excellent chance at taking down deer.

Different plants thrive in various areas of Bryce Canyon, including sagebrush in the high desert meadows and white fir, aspen, and spruce trees at the higher elevations. Wildflowers bloom seasonally in the fertile nooks and crannies of the exposed Pink Cliffs. One of them, a vibrant fuchsia flower called the Bryce Canyon Paintbrush, grows nowhere else on earth.

The Namesake

For many millennia before white settlers arrived in Bryce Canyon country, indigenous people foraged for pine nuts on the plateau and hunted rabbits in the area. Named for the Mormon pioneer Ebenezer Bryce, who brought his family to the area in 1875, Bryce Canyon became popular as farmland because Bryce and other pioneers diverted water from the top of the plateau via a 10-mile ditch, making the valley below lush enough to support crops in the 1890s. These pioneers established the town of Tropic, Utah.

A U.S. Forest Service supervisor, J. W. Humphrey, first saw the canyon in 1915 and was enraptured by its beauty. He started promoting the area, giving movies and photographs to officials in Washington, D.C. In 1919, the Utah legislature also urged leaders in the nation's capital to set aside this 56-square-mile parcel and suggested it be dubbed Temple of the Gods National Monument. The canyon was established as a national monument in 1923, and the area was upgraded to a national park when

Calvin Coolidge signed legislation in 1928. Somehow, Ebenezer Bryce's name stuck.

Today, about 1.5 million people visit Bryce Canyon on an annual basis, thanks to improvements made by the railroad industry and the New Deal's Civilian Conservation Corps. Despite the relative ease of accessibility the park offers modern travelers, this is still one of the most remote places on the continent. The region enjoys some of the clearest and cleanest air on the planet— allowing for views that stretch for 200 miles— and incredible night skies for stargazing, planet-gazing, and even galaxy-gazing.

Below: *Technically an arch, Natural Bridge owes its bright red hue to an abundance of iron oxide. The timeworn window offers a keyhole view of the Ponderosa pine forest in the canyon below.* Opposite: *Thor's Hammer, an example of Claron Formation limestone and more commonly known as a hoodoo, stands sentinel near Sunset Point.*

Canyonlands National Park

A serendipitous, surreal masterwork of natural beauty, Canyonlands National Park encompasses a vast and endlessly changing sandstone wilderness crisscrossed by great chasms and gorges. From all appearances, this is one of the most arid places on earth, yet it was forged by water. Here, in southeastern Utah, the combined energy of two unusually abrasive rivers has created what is surely one of the most spectacular examples of the power of erosion anywhere on earth.

The rugged landscape of Canyonlands is one of deep-shadowed canyons, bright orange mesas, rust-colored pinnacles, and maroon buttes—an intense palette of natural colors that comes alive in the rays of the setting sun. The terrain here is so unique, unlikely, and unusual that it looks as though it might have been painted by Salvador Dalí.

The wild array of arches, sandstone pillars and needles, canyon mazes, and scarps that make up the otherworldly terrain of Canyonlands is the work of the Colorado and Green rivers. They meet in the heart of the park at a spectacular site called the Confluence. Here, the rivers form a great Y, cutting 1,000 feet into the brilliantly hued sandstone. From the Confluence, the rivers roll on as one.

The Mighty Colorado

Over the 20 million years of its existence, the Colorado River has gradually carried away solid rock from an area the size of the state of Texas, two miles deep. The abrasive power of all this sediment, accelerated by wind, precipitation, and frost, has carved out the park's trademark canyons, stark mesas, and high buttes, all of which are unlike any seen elsewhere.

The remarkable stripes that run through the nearly unbelievable shapes of these figures are the result of the way in which different kinds of stone have resisted the constant aggression of these natural sculpting agents. Each of these differently hued stripes indicate a different chapter in geological history. The lowest layers exposed in Canyonlands, those of the Paradox Formation, date back more than 300 million years. Many of these ancient layers feature *grabens*—German for graves—which are ditches that were etched in the surface of the earth as the underground strata of salt receded toward the Colorado River. The grabens are some of the youngest geological features in Canyonlands—only about 50,000 years old—and continue to grow at a rate of an inch a year.

The perpendicular landscape of the region was also shaped by the geological uplift of the Colorado Plateau as well as the underlying deposits of salt. Under great pressure from the rock above, the salt formed into huge domes that eventually caused the surface to buckle and fracture.

The two rivers that flow together in the park divide it into three sections: Island in the Sky, the Needles, and the Maze. In the north, a high mesa called Island in the Sky rises 2,000 feet as a great scarp several miles from the Confluence. In the east is the district known as the Needles. Here, giant pinnacles banded with alternating white and red stone rise 400 feet above the grassy floors of valleys ringed by perpendicular cliffs.

Southeastern Utah
Established September 12, 1964
525 square miles

Things to See: *Islands in the Sky; the Needles; the Maze; Chesler Park; Green River; Devil's Kitchen; Horseshoe Canyon; Colorado River; Butler Flat; Peekaboo Spring; Cataract Canyon*

Things to Do: *Hiking; Boating; Backpacking; Horseback riding; Climbing; Biking; Camping*

What's Nearby? *Glen Canyon National Recreation Area; Arches National Park; Natural Bridges National Monument; Capitol Reef National Park; Hovenweep National Monument; Rainbow Bridge National Monument; Colorado National Monument; Yucca House National Monument; Mesa Verde National Park*

Right: *Downriver from the Confluence of the Green and Colorado rivers, Cataract Canyon is a standout in this land of superlative canyons, renowned by paddlers for its whitewater.* Opposite: *Canyonlands National Park in Utah is rife with panoramic views of the Green and Colorado rivers, as well as of the remarkable byproducts of their waters' unyielding and erosive power, the canyons themselves.*

Above: *The Green River Overlook offers a sweeping vista of the park's bleakly beautiful red-rock landscape, all the way to the Maze and the Land of the Standing Rocks.* Below right: *Millennia of wind, water, and ice has sheared away the softer sandstone and left behind a landscape populated with arches and other formations such as the pictured Molar Rock and Angel Arch.*

migrate from the high country into the park's gnarled red topography. Near perennial water sources, there are frogs, toads, and even one salamander species. The Colorado River basin is also home to 14 species of native fish (and three times that many species of nonnative fish).

Into the Wild

Canyonlands is mostly wilderness, with paved highways penetrating only its periphery. Trails and jeep roads lead into some of its most scenic and geologically flamboyant places. They meander along the rims of high plateaus and then plunge dramatically down steep canyon walls where the rate of descent or ascent can be as great as 40 percent. As you drop into Canyonlands, the ground falls away from you in giant stair steps—stair steps that usually end abruptly in rock walls.

The eerie look of a landscape so wild and a terrain so treacherous caused late 20th-

Getting Lost in the Maze

To the west of the Confluence lies the third section of the park, the isolated, unforgettable wedge of canyon country known as the Maze. At the end of a 14-mile trail, the Maze Overlook offers a spectacular vista of rivers, spires, clefts, and canyons. Many believe that this is the finest view in the Southwest—and it's hard to argue with that after you've watched the sun rise over the incomparable geological labyrinth. Down below the overlook, the floor of the Maze is a rarely visited world of dry washes, shifting sand, and looming red-rock walls. Not too surprisingly, a trail map is an absolute necessity for hikers and backpackers who venture down into this geological analogue to a spider's web.

In and around the Maze and elsewhere in the park, there are naturally occurring "potholes," divots in the rock that fill with water after the rare rainstorm and then provide habitat for a whole host of plants and animals. Most of the animals in Canyonlands are nocturnal or crepuscular, which means they're most active at dawn and dusk.

Animals that visitors are most likely to glimpse in Canyonlands are birds: 273 species have been spotted here, including common ravens, western meadowlarks, and great blue herons. Reptiles, particularly lizards, are also quite visible scrambling amidst the rocks. Mammals include mule deer, desert bighorn sheep, kangaroo rats, and mountain lions. In the fall, black bears

century writer Edward Abbey to describe Canyonlands as the "most arid, most hostile, most lonesome, most grim, bleak, barren, desolate, and savage quarter of the state of Utah—the best part by far." Although Abbey worked as a ranger at nearby Arches National Park, he set the climactic scenes in his 1975 novel *The Monkey Wrench Gang* in and around the Maze because of its utter remoteness.

Long before Abbey lurked in southeastern Utah, nomadic hunter-gatherers frequented what is now Canyonlands as long as 10,000 years ago. Ancestral Puebloans settled the Needles District around A.D. 1200, but the dearth of water drove them out about a century later. In the 18th century, Spanish explorers first circled the area, leading up to the establishment of the Old Spanish Trail through modern-day Moab. In 1869, Major John Wesley Powell led a party on the Green and Colorado rivers from Wyoming to the Grand Canyon in Arizona, marking the first official exploration of the Canyonlands.

After Mormon settlements appeared in the region in the 1880s, ranching and mining emerged as economic mainstays. In the 1950s, a uranium boom gripped southeastern Utah, but before the park's natural wonders could be plundered by industry, Congress established Canyonlands National Park in 1964, setting aside about a quarter of a million acres of land in the process. In 1971, the park was expanded to its present size of 337,598 acres.

In all of this wide-open and wild real estate, there is plenty of room for humans to roam and truly get away from it all—but you'll need a serious four-wheel-drive vehicle if you want to navigate the undulating, rocky dirt roads around the Maze. On solid ground, mountain biking, hiking, and backpacking are prime pursuits of visitors to the park, and on the Colorado River, rafting is the recreational activity of choice. Either way, the remarkable landscape of Canyonlands National Park is the real draw.

Desert Plant Life: The Will to Survive

In the desert, it takes more than just strength and will to survive: It takes water. With arid climates, temperature extremes, and poor soil conditions, it's no wonder that deserts have a reputation for very little life. While survival is difficult, many species—both plant and animal—have found ways to adapt and even flourish.

The wildflowers of the desert are many and varied. When they bloom, their petals light up the desert floor with bright pinks, purples, whites, yellows, oranges, reds, and blues. Flower gardens such as these exist due to their seeds' ability to go dormant. When water is available, the seeds gather it in and sprout in a riot of color. In unusually dry periods, however, they remain as seeds, waiting for the opportunity to sprout again. These types of plants are called *drought escapers* because they lie low and ride out the storm—or lack thereof.

Other types of desert plants are those, obviously, that are typically associated with deserts, the *drought resistors.* These are cacti and yucca, and even moss. The yucca gets around the heat by having deep taproots to capture groundwater. Cacti store water (certain cacti can even be harvested for water by lost hikers) and use their long, slender, needlelike leaves to reduce radiation from the sun. Moss is simply able to go without water indefinitely, waiting patiently for water to arrive and coming back to life when the rains come. The difference between moss and the flowering escapers is that moss is a perennial, an established plant that exists year-round, whereas the escapers are annuals, growing new plants from seeds each year.

One last group of desert plant is called *drought evaders.* These are plants that grow only where water is plentiful in the desert—near hidden shaded springs, streams, and pools of water. While getting their water this way may seem like cheating, the evaders do something very useful: They alert desert wanderers to where water can be found.

Capitol Reef National Park

From a distance, parts of this park look like a swell of gigantic ocean waves, but the Waterpocket Fold, of which Capitol Reef is a segment, is an immense pleat in the earth's crust that rises in great parallel ridges for 100 miles across the starkly beautiful desert landscape of southern Utah.

The landscape of Capitol Reef National Park is defined by this dramatic warp in the earth's surface. The west side of the fold is 7,000 feet higher than the east side, thanks to a major geological event that took place about 60 million years ago: Mountains emerged and reactivated an ancient fault, sending the east side of the fold down while seesawing the west side skyward.

The resulting awe-inspiring formation is not actually a reef but is rather a ridge of limestone that once existed in an ocean. Waterpocket Fold is one of the world's largest and finest monoclinal flexures. In these unusual places, earth's crust has buckled upward. Early pioneers, who were not geologists, called any rocky barrier to their travel a reef, and this reef's sheer cliffs, which are nearly 1,000 feet high in some places, blocked the east-west travel in this region for decades.

Peering into the Past

Over the centuries, the exposed edges of the uplift have eroded into a slickrock

Southern Utah
Established December 18, 1971
375 square miles

Things to See: *Cathedral Valley; Freemont River; Temple of the Sun Rock Formation; Waterpocket Fold; Behunin Cabin; Historic Gifford Homestead; Fruita Rural Historic District*

Things to Do: *Camping; Hiking; Backpacking; Rock climbing; Horseback riding; Fishing*

What's Nearby? *Glen Canyon National Recreation Area; Bryce Canyon National Park; Natural Bridges National Monument; Canyonlands National Park; Cedar Breaks National Monument; Rainbow Bridge National Monument; Arches National Park; Hovenweep National Monument; Zion National Park*

Left: *Centered on the massive Waterpocket Fold, the geology of the park is notably diverse. Rugged and undulating grey slopes offer a contrast to the red and white sandstone of Capitol Reef itself.* Opposite top: *Capitol Reef National Park's geology is marked by countless buttresses and outcroppings left behind when softer sandstone eroded away, leaving behind harder red Wingate sandstone and other tough material.* Opposite bottom: *Cathedral Valley, one of the most scenic areas in this spectacular park, attracts the lion's share of park visitors to the 60-mile loop drive that passes such formations as Glass Mountain and Temple of the Sun.*

wilderness that encompasses most of the park's scenic splendors. Layer upon layer of brightly colored sandstone is cut by deep, serpentine canyons or eroded into natural bridges or massive domes. The eons of erosion created basins, known as *waterpockets,* all over the surface of the fold.

At Capitol Reef, some 10,000 feet of sedimentary layers are exposed, representing about 200 million years. Rocks as old as 280 million years populate the lowest strata, well below the park's youngest rocks, which are a mere 80 million years old. Each layer represents a different chapter in the area's environmental history, from its undersea era to rivers and swamps to deserts. Looking a bit out of place, black basalt boulders dot the otherwise red and tan canyon floors as well as assorted mesas and plateaus throughout the park, the result of landslides and subsequent "debris flows" in the Fremont River and its tributaries.

While it has been much more accessible to the general public since a paved road

arrived in the 1960s, the park is in such a remote corner of the Colorado Plateau that the nearest traffic light is about 80 miles away. But for centuries, Capitol Reef has been known as a place of dramatic beauty that has drawn visitors to gaze at its wonders or reap its bounty. Ancient petroglyphs, often figures of bighorn sheep and other animals, were cut into rock walls by people who inhabited this area more than 700 years ago. The people who carved these figures once plowed fields in the

central area of today's park, where towering cliffs contrast with a green oasis along the Fremont River.

In the 19th century, Mormon pioneers farmed and planted orchards in the valley, leaving behind the roughly 2,600 apple, peach, and apricot trees that are still there to this day. (Modern park visitors can even pick fruit during harvest season for a nominal fee.) In the 1920s, Ephraim Portman Pectol earned the nickname "The Father of Capitol Reef National Monument" by promoting what is now the national park as "Wayne Wonderland"—named for the park's home county—and organizing a local club for support. Pectol, in fact, personally contacted President Franklin D. Roosevelt in 1933 to lobby for the creation of a national monument. Four years later, Pectol's favored name was jettisoned but his vision realized when Roosevelt set aside nearly

40,000 acres as Capitol Reef National Monument. President Lyndon B. Johnson added more than 200,000 more acres to the monument as he left office in 1968, and Congress in 1971 passed legislation granting Capitol Reef its national park status.

Fremont Art and Architecture

The Fremont River runs through the center of Capitol Reef. It was here several hundred years ago that the Fremont people arrived and flourished in the river's canyon. From A.D. 700 to about 1300, the Fremont people roamed through modern-day Utah and its neighboring states. What happened to the Fremont, no one really knows for sure. Modern researchers do know that, instead of being killed off in one fell swoop, the culture seems to have dwindled from the year 1300 to nonexistence in 1500. Scientists believe that disruptions in trading patterns, small-time warfare, and the movement of neighboring tribes all contributed to the slow decline of this dynamic people.

The Fremont thrived on hunting and gathering and were spread all throughout the Utah area of today. They were not, however, nomadic, having agricultural systems in place to tide them over through bad hunting seasons. They lived very much with the land, building housing to suit their needs in the varying landscapes and seasons. Some used the towering rocks and caves for shelter, while others built huts, and still others dug into the cool ground and built roofs over the pits for shelter.

Likely stemming from their religious life, the Fremont people had a deep sense of art. Great skill can be seen in the humanoid clay figures they made, particularly in the detail of the faces and the artifacts on the figures, such as lavish necklaces and earrings. These skills extended to elaborate basket weaving with regional fibers, including yucca, willow, and milkweed. The Fremont also made pottery from gray clays with smooth surfaces on

the inside for cooking and storing food. These were often decorated with pinch patterns on the outside.

The most visible relics of the Fremont people, however, are the *petroglyphs* still to be enjoyed at the park today. Petroglyphs are figures carved into the rock (unlike pictographs, which are painted). The Fremont petroglyphs show figures with human bodies and animal heads, as well as other figures that are purely human or purely animal. These figures can represent any number of things, including religious or mythological information, hunting parties, food storage information, and much more. Not a lot is known about the exact meanings of the glyphs, but one thing is certain—they were more than just art to the Fremont. Because of these artifacts, the park has one important rule: Do not touch! As the years go by, erosion can happen from wind, rain, or simple carelessness. So much of the culture has been lost already, to lose more would be tragic.

Park Landmarks

The last year-round residents left the park in the early 1960s, but cattle drives through its boundaries still bring back the feeling of frontier days. In the southern end of the park, wilderness trails wind through places with poetic names such as Muley Twist Canyon. This path is so narrow that, in pioneer days, mules had to slither through the canyon walls. In various other parts the pioneers descriptively dubbed the terrain Poverty Flat, Fern's Nipple, Tarantula Mesa, and Dogwater Creek.

To the north, the unforgettable Cathedral Valley reveals eroded spires of Entrada sandstone that rise 50 stories from the valley floor. Here, a narrow four-wheel-drive road loops among stark and bizarre forma-

A balanced rock perches precariously on a sandstone pillar in the Hartnet Draw. As the red sandstone is eroding more rapidly than the rock, the formation will inevitably collapse.

tions with such names as the Walls of Jericho and the Temple of the Sun. The Entrada sandstone formations feature nearly horizontal layers, much different than the skewed strata closer to the center of the park. Many of these reddish towers are capped with the green sandstone of the Curtis Formation. More recent erosion has created Gypsum Sinkhole and Glass Mountain, and a volcanic period just a few million years ago also left its mark on the valley.

Sometimes lucky park visitors encounter a herd of desert bighorn sheep. The last sighting of a native bighorn was in 1948; park officials believe that the animals disappeared because of diseases transmitted by domesticated sheep. The park's staff reintroduced the desert bighorn in 1984, and the animals have since established several populations on park land.

Beyond the bighorn, Capitol Reef is a bird-watcher's paradise, with numerous different habitats attracting both migratory and nonmigratory species. From loons, grebes, and pelicans to bald eagles, peregrine falcons, and great horned owls, the variety in Capitol Reef's feathered and winged population is just about endless. Numerous mammals—including shrews, bats, badgers, black bears, and mountain lions—also live

here, as do several fish, amphibian, and reptile species. Plant life is sparse in the red-rock canyons, with numerous federally endangered species found in the park.

The modern-day Capitol Reef biosphere is radically different than what it was in epochs past. Fossils preserved in various layers range from cyanobacteria, which proves that the desert here was wetter than the Sahara, to fin marks left by ancient fish. Many predinosaur reptiles also thrived in the region during the early Triassic period.

Fringed by cottonwood trees, the Fremont River courses through a gorge of layered sandstone.

Today, the layers of past millennia are exposed like open chapters of a long history book. The dynamic geological processes that shaped the stirring panoramas of Capitol Reef National Park still sculpt the land today at a nearly imperceptible rate. This snapshot today is certain to shift and evolve in the future: As has been proven here over and over again, nothing in this world is permanent.

Carlsbad Caverns National Park

Every sunset on summer evenings, in a corner of the Guadalupe Mountains in southeastern New Mexico, a dark cloud swirls out of the ground and rises into the dusk. What at first appears to be a ghostly tornado is actually 400,000 bats flying out of an immense opening in the earth. The bats fan out over an area 100 miles wide, catching and devouring flying insects. At dawn they return to their subterranean home.

This nightly exodus of Brazilian free-tailed bats led to the modern rediscovery of Carlsbad Caverns around 1900. This great cave system—consisting of 300 separate rooms—comprises one of the largest caverns in the world. The size and boldness of its huge vaulted underground chambers are truly awesome. The cave contains formations of such startling shapes and colors, and of such monumental proportions, that country humorist Will Rogers called this underground wonderland "the Grand Canyon with a roof over it" when he visited the park in 1931.

People have known about the spectacular caverns of Carlsbad Caverns National Park for thousands of years. According to archaeological evidence, nomadic hunters and gatherers used the cave's enormous mouth for shelter. Apparently, however, they didn't penetrate far inside. Shortly after its turn-of-the-century rediscovery, miners began excavating the cave for its huge deposits of bat guano, which were shipped to Southern California for use as a fertilizer in citrus groves.

One miner, a young local man named James Larkin White, was so intrigued by the cave that he undertook a serious exploration of the labyrinthine caverns beyond Bat Cave. His passionate interest in the cave garnered the publicity that helped establish Carlsbad Caverns as a national monument in 1923 and a national park seven years later. White served as its chief ranger.

Southeast New Mexico
Established May 14, 1930
73 square miles

Things to See: *Bat Caves; Giant Dome; King's Palace; Big Room; Hall of the White Giant; Spider Cave; Guadalupe Mountains*

Things to Do: *Caving; Hiking; Back Country Camping; Bat viewing*

What's Nearby? *Guadalupe Mountains National Park; White Sands National Monument; Fort Davis National Historic Site*

The full extent of the caverns has still not been fully explored. To date, approximately 30 miles have been investigated and mapped. Three of the most spectacular miles, which include the great vaulted chambers known as the King's Palace, the Queen's Chamber, and the Green Lake Room, are open to park visitors. Throughout the caverns there is a profusion of multicolored rock formations, such as Iceberg, Boneyard, and Rock of Ages, that owe their startling hues to iron oxide deposits.

Origins

The same escarpment that forms the Guadalupe Mountains also spawned Carlsbad Caverns. Over

Carlsbad Caverns' Natural Entrance provides entrée to self-guided tours, allowing park visitors to discover the cave at their own pace and level of comfort.

A variety of limestone formations can be found in Carlsbad Caverns. Hanging from the ceiling in Doll's Theater are soda straws, so called because their width never changes from end to end.

time, fractures in the limestone sedimentation appeared, allowing mineral-laden water to cut through rock and form the caverns. The cave's stunning interior decoration is also the work of limestone-carrying water. Over millennia, dripping water has built a nearly unbelievable array of formations: Some are six stories tall; others are as delicate as lace.

The process by which a cave forms, which is known as *speleogenesis,* typically depends on rainwater flowing downward through the limestone, cutting open chambers, and creating stalactites and stalagmites. The creation of Carlsbad Caverns and the adjacent caves in the Guadalupe Mountains is unique, as it also involves the

upward flow of underground springs rich in hydrogen sulfide. The rainwater and the spring water mixed and formed sulfuric acid, which proved especially effective at speleogenesis. The caves in the park were formed between four million and six million years ago, as this phenomenon has long since ceased in this area.

The Giant Dome and Twin Domes stalagmites are just a few of the many sights to be found in the Big Room.

so tall that you could build a 30-story building inside it. Below the Big Room, at the 830-foot level, are other large rooms: the King's Palace, with its statuesque stalagmites, and the lovely Queen's Chamber, with rock that seems to flow like draperies.

Such stalagmites and other cavern formations are known as *speleothems.* Besides the well-known stalagmites and stalactites, other speleothems in Carlsbad Caverns include soda straws,

When you ride an elevator into the depths of Carlsbad Caverns or walk down well-made trails into the cave, remember that the first visitors descended into the caverns in guano buckets lowered by pulleys. Tours used to begin in the uppermost of the cave's three largest chambers, the Bat Cave, but this area is now closed to everyone except the bats—as their numbers have plummeted in recent decades.

Size Matters

At a level 750 feet below the surface, the Hall of the Giants contains the cavern's biggest stalagmites: the Rock of Ages, the

Giant Dome, and the Twin Domes. These monster monoliths seem to be straining toward the great vaulted ceiling hundreds of feet above them. On this level you can also tour the Boneyard, which is filled with structures that only slightly resemble bones, and Iceberg Rock, by conservative estimates a 100,000-ton hunk of stone.

Dwarfing every other room within Carlsbad Caverns is the Big Room, the largest known underground cavity in the Western Hemisphere. This immense, aptly named chamber is about 1,800 feet long and up to 1,100 feet wide. It is so vast that it could contain more than a dozen football fields; it is

ribbons, flowstone, lily pads, and shelves. All of these are the result of water dripping into the cave and evaporating, leaving behind calcite that gradually solidifies into a formation. Today, such activity has stopped—at least for the time being. The surface climate's shift from wet to dry in the last few million years is responsible for the slowdown in speleothem formation.

The park's most-visited rooms merely scratch the surface of Carlsbad Caverns' subterranean world. Until recently, Lechuguilla Cave was thought to be an insignificant dead-end cavern system in the park's backcountry. In 1986, a group of spelunkers from Colorado made a breakthrough, discovering large walking passages below rubble that stretched into a serpentine, 120-mile network of caves. Not only did Lechuguilla Cave prove vast, it also offered an entirely new bounty of geology and biology to study. The former group included unique gypsum formations that looked like hair, rock balloons, and iridescent globes known as cave pearls. The novel life forms that find habitat in Lechuguilla Cave are thought to include heat-loving thermophiles, rock-eating bacteria, and other microbes. However, park officials have designated this cave off-limits to casual visitors—only scientists and surveyors are allowed.

Living Below Ground

Besides the bats that roost there, the underground world of Carlsbad Caverns offers habitat for a number of dark-loving crustaceans, insects, centipedes, spiders, and other invertebrates. Cave crickets, like the bats, leave the caves nightly in search of food. In this behavior, the cave crickets provide a link of outside sustenance for the food chain of full-time cave dwellers.

On the surface, the Chihuahuan Desert—an entirely different ecosystem—is home to a wide range of plant and animal life, including spadefoot toads, rattlesnakes, javelina, numerous rodents, and elk. The surface area of the park also has a wide range of plants, especially cacti, as well as vast patches of living earth, also known as microphytic crust, comprised of symbiotic strains of algae, fungi, lichens, and mosses.

While hiking and camping are popular above-ground activities, the park is naturally focused on what's below the surface.

The self-guided tours of Carlsbad Caverns include routes that traverse the Big Room and the Natural Entrance's Main Corridor (which descends 750 feet to the Big Room). Rangers also offer more diehard visitors a number of guided cave tours that often require crawling on one's belly through a narrow opening—those suffering from claustrophobia should not apply. But for the adventurous, these expeditions offer a glimpse into a subterranean world that few people ever see.

The Bats of Carlsbad Caverns

For many Americans, the idea of bats conjures up images of blood-sucking vampires; nights in haunted castles; and dark, foreboding places. While the last of these may have some truth to it, bats for the most part get the short end of the stick when it comes to animal reputations. In many Asian cultures, bats are seen as symbols of good luck, similar to ladybugs in America, thanks to their beneficial roles in consuming insects that might otherwise damage crops.

Scientists believe that bats first came to Carlsbad Caverns about 17,000 years ago, calling the vaulted ceilings of the upper chambers home long before the first known humans came around to bother them. The number of bats that fly in and out of Carlsbad nightly varies based on everything from the time to the weather and the season. They go wherever their search for food takes them. Bats are incredibly helpful as a natural means of controlling insect populations. One hundred thousand bats can eat up to 1,000 pounds of insects every night.

The Brazilian free-tailed bats in Carlsbad Caverns eat up to half their body weight in insects nightly. In fact, pregnant and lactating females may eat up to 100 percent of their body weight! Insect activity is at its peak during the spring, summer, and fall, which means that this is when bats will be found in the park. Of the 17 different varieties that live in Carlsbad Caverns National Park, three roost in the cave. Other species stay in trees or bushes, nabbing crop-damaging insects at nearly 10,000 feet.

During these seasons, every evening at dusk, the Brazilian free-tailed bats perform their most famous feat against the setting sun: All 400,000 of Carlsbad's bats exit the cave in one spectacular streaming cloud in search of food. This happens at a time called civil twilight, 28 minutes after sunset, which means that the precise time of departure differs from day to day. It's a mystery to scientists why the bats choose that time to leave as one.

What scientists do know, however, is that the bats are extremely sensitive to their environment and to human activity. If average observers think that the sight of 400,000 bats flying as one is impressive, they should take the time to imagine what an outflight must have looked like when 12 million bats called the caverns home. Over the years, due to the increased use of insecticide, the bat population has dropped drastically, leaving some of the caverns' oldest inhabitants a shadow of what they once had been.

Channel Islands National Park

Blue whales absolutely love the Santa Barbara Channel, less than 100 miles northwest of one of the biggest cities in the world, Los Angeles.

For human passengers crossing the channel on the ferry to Channel Islands National Park, blue whale encounters are not uncommon. In fact, this is one of the best places on the planet to spot these huge beasts, the largest animals on earth, as they languidly crest on the ocean's waves, revealing an empathic eye, a spouting blowhole, then at last their trademark tail. About 2,000 of the endangered cetaceans roam the waters of the northeastern Pacific, perhaps a third of the world's total.

The statistics, delivered via the boat's loudspeaker, are amazing. A blue whale's heart is the size of a Volkswagen Beetle. They can swallow a swimming pool in a single gulp. An individual whale can weigh more than 300,000 pounds.

All this information, and the boat hasn't even reached the dock yet.

Only 90 minutes by boat from the beaches of Southern California is the aptly named Arch Rock, a 40-foot semicircle jutting out of the Pacific off Anacapa Island and the de facto gateway to the Channel Islands. The national park comprises the five northernmost islands of this eight-island chain.

The chain's four largest and northernmost islands—San Miguel, Santa Rosa, Santa Cruz, and Anacapa—are two to five miles apart, and the fifth, Santa Barbara, is about 30 miles to the southeast. These comprise the park. The chain also includes the famous Santa Catalina Island as well as the lesser known San Clemente and San Nicolas. While most of Catalina remains undeveloped, it is not part of the national park.

The islands are strung like great peaks of a range lost long ago to the relentless sea, and are in fact remnants of ancient mountains that once were the western extension of the Santa Monica Mountains. Today, only the eroded peaks of the range rise above the ocean, but the same geologic upheaval that created the mountains on the mainland

Seals and sea lions use this part of Anacapa Island for breeding areas and nurseries. As a result, the nearby waters attract some of the largest great white sharks in the world.

Off the Southern California coast
Established March 5, 1980
390 square miles

Things to See: *Anacapa Island; Santa Cruz Island; Santa Rosa Island; San Miguel Island; Santa Barbara Island; Arch Rock*

Things to Do: *Hiking; Snorkeling; Kayaking; Scuba diving; Boating; Camping*

What's Nearby? *Santa Monica Mountains Natural Recreation Area; Joshua Tree National Park; Cabrillo National Monument*

Wildflowers surround this lighthouse, which warns recreational and commercial vessels away from the deadly reefs and offshore shoals. Not all craft have navigated the area successfully.

water surrounding the islands is the territory of a number of species of dolphins, porpoises, and whales—including blues, grays, and the occasional pod of orcas.

These waters are home to vast undersea kelp forests that provide habitat for numerous other plants and animals. These forests grow at depths up to 100 feet, attached to the floor in a rootlike structure, with a dense green canopy of kelp fronds above. Among the denizens of the kelp forests is the enormous black sea bass, topping out at seven feet and 700 pounds, as well as California spiny lobsters, rockfish, sea cucumbers,

was also responsible for the islands. It takes little imagination to picture their bases on the seafloor, surrounded by foothills and valleys.

America's Galapagos

About half a million years ago, violent and extensive earthquakes gradually separated the islands from the mainland; over time, wind and water eroded them to the outcroppings of today. Thanks to this separation, distinct branches of the evolutionary tree are represented in the island's keenly adapted plant and animal populations—biologists have nicknamed the Channel Islands "America's Galapagos." Many of the park's furred and feathered denizens are smaller than their counterparts on the mainland. There are only 23 vertebrate species on the five islands, but many of them are distinct subspecies on each of the islands where they are found. The island fox is smaller than any other North American canid, weighing in at a mere five pounds, the size of a typical housecat. Both the island fox and the island deer mouse have evolved into unique subspecies on each island.

Beaches, rocky harbors, and inlets provide a habitat for a wide range of aquatic wildlife. A marine sanctuary extends for six nautical miles around each island, protecting habitat for thousands of species of fish and marine mammals, as well as many unusual marine plants. The seaweed here can seem like a multihued carpet on the sea floor, with sea anemones nesting together in small colonies that resemble wildflower beds. The

and sea urchins. Because they are at the confluence of warm South Pacific water and cooler water from the north, the kelp forests are home to an unusually diverse undersea menagerie.

While snorkelers and divers get a good look at the landscape under the sea, sea kayaking is the true sport of choice in Channel Islands National Park. The islands' coasts are dotted with sea caves, including Painted Cave on Santa Cruz Island, one of the world's largest. But these caves are dangerous places, and every year brings reports of accidents involving kayakers get-

ting caught in a cave as it is deluged by a powerful wave.

Like the caves, the park's tidepools exist in a state between sea and land. They can be found along the craggy shoreline of the islands, and each is a bustling little eco-system. Occupying a space known as the intertidal zone, these pools are recharged with frothy saltwater twice a day, and are full of starfish, sponges, periwinkles, crabs, barnacles, and limpets.

But Channel Islands National Park is perhaps most renowned for its pinnipeds, better known as seals and sea lions. Point

Bennett, the westernmost tip of San Miguel Island, attracts hundreds of thousands of pinnipeds to breed throughout the year. Visitors who make the boat trip (and hike) in June get to see hulking sea lions give birth to their young while vying for space on the rocks with the huge northern elephant seals.

Of the five islands that comprise Channel Islands National Park, Anacapa Island is the closest to the California coast, just 12 miles from the harbor in Ventura.

The Sinking of the *Winfield Scott*

The trip across the United States in the 1800s took longer than most Americans can imagine traveling today. From New York to San Francisco, the voyage was set in three stages—one steamboat from New York to Panama; a one-month waiting period in Panama when, in the days before there was a Panama Canal, travelers would cross overland from the Atlantic to the Pacific; and then another steamboat to San Francisco. To go back required the same itinerary in reverse order. To shorten an already lengthy trip on the Pacific side, experienced captains would often cut through Santa Barbara Channel, the thin stretch of water between California and the islands, instead of going around the islands. In this part of the world, the weather was fickle and the way was narrow, with shallow reefs and small islands making for treacherous sailing.

On December 1, 1853, the *Winfield Scott* set sail from San Francisco carrying more than 300 passengers, mail (a very precious commodity in those days), and more than $1 million in gold. Fog crept over Santa Barbara Channel on December 2. Even so, Captain Simon F. Blunt had traveled the way many times and did not think himself in danger of striking the islands. Perhaps it was that confidence that did him in—he turned too soon and hit Anacapa Island at full force. All passengers were saved either on long boats or by other passing ships, but the *Winfield Scott* itself was lost.

It is estimated that at least 33 ships went down in the Santa Barbara Channel in the last half of the 19th century. Visitors to the islands can still snorkel or dive the *Winfield Scott* and other wrecks today. They should, however, be warned: Most of the valuables have long since been rescued. Even if something attractive does catch their eye, it is illegal to "salvage" anything from the site, so treasure hunters will have to find somewhere else to dig.

Just off the coast of Santa Rosa Island are the rusted remains of the shipwrecked Chickasaw, *a freighter full of children's toys that ran aground here in 1962.*

Coming and Going

Many of the islands' animal populations are migratory. In the spring, double-crested cormorants, brown pelicans, pigeon guillemots, surfbirds, and oystercatchers prowl along the coast. Each December, great gray whales stop by the islands on their annual trip south. The great blue whales are less predictable but can most often be seen in the park's waters in the summertime.

Always a sanctuary for wildlife on both land and the surrounding sea, the islands were inhabited many thousands of years ago by the Island Chumash people, who left behind a cooking pit that still contains the burned bones of a pygmy mammoth. How people and mammoths got to the islands remains something of a mystery—the theory on the latter is that they swam while humans probably took some kind of boats—but it happened quite some time ago. The oldest human remains found in North America—dated at 13,000 years old—were unearthed on Santa Rosa Island in 1960. On Santa Cruz Island, there are also remnants of villages built by later inhabitants.

Spanish explorers claimed the Channel Islands in the 16th century. The territory fell under Mexican rule in 1821 and then that of the United States in 1850. Each of the islands that now comprise the park was used for sheep and cattle ranching in subsequent years. The remnants of Scorpion Ranch on Santa Cruz Island provide an interesting glimpse into this period in history. The islands were under the control of the U.S. Coast Guard, Army, Navy, and Air Force later in the 20th century. The establishment of Channel Islands National Monument in 1938 included only Anacapa and Santa Barbara islands, but the creation of Channel Islands National Park in 1980 included the three remaining islands and made for a focus on conservation over other interests.

The nonprofit Nature Conservancy owns 75 percent of Santa Cruz Island, the largest in the park, and public access is limited. The aforementioned Scorpion Ranch left its mark on the park land in the form of feral hogs and sheep, which were eradicated because of their negative effect on the park's grasses. Overgrazing by the sheep led to erosion and loss of cover for the island fox, which were increasingly targeted by predators—namely golden eagles—and saw their numbers plummet by more than 90 percent in the 1990s.

Becoming and Staying Green

The path to ecological recovery is tricky: The fox's nemesis, the nonnative golden eagle, owes its dominance here to the decline of the bald eagle, Channel Island natives that were largely wiped out by the pesticide DDT by the 1950s. Bald eagles don't hunt island foxes like golden eagles do, so the replacement of golden eagles with bald eagles has proven to help boost the park's island fox populations. The removal of the feral livestock that once ravaged the islands' foliage has also helped.

The difficulty of restoring an ecosystem to its original state has thus emerged as the prime modern narrative of the Channel Islands, with their longer-standing status as America's Galapagos in danger if the island fox and other unique species become extinct. But there is hope for the future: The park's island fox population, which once numbered in the thousands before crashing to just 15 in the late 1990s, is on the rebound. With most of the golden eagles having been transplanted to Northern California and the feral sheep long gone, there are now hundreds of foxes in the park.

With the resurgence of the island fox comes proof that the mistakes of the past can be undone, but only at a high price and numerous unintended consequences. In Channel Islands National Park, there is a lesson to be learned about ecological balance: It's much easier to keep a scale balanced than it is to fix a broken scale.

Arch Rock, at the far eastern end of Anacapa Island, is one of the first sights visitors to Channel Islands National Park experience when arriving by boat.

Congaree National Park

South Carolina's rivers once were bordered by more than one million acres of old-growth bottomland hardwood forests, which, in fact, blanketed almost 30 million acres across the Southeast. Now almost all of the old growth forest that's left in the United States is preserved by Congaree National Park.

Congaree contains a majestic and complex combination of hardwood floodplain forest, vast forest canopy, swamp, and uplands area. The 22,200-acre park is one of the globe's best remaining examples of a mature forested southern floodplain. It contains hundreds of types of plants, as well as 41 mammal, 53 reptile or amphibian, 52 fish, and 175 bird species, including eight species of woodpeckers—even the endangered red-cockaded woodpecker. South Carolinians have long called Congaree, formerly the Congaree Swamp National Monument, their state's best-kept secret. "The Congaree is our most under-utilized national treasure," said South Carolina's Senator Ernest Hollings in 2003 testimony on the legislation that led to Congaree's elevation to national park status. "Many people outside my state have never heard of it, and when they do they think it is a nasty swamp with a bunch of standing water. So Americans are missing out on a majestic hardwood forest that has more types of trees, plants, animals, and birds than a person will see in a lifetime," the senator added.

While many of Congaree National Park's record-sized trees fell in Hurricane Hugo in 1989, the park remains the home of huge sweetgum, oak, loblolly pine, and bald cypress trees.

About 135,000 visitors per year see Congaree National Park, many more than in its days as a national monument. But that number still places the gorgeous park and its canopied hardwood forests, one of the world's highest natural canopies, in the category of "under-discovered gem."

Tales of the Swamp

Senator Hollings certainly was correct about the Congaree swamps having a wholly undeserved image problem outside of South

Carolina. Take the case of one of the state's most famous figures, Brigadier General Francis Marion, the "Swamp Fox" of the American Revolution. Marion became a folk hero for many reasons, including a 1959–61 TV series based on his exploits; but his fame primarily rests on historians' agreement that he was one of the inventors of guerrilla warfare. In 1776, Marion commanded an irregular group of militiamen, "Marion's Men," who often supplied their own food, arms, and horses and fought without pay. Marion's forces often fought the British by surprise attacks and then losing pursuers in the maze of paths through the swamps.

And all of this is true, it seems, except for the fact that swamps of South Carolina are dry for much of the year. Or, to be more precise, they're not really swamps. The glory of the area is its old-growth floodplain forest. The Congaree River indeed does overflow its channel and flood—about ten times each year and most frequently in February. At those times, the floodplain turns swampy, spreading nutrient-rich sediments around the forest floor. In any case, it appears that General Marion, the Swamp Fox, knew there was more to the region than the swamps that so well protected him: There were also the trees. "I look at the venerable trees around me and I know that I must not dishonor them," he wrote in his journal.

The Congaree River has this particular ecosystem because much of South Carolina is a great watershed. The Congaree River is formed in South Carolina's Richland County with the confluence of the Saluda and Broad rivers. The Saluda and the Broad drain 8,032 square miles of northwest South

Carolina and western North Carolina. About 60 miles downstream, the Congaree joins the Wateree River to form the Santee River. Flooding almost monthly, the Congaree River twists and turns so actively, it sometimes doubles back on itself, forming a river bend called an oxbow. One oxbow is Weston Lake, located due north of the park near the South Carolina state capital, Columbia. A former bend in the river, Weston Lake now sits two and a half miles from the Congaree.

A Tough Area to Develop

The river region was inhabited by ancient people who fished its waters and hunted its forests. Later, the area's first regular residents were the Congaree, who were noted by Spanish explorer Hernando de Soto when he reconnoitered the region in 1540. Smallpox destroyed the Congaree by the mid-18th

Central South Carolina
Established November 10, 2003
35 square miles

Things to See: *Cedar Creek; Congaree River; Boardwalk Trail; Congaree River Blue Trail*

Things to Do: *Boating; Hiking; Fishing; Camping; Canoeing; Kayaking*

What's Nearby? *Ninety Six National Historic Site; Charles Pinckney National Historic Site; Fort Moultrie National Monument; Fort Sumter National Monument; Kings Mountain National Military Park; Cowpens National Battlefield*

Congaree's lion's mane mushroom—also known as bearded tooth mushroom, hedgehog mushroom, and the pom pom mushroom—illustrates the lush vegetable life that flourishes under the park's canopy of trees.

A path leads visitors through a stand of oak in a Congaree forest. The park hosts the United States' largest remaining old-growth bottomland hardwood forest.

their final chance to save the last portion of old-growth hardwoods forest that remained. Together with the Sierra Club, residents convinced Congress in 1976 to designate the area Congaree Swamp National Monument. In 1983 the national monument was designated an International Biosphere Reserve.

The next major stage in park history was not an act of Congress but a devastating act of nature, Hurricane Hugo. In September 1989 Hugo smashed the Congaree forests, including numerous national champion trees, such as the national champion Shumardoak. A 1996 arboreal survey identified four national and 19 South Carolina state record trees remaining within the park—it recorded more than 150 trees larger than 12 feet in circumference, with great specimens of sweetgum, oak, loblolly pine, bald cypress, and other huge trees remaining.

Perhaps paradoxically, the apparent disaster led to new life for the forest. With its famous canopies torn and punctured by the hurricane, sunlight streamed over all those forest-floor nutrients, and a vital new generation of forest began growing. The year 2001 was huge for Congaree: The monument area was designated a Globally Important Bird Area, its Harry Hampton Visitor Center was dedicated, and the 25th anniversary of Congaree Swamp National Monument was celebrated. In November 2003, President George W. Bush signed the bill designating Congaree National Park the nation's 57th national park.

Varying Terrain

Like other Southern cities such as Raleigh, North Carolina; Richmond, Virginia; and

century. White settlers quickly began looking for ways to farm the swampy land, but success was elusive, and they quit in droves.

In the early 20th century, loggers attempted to cut the river region's mighty bald cypress trees, but they too were frustrated by the inaccessibility of the Congaree floodplain and left within a decade. More than 50 years after that, in the 1960s, lumber prices had soared to the point that private landowners wanted to have another go at logging. But South Carolinians knew that the area represented

Washington, D.C., Columbia is built on the *fall line,* the transition zone between the granite rocks of the Piedmont and the sedimentary deposits of the Coastal Plain. The fall line is where bedrock waterfalls in river channels vanish in favor of straight, rocky river channels with rapids. Below the fall line, rivers flowing over the coastal plain broaden and bend back and forth as they flow. The fall line in question crosses the Congaree River in Columbia, where the scenery can change from rock outcrops in the river to riverbanks of coastal vegetation in just a few blocks.

Favorite ways to see the park are by foot or by canoe. Most parkland here is hardly ever traveled, by foot or by water, but a limited part of the park offers six hiking trails totaling 18 miles. The Boardwalk Loop at Congaree National Park, a boardwalk raised about eight feet off the ground, takes travelers about two and a half miles through hardwood forests roughly three miles from the Congaree River. The loop floods over every few years. Cedar Creek offers a marked canoe trail, but the Congaree River Blue Trail is the canoeing king. The Blue Trail is a 50-mile designated recreational paddling trail extending from Columbia downstream to Congaree National Park. Paddlers begin with an urban adventure experience, canoe on to encounter the wandering river and its countless sandbars, and then discover the handsome high bluffs and floodplain habitats of Congaree National Park. There, canoeists usually put down their paddles and either hike, camp, fish, bird-watch, or simply enjoy nature in the beautiful, often underestimated, park.

The Sierra Club Puts Grass Roots in the Swamp

The Sierra Club has been an integral part of the American conservation movement for well over 100 years. In fact, it's the oldest and largest grassroots organization in the United States. Formed by John Muir and Joseph LeConte in the late 1800s, the club inspired members to rally around the idea of coming together to celebrate and preserve the beauty of nature. Early in the club's inception, great numbers of scientists flocked to it, often to help explore the uncharted wilderness and conduct scientific studies in remote locations.

Over the years, millions more joined the scientists in delighting in the parks system that the Sierra Club eventually helped to create and expand. One artist, especially, became the visual spokesperson for the Sierra Club and everything it stood for. Ansel Adams signed on as the official club photographer, using his talents to reach out to those who had never before been  able to experience the natural splendors of America. By connecting with everyday folk, the club was able to spread its roots that much further.

Not only was it able to begin charting efforts, the club became involved politically, first using its large and diverse membership base to oppose a bill that reduced the boundaries of Yosemite National Park, and later discovering the awesome power of grassroots planning. The Sierra Club continued to grow and expand, using its sway in support of bills introducing the Grand Canyon and Mount Rainier for consideration as national parks.

More recently, the club negotiated a victory for Congaree. In 1969 prices in the logging industry were beginning to rise. A major effort was put forth to allow logging in the old-growth forest of the Congaree area. The Sierra Club was there to help organize the community, not only keeping logging efforts at bay, but establishing Congaree as a national monument. This paved the way to national park status.

Though originally founded to "make mountains glad," the club has been extending happiness to lowlands and highlands alike for decades—and will continue to do so for decades to come.

Crater Lake National Park

Southern Oregon's Crater Lake National Park, centered on the idyllic blue lake of its namesake, is one of the grandest sights on the continent. There is little in the lake's surroundings, however, that prepares the visitor for the most sublime panorama of the Cascade Mountains. After approaching the lake on a road that gradually rises, twisting and turning its way up the side of a mountain clothed in forests of Shasta red fir, hemlock, and pine, the pavement plunges downward into a great basin, and there is the vast and mirrorlike surface of Crater Lake, 25 square miles of water so blue that it looks like India ink, circled by steep slopes, mountains, and great cliffs that form a vast natural amphitheater.

Several natural features add to the spectacle of this remarkable lake. The Phantom Ship is an island made of lava, with 160-foot-high ridges and peaks that resemble an ancient sailing ship. Discovery Point is the place where, on June 12, 1853, a band of prospectors looking for gold first gazed on the lake. Hillman Peak is a 70,000-year-old volcanic cone, named for one of the prospectors, and Wizard Island is a volcanic cinder cone that rises about 700 feet above

Southwestern Oregon
Established May 22, 1902
285 square miles

Things to See: *Crater Lake; Wizard Island; Phantom Ship; Mount Scott; Watchman Overlook*

Things to Do: *Hiking; Backcountry camping; Boating*

What's Nearby? *Winema National Forest; Rogue River National Forest; Umpqua National Forest; Oregon Caves National Monument; Lava Beds National Monument; Redwood National Park; John Day Fossil Beds National Monument*

Right: *The Pinnacles, accessible only during summer via a paved six-mile offshoot from Rim Drive, are eroded towers of hardened volcanic ash populating the banks of Sand and Wheeler creeks.* Opposite: *Wizard Island sits majestically in the striking blue expanse of Crater Lake, which owes the purity of its color to the pure snowmelt.*

the lake's surface. The name Wizard Island refers to the pointed hat worn by sorcerers, which it resembles, but there is also no doubt that plenty of magic exists in this stunningly beautiful place.

The Park's Beginnings

One of the lake's loveliest inlets, Steel Bay, was named in honor of William Gladstone Steel. Born in Ohio in 1854, Steel became intrigued by the lake from a newspaper article he read as a schoolboy. He finished high school in Oregon and went on his first trip to the lake in 1885. "Not a foot of land about the lake had been touched or claimed," Steel wrote after the trip. "An overmastering conviction came to me that this wonderful spot must be saved, wild and beautiful, just as it was, for all future generations."

After returning to Portland, Steel worked tirelessly to make Crater Lake a national park. He lobbied for 17 years and appealed to President Theodore Roosevelt. Finally, in 1902, the nation's sixth national park was created, more than 200 square miles of

wilderness with the lake as its centerpiece. Steel's work later contributed to the construction of Crater Lake Lodge (opened in 1915) and Rim Drive, which circumnavigates the lake (opened in 1918).

The distance from the surface of the lake to its bottom is 1,932 feet, which makes it the deepest lake in the United States. Water has accumulated here over centuries as rain and snowmelt filled in the huge caldera. Because no water flows into or out of the lake via streams or rivers, its waters contain

few minerals and almost no impurities. The lake's only fish, rainbow trout and kokanee salmon, were introduced by people.

On the lake's shores and the surrounding slopes, a wide range of different habitat attracts many different animals. Seasonal and year-round mammalian residents include elk—a summer herd grazes the meadows at the base of Union Peak—as well as black bears, wolverines, weasels, flying squirrels, pronghorn antelopes, and pikas. The bird checklist is even longer, including endangered peregrine falcons and bald eagles as well as lots of ducks, grebes, hawks, and owls. The park is also home to a surprising number of reptiles and amphibians specially adapted to the harsh winters and 500 inches of snow that blanket Crater Lake each year.

The Mystery Remains

Scientists today still do not fully understand the ecological character of the lake. Evidence of hydrothermal venting near the lake's bottom was discovered by manned submarines in 1989. This hot water may play an important role in the lake's ecology. Recently, scientists have found green algae, which requires sunlight, growing at a record depth of 725 feet. This indicates to scientists that the sun's rays may penetrate deeper in Crater Lake than in any other body of water in the world. The lake's purity and its depth also account for its startling blue color.

Issued by the U.S. Postal Service in 1934, 32 years after the establishment of Crater Lake National Park, this dark blue stamp's color was matched to that of the lake.

Geologists believe the story of the lake began long ago when a great 12,000-foot volcano called Mount Mazama formed as part of the Pacific Northwest chain of volcanoes that also includes Mount Shasta and nearby Mount St. Helens. Like all of the Cascade Mountains, the peak was built of lava flows, ash, and debris from repeated eruptions over the eons.

Klamath legends of quarrels between the deities of the sky and of the netherworld *(see sidebar)* have helped geologists construct a reasonably accurate timetable of the land, as the legends parallel Crater Lake's geological history. About 8,000 years ago, Mount Mazama erupted for the last time. This gigantic explosion catapulted volcanic ash and smoke miles into the air. After the blast, Mazama's peak remained as a shell over a hollow interior. Apparently, the ancestors of the native people who knew the legend of Mazama watched as the summit finally collapsed with a deafening roar. This geologic event created a huge smoldering caldera.

Klamath Creation Myths

The Klamath people of Crater Lake were one of four cultures that shared this area. While the others died away with the coming of outsiders, the Klamath culture survived. As a result, many of their stories of Crater Lake have survived as well.

Like other aboriginal religions, that of the Klamath had a few gods but was greatly animistic, which means that the Klamath believed spirits could inhabit natural objects such as rocks, trees, and bodies of water. Existing for many hundreds of years, the Klamath were present during the volcanic eruption that eventually formed what is now Crater Lake. Its creation had such a profound effect on the culture that the event soon found its way into Klamath legend.

The legend of Crater Lake began, as many such do, with a woman. The chief of the underworld, Llao, fell in love with the daughter of a Klamath chieftain. When the daughter spurned Llao, he became so angry that he tried to destroy all of the Klamath people with a rain of fire. Skell, the chief of the overworld, saw the merciless treatment of the humans and battled Llao on top of the mountain. This provides an understandable rationale for the great blasts and mighty eruptions the Klamath ancestors experienced. Finally, Skell of the overworld won the quarrel. He drove Llao back to his home under the mountain and then made it collapse on top of the underworld chief. Thus, says the legend, Crater Lake was formed.

Another legend tells of how Llao was tricked by Skell after a long-standing feud. Skell cut up Llao's body and fed it to the crawfish of the lake. Finally, he threw Llao's head into the lake, where it lodged only half-covered by water. Today, this is called Wizard Mountain. Llao Rock and Skell Head are two more lake landmarks that harken back to the Klamath war of the gods.

Other legends tell of spirit journeys made by the Klamath people to the lake. They believed that spirits lived under the vast waters and that swimming in these waters could bring spiritual understanding—understanding profound enough to make one a shaman. Given these tales, it's little wonder that Crater Lake became the spiritual center for the Klamath people.

Since that eruption, the Klamath have considered this remote lake a sacred spot. Many undertook the dangerous trek to the lake as a spiritual quest. Believing that godlike spirits lived in its waters, these searchers would swim in the lake under the cover of night in search of revelation. The floor of the lake was rumored to be a different world.

Opening to the Modern World

Crater Lake remained a secret of the Klamath people until white prospectors stumbled upon it in 1853, named it "Deep Blue Lake," and promptly continued their search for gold. Soon thereafter, Captain Clarence Dutton first surveyed the lake from the deck of the half-ton *Cleetwood,* estimating the deepest point at 1,996 feet. Dutton's estimate—conducted with a piece of pipe and a piano wire—proved very close to the modern sonar-based measurement of 1,932 feet, established in 1959.

Today Rim Drive and paved roads make the lake much easier to visit than it had been in the days of the Klamath vision quests. The landscape remains sacred, however, as ritual quests continue. Modern visitors to Crater Lake should pay heed to Klamath legend. This will always be a great spot for any person to go on a spiritual quest, as it has been for thousands of years.

Park godfather William Gladstone Steel shared a similar idea of the place. Four years before his passing in 1934, he was quoted as saying, "Plundering through this wilderness of sin and corruption, tasting of its wickedness, forgetting my duty to God and man, striving to catch bubbles of pleasure and the praise of men, guilty of many transgressions, I now look back on this, my 76th birthday, and my heart bounds with joy and gladness, for I realize that I have been the cause of opening up this wonderful lake for the pleasure of mankind." Reading these words, it seems Steel's own personal redemption came through the preservation of Crater Lake.

Finding purchase in the nutrient-rich volcanic debris, the lush forests below Crater Lake are perpetually wet, shrouded by some 500 inches of snow in the winter that barely have time to melt during the park's short summer.

Cuyahoga Valley National Park

Traveling Cuyahoga Valley National Park, which lies in Ohio almost equidistant between Akron and Cleveland, is an adventure in the park service's most urban-friendly environment. The park preserves 33,000 acres along the Cuyahoga River, appropriately called "crooked river" by the Mohawk people. Within its bounds,

Cuyahoga Valley National Park contains an astonishing array of fauna and flora, recreational opportunities, boundless varieties of forests, plains, streams and ravines, breathtaking waterfalls, and historic excursions. Those looking for activities can find hiking, biking, boating, railroading, canoeing and kayaking, bird-watching, fishing, golfing,

horseback riding, and—in winter—downhill skiing, cross-country skiing, snow tubing, snowshoeing, sledding, and ice fishing.

A Prosperous Past

Much but by no means all of this activity is happening in, on, and along the backbone of the national park, the Cuyahoga River.

Northeastern Ohio
Established October 11, 2000
51 square miles

Things to See: *Cuyahoga River; Ohio & Erie Canalway; Towpath Trail; Frazee House; Cuyahoga Valley Scenic Railway; Brandywine Falls; Beaver Marsh; Blue Hen Falls*

Things to Do: *Hiking; Bicycling; Canoeing; Kayaking; Picnicking; Bird-watching; Camping; Fishing; Golfing*

What's Nearby? *David Berger National Memorial; James A. Garfield National Historic Site; First Ladies National Historic Site; Perry's Victory and International Peace Memorial*

When visitors glide down the Cuyahoga, it must seem so very easy for them to imagine themselves back in the middle of the 19th century riding in a packet, a sleek passenger boat, along the Ohio & Erie Canal Towpath.

"These boats are about 70 feet long, and with the exception of the Kitchen and bar, is occupied as a Cabin," explained Thomas S. Woodcock, a passenger on the Erie Canal in 1836. "The forward part being the ladies' Cabin, is separated by a curtain, but at meal times this obstruction is removed, and the table is set the whole length of the boat. The table is supplied with every thing that is

Right: *Blue Hen Falls tumbles over a hard rock shelf composed of Berea sandstone, which sits atop softer Bedford shale making up the waterfall's shelf. The falls is a favorite hiking destination.* Opposite: *Much of the deep water of beautiful Beaver Marsh is dominated by the spatterdock plant, also called cow lily or yellow pond. Beaver Marsh features a popular boardwalk, visible in the photograph.*

necessary and of the best quality with many of the luxuries of life."

You can almost hear the canawlers, the canalboat men, crying out, "Low bridge!" as they all hit the deck to avoid a bridge with little headroom, built that way to save money. You could see why the canawlers seemed weary: They were "trippers," long-haul workers who toiled and traveled up and down the canal. And they were often hauling a hoodledasher, two or more empty boats tied to a full-cargo boat, pulled by one team of mules. The canawlers grew tired of ducking under bridges all through New York, Ohio, and Pennsylvania.

"The Bridges on the Canal are very low, particularly the old ones," Woodcock wrote. "Indeed they are so low as to scarcely allow the baggage to clear, and in some cases actually rubbing against it. Every Bridge makes us bend double if seated on anything, and in many cases you have to lie on your back. The Man at the helm gives the word to the passengers 'Bridge,' 'very low Bridge,' 'the lowest in the Canal,' as the case may be."

Despite some serious, even fatal, accidents, a low bridge generally "affords amusement to the passengers who soon imitate the [helmer's] cry, and vary it with a command, such as, 'All Jackson men bow down,'" he wrote. "After such commands we find few aristocrats."

Community Organization

The story of Cuyahoga Valley's beginning is inspirational. The modern-day park came together in small waves, with bits and pieces falling in place over the years. Finally, after nearly a century of work and the help of countless local citizen activists, the park took on the national park status it holds today.

Visitors have journeyed to Cuyahoga Valley since the 1870s in search of an escape from the rigors of everyday urban life. They were attracted to the natural splendor of the area—its unspoiled lakes and pollution-free air. By the 1910s, with the help of the Cleveland and Akron park districts, officials began developing pieces of land as county parks. In the late '20s and early '30s, the area received another couple of boosts. One was from an area businessperson named Hayward Kendall, who donated 430 acres to the growing collection of parks in honor of his mother, Virginia; the other was from the Civilian Conservation Corps, Franklin Delano Roosevelt's army of young people who swept the nation during the Great Depression, creating parks and roads for Americans to enjoy. The CCC planted more than 100 acres of trees and built lodges, shelters, and Kendall Lake. These buildings now make up most of the park's welcome centers and recreational areas.

Over the years, many new pieces, including golf courses and a ski lodge, have been added, and the whole area grew to be a large series of regional parks. The citizens of Ohio, however, didn't feel that their parks were safe from the encroaching population and its pollution: Urban sprawl was at the doorstep. The solution to this was found to be involvement on the national level.

In the '60s and early '70s, National Park Service opposition to the idea ran high. The federal agency believed that bringing Cuyahoga into its fold would mean taking money away from larger parks, such as Yellowstone. In response, local citizens and private organizations began working together in a loose collective of foundations, though it took several years before legislation was passed to protect the area. Finally, legislation was signed by President Gerald Ford in 1974 to bring the park into the service as Cuyahoga National Recreation Area. In the year 2000, the park designation and name were changed to formally recognize it as Cuyahoga Valley National Park. Thus, this park is a shining example of how a community can come together over generations to protect its natural resources and provide green spaces for its citizens.

A Refuge from the City

Floating down the river today is more likely to mean motoring in an excursion boat built for 1,000 with catering and live music than it is drifting behind a mule team pulling a packet boat, but the romance of the Cuyahoga River has not abated. Visitors still see steelhead trout and bullhead stirring the waters beneath. In the span of a few minutes, they might see a gray fox dash to the water's edge, and what looks to be a mink. Behind it all sounds the resonant "rumm-rumm-rumm" of the bullfrog and the rapid "peep-peep-peep" of the spring peeper. What hasn't changed is the tranquility of the park's rolling hills, narrow ravines, placid floodplain, and meandering river scenery, which draws about 2.5 million visitors yearly.

The woods and wetlands support 56 butterfly species, almost 200 bird species, and 32 mammal species. The latter include the endangered Indiana bat, first discovered in the park in 2002.

The 51-square-mile park is dominated by a 22-mile stretch of the Cuyahoga River and the almost 200 miles of streams that course through it. Ohio's only national park, Cuyahoga Valley abounds in marshes and waterfalls—the tallest being 65-foot-high Brandywine Falls—and amazing geological features such as the skyscraping Ritchie Ledges. The Beaver Marsh, a beaver dam built along the defunct Ohio & Erie Canal, is a favorite short hike.

Cuyahoga Valley National Park has no roads but plentiful bike and hiking paths. The 20-mile Towpath Trail, the route along which those mules and canawlers pulled the river's packets, is one of the park's most popular stretches. This trail remains a

The only remaining covered bridge in Summit County, Ohio, Everett Road Covered Bridge was once one of about 2,000 such bridges in the state.

work in progress; plans call for it eventually to follow the route of the original canal for more than 100 miles, from Cleveland to New Philadelphia.

The park's roots, more so than those of any other national park, lie as much in the

human history of the Cuyahoga Valley as they do in its natural beauty and scientific value. In the 1870s people came to the park for carriage rides or boat trips along the canal. In 1880, the Valley Railway—the advance version of today's Cuyahoga Valley Scenic Railroad—began operations.

Park development per se began with the establishment of Cleveland and Akron metropolitan park districts in 1917 and 1921, respectively. In 1925, the Olmsted Brothers landscape architecture firm—formed by stepbrothers John Charles Olmsted and Frederick Law Olmsted Jr., who went on to influence the founding of the National Park Service—readied a report on the Cuyahoga Valley for Akron and Summit County parks. "It is in the valley that one can realize most effectively a sense of isolation and freedom from the sights and sounds of all the multitude of circumstances which go to make the modern city—and when all is said and done that is the justifying purpose of a country park," the study said. Yet, even though much of the valley was under state or local protection, by the 1960s it became clear that urban growth would not spare the area much longer, which could spell catastrophe. In June 1969, an oil slick and debris in the Cuyahoga River caught fire in Cleveland, drawing national attention to Ohio's environmental woes. Pressure mounted, and

Probably the best-loved, most-photographed feature of Cuyahoga Valley National Park is Brandywine Falls. The 60-foot-high falls are approachable head-on by boardwalk, which provides an opportunity for great photos and a close-up of its geological features.

in 1974 the park was established as a U.S. national recreation area, then redesignated a national park in 2000.

Restoring the Natural Order

The Cuyahoga River still suffers at times from excesses upstream, but it is probably also the National Park Service's most potent symbol of hope for the restoration and conservation of despoiled lands. A portion of the park is a reclaimed automobile junkyard—a large beaver population, formerly extirpated in the park region, now resides in that area. The former Richfield Coliseum—once home to the NBA's Cleveland Cavaliers, the WHA's Cleveland Crusaders, the NHL's Cleveland Barons, and other teams—was also located on land now reclaimed for the park.

Long before any of them, in 1814 to be precise, a man named George Wallace built a sawmill next to Brandywine Falls. He dreamed up the idea of a place called Brandywine Village and encouraged others to

move there. Many did, including his brother-in-law, who built a gristmill across the falls from Wallace. Today, the falls and village are arguably the national park's two top attractions, although only a couple of buildings remain from the village.

Many consider the majestic 60-foot Brandywine Falls, sculpted by Brandywine Creek, the centerpiece of the area. Geologically, Brandywine Falls is a classic waterfall,

Above: The home of James and Adeline Wallace, built in 1848, still sits adjacent to the Brandywine Falls. Listed on the National Register of Historic Places, today it serves guests of the park as a bed and breakfast. *Left:* Sunshine pierces ledges of stratified rock in Cuyahoga Valley National Park. The valley is characterized by rocks carved by the thousands of miles of rivers and streams that flow through it.

capped by a layer of hard Berea sandstone that protects the softer layers of rock below, which themselves are 350-million- to 400-million-year-old Bedford and Cleveland shales formed from mud on the seafloor that covered the valley at the time. A boardwalk leads most of the way to the waterfall's gorge for a head-on view of the falls. It also offers a close view of the grains of sand from that ancient sea that compose the Berea sandstone.

Death Valley National Park

In remote eastern California, Death Valley National Park holds the record for the highest temperature ever recorded in the Western Hemisphere: The mercury sizzled its way up to 134 degrees Fahrenheit in July 1913. Formerly a world record, that temperature was commemorated in the form of the world's tallest thermometer in the nearby town of Baker, California, but it was ultimately eclipsed by a scorcher in Libya that hit 136 degrees. But world record or not, it's still very hot here—in 2001, the daily high exceeded 100 degrees for an amazing 154 days in a row.

Extremes

Not surprisingly, Death Valley is not only the hottest but the driest place in North America. The evaporation rate at the bottom of Death Valley is capable of drying up 150 inches of water a year—enough to evaporate the annual average rainfall of two inches many times over. And there have been many years that have come and gone without any recorded rainfall at all.

But the superlatives do not begin and end with hot and dry. The park also owns the distinction of having the lowest elevation in the Western Hemisphere, bottoming out

East central California
Established October 31, 1994
5,270 square miles

Things to See: *Badwater Basin; Telescope Peak; Zabriskie Point; Furnace Creek; Stovepipe Wells; Scotty's Castle; Panamint Springs; Ubehebe Crater; Eureka Dunes*

Things to Do: *Hiking; Backpacking; Backcountry camping; Biking; Bird-watching*

What's Nearby? *Manzanar National Historic Site; Sequoia & Kings National Parks; Devils Postpile National Monument; Mojave National Preserve; Yosemite National Park; Santa Monica Mountains National Recreation Area; Grand Canyon National Park*

at 282 feet below sea level in the Badwater Basin. A land of geographic extremes, Death Valley also encompasses Telescope Peak, on the other side of the spectrum with an elevation of 11,049 feet above sea level. This 11,331-foot difference between the summit and the valley floor represents one of the greatest vertical rises in the lower 48 states. At the higher elevations, desert fir, spruce, and quaking aspen are found in abundance, providing stark contrast to the desert floor of the valley, which is devoid of plant life.

More than two vertical miles below the park's highest point, the Badwater Basin is clad in the vast white expanse of 200 square miles of salt flats. The valley floor primarily owes its sub-sea-level elevation not to erosion but to seismic faults that lifted the mountains higher while pushing the valley

With ominous thunderclouds looming on the horizon, the parched valley floor at Badwater Basin is a patchwork of salt and other remnants of an ancient, long-dry sea.

floor lower. Known as strike-slip, or trans-verse, faulting, this phenomenon took place over hundreds of millions of years.

Death Valley is as vast as it is hot. This is the largest U.S. national park outside of Alaska. At 3.3 million acres, it is even larger than Yellowstone National Park. Its landscape encompasses numerous eco-systems and destinations of interest, includ-ing salt and alkaline flats that stretch for miles, broad regions of sand dunes, winding ancient canyons, multicolored rock cliffs

Eureka Dunes, which rise to a height of nearly 700 feet above the valley below, are California's largest sand dunes.

and ridges, and historical sites. Although, as previously noted, the average annual rainfall is less than two inches, Pacific storms occasionally roar in and cause flash floods that wash out roads, trails, and campgrounds. On most days of the year, however, Death Valley is a sunny paradise where one can experience great solitude and tranquility. In the wintertime, it is a haven for "snowbirds" who park their recreational vehicles and stay for weeks, sometimes even months.

The Panamint City and Rhyolite Ghost Towns

Death Valley has its name for many reasons, though the greatest has to be the weather. In death, however, life is always possible. Many things in the Wild West lived and died quickly, and many things that died lived on in memory, their shells preserved by the hot and dry desert. Those that lived were products of the great gold and silver mines that once dotted the region. Death Valley was known for its pockets of ore, quickly found and quickly dug up. Where there were mines, there were towns, and life and busy streets ringing with prosperity. More often than not, though, the mines became played out, and the towns disappeared, leaving barren shells of what they once had been. Death Valley National Park has more than its share of these. Visitors can now walk the towns, like ghosts haunting a dead and sunken ship.

Panamint City, named for the Panamint Mountains, was known as a den of thieves. As rough as they come, Panamint was the site of shootings and crime, a hideout of outlaws and bandits, where only those of great courage (or great corruption) were willing to go. The discovery of a silver vein changed all of that. Rough and tumble citizens were, for once, finding out that honest work was more profitable than crime. By 1874, the town was a booming and industrious place. In 1875, however, the silver ran out, and so did the people.

Rhyolite, Nevada, just outside the park, thrived three decades later, first coming alive in 1904 when gold was found nearby. Called the "Queen City," its population neared 10,000 at its height over the next few years. Rhyolite was home to a stock exchange, an opera house, and an estimated 50 saloons. The gold mine was greatly diminished by 1910, however, and closed in 1911. The lights went out in 1916, when power to the town was cut off. Pictured here is what remains of the three-story Cook Bank Building.

Stories like these were all too common in the gold rush days. Mines and accompanying towns would spring up everywhere and fall away just as easily. Death Valley National Park holds the remains of eight ghost towns, all of which have their own amazing histories of boom and bust. These fascinating studies in mortality can be reached by hikes or car rides from the main park.

Out of This World

In the end, Death Valley is a realm unlike any other. The park is a place where life has largely been stripped away and earth's original surface can be seen, naked and bare, in its pure and elementary shapes. Climate reigns here, not humans, beasts, or plants. Death Valley will forever be the domain of the sun, sand, wind, and rock. There are rocks here that formed when life first trafficked among the tides of the moon; the mountain ranges will stand into the far distant future.

In one corner of the park is the cracked bottom of a dry lake called the Racetrack. This mysterious spot earned its nickname from the sizable boulders that race around the area, leaving serpentine trails in their wake. No one, however, has actually ever seen the rocks race. The prevailing theory about them holds that a thin layer of ice on the shadowy undersides of the rocks enable them to slide on the Racetrack when a stiff wind blows.

While the Racetrack is down a long road full of jagged rocks that's not recommended for even four-wheel-drives with industrial-strength tires, there are plenty of more accessible geological wonders in the park. A nine-mile loop drive takes visitors through the multicolored volcanic landscape known as Artist's Palette, where rolling multicolored hills of purple, green, blue, and brown provide an otherworldly backdrop—which is perhaps why George Lucas used it as a filming location for the sci-fi classic *Star Wars*.

Part of the Amargosa Mountains, Zabriskie Point offers a remarkable viewpoint of the gnarled landscape that was Furnace Creek Lake—until it dried up some five million years ago.

While sand dunes do not dominate the valley floor like the salt flats, there are several captivating dune-fields in the park, the eternal works in progress of an unseen creator: the wind. The best known, the Eureka Dunes, are some of the tallest dunes in North America—cresting more than 680 feet above the dry lakebed at their feet—and are known for a very odd phenomenon: singing sand. A low note that sounds like a motor or an organ accompanies the avalanches of sand that surge down the steepest face of the dunes.

Also on the north side of the park, the fire gods have left their mark on the landscape in the form of Ubehebe Crater. This vivid orange, red, and white scar is the result of a recent eruption of a volcano here; geologists estimate it blew its top only a few hundred years ago. Park visitors can view this spectacular sight from the safety of the parking lot, or they can hike the mile-long trail that circumnavigates the crater. Adventurous hikers can even scramble down the trail rarely taken to the crater floor about 500 feet below the rim—the inverted perspective is worth the strenuous hike back out.

Another notable below-ground formation on park land, Devils Hole is a half-million-year-old, 300-foot-deep limestone cavern filled with water that flows from a fed geothermal aquifer. The resulting 92-degree Fahrenheit waters are ideal for the endangered Devils Hole pupfish, who thrive here and nowhere else on earth. But Devils Hole

Left: *Dante's View offers this vista of the Black Mountains and the valley at their feet.* Below: *Manly Beacon rises over the Badlands but is itself dwarfed by the Panamint Mountains in the distance.*

But it wasn't until the California gold rush of 1849 that a party of disoriented pioneers took a wrong turn and revealed this superlative desert valley to the general public. Although only one person in the party died (and an elderly one at that), this is the expedition that gave the valley its lasting, and not entirely appropriate, name.

A different kind of mineral rush followed in the 1870s and '80s, after miners discovered silver and borax. Boomtowns dotted the landscape as famed 20-mule teams hauled huge wagons packed with borax to the railroad, 165 rugged miles away. While the teams only ran from 1883 to 1889, they became an enduring icon of the Old West,

is not technically in Death Valley. Its location east of the main park in Nevada's Amargosa Desert means that Devils Hole is part of the park officially but not contiguously.

Abounding Life?

While the landscape often appears lifeless, the park's name is ultimately a misnomer. Beyond the pupfish, Death Valley is home to a wide variety of plants and animals, including more than 50 mammal species, about 300 kinds of birds, and nearly 40 different reptiles and amphibians. Bats, shrews, and mice survive on the thriving invertebrate populations; mountain lions prowl for mule deer. The longest-lived residents of the park are desert tortoises, who spend most of their 80-year lifespans bur-

rowed into the ground, dozing away.

No such luck for the humans, whose history in Death Valley is nearly as rich as the park's geological past. The Timbisha Shoshone were the first people to call what is today the park home, centuries before the first European settlers arrived, and a community of Timbisha Shoshone people still lives on private land within the park's boundaries.

thanks to 20-Mule-Team Borax Soap's long-running advertising campaign.

President Franklin D. Roosevelt established Death Valley National Monument in 1933 (it became a national park in 1994), and the 1930s brought federal investment to the park in the form of roads, water lines, and buildings. There are other historic structures in the valley: the Furnace Creek Inn, a regal lodging that opened in 1927, and those that make up the numerous ghost towns that still remain in the park today.

And no trip to the park would be complete without a visit to Scotty's Castle, a 25-room palace at the foot of the Grapevine Mountains. Take a tour of the Mediterranean-inspired castle and learn the tale of Walter Scott, aka "Death Valley Scotty," the eccentric who infamously swindled Chicago tycoon Albert Johnson into staking his nonexistent mine, only to later win Johnson's lifetime friendship thanks to his larger-than-life personality. Built in the 1920s and '30s but never completed, the castle was Johnson's, although Scotty told anybody within earshot that it was his own. Today, costumed tour guides offer colorful interpretations of the story as they walk visitors through the nicely preserved interior.

The floor of Death Valley is home to numerous perpetually changing dune fields. Countless tiny grains of quartz, whittled from rock over the eons, comprise the dynamic landscape.

Scotty is buried on the hill behind the castle that bears his name, alongside his faithful mutt Windy. After the tour, the climb to the top is worth it, not only to pay respects to Scotty—and to rub the well-worn nose on a bronze facsimile of his smiling mug—but for the view of the surrounding desert wonderland that is Death Valley National Park.

Denali National Park and Preserve

Like Mammoth Cave or the Grand Canyon, Denali National Park and Preserve—and its centerpiece Mount McKinley—are so immense that they seem to exist in another dimension of sheer size. The park spans a breathtaking 6,075,107 acres, yet Denali is dominated by the 20,320-foot Mount McKinley, which the Athabaskan Indians simply call "Great One." It's easy to see why. Mount McKinley is the highest peak in North America, and even that singular fact can't correctly express its size, which in some ways makes it larger than Mount Everest.

Mount Everest has a "real vertical rise" of about 12,000 feet. Mount McKinley starts

Central Alaska
Established December 2, 1980
9,500 square miles

Things to See: *Mount McKinley; Wonder Lake; Primrose Ridge; Muldrow Glacier; Mount Foraker; Polychrome Overlook*

Things to Do: *Hiking, Snowshoeing, Cross-country skiing; Backpacking; Wildlife viewing; Fishing; Camping; Rafting; Horseback riding*

What's Nearby? *Lake Clark National Park and Preserve; Kenai Fjords National Park; Yukon–Charley Rivers National Preserve; Wrangell–St. Elias National Park and Preserve*

from its ground level plateau at an altitude of 2,000 feet then rises 18,000 feet to its peak. The mountain's enormous snowy face, flanked by five giant glaciers, towers over a 200-mile Alaskan landscape all the way to Fairbanks and Cook Inlet, crowning the majestic peaks of the 600-mile-long Alaska Range.

On a summer day, when there is up to 24 hours of sunlight, visitors to Denali see

Left: Arctic Lupine flowers into blue blossoms, sometimes with pink and white highlights. The wildflowers thrive at high altitudes by glaciers and on dry slopes, meadows, and tundra. Far left: Armed only with chocolate doughnuts and a thermos of coffee, several local men first climbed Mount McKinley, pictured here behind Wonder Lake, in 1913.

Denali National Park's 2,363-foot Broad Pass is a favorite of photographers. The Alaska Railroad's flagship train, the Denali Star, climbs through this pass to reach the railroad's highest elevation.

sights they will remember for the rest of their lives. A huge herd of caribou migrates through a pass below Mount McKinley, heading toward its summer feeding grounds. On a green meadow on Primrose Ridge, a band of two dozen pure-white Dall sheep pause briefly as they make their way to the high alpine crags where they prefer to spend their summers. A golden eagle soars off a cliff along Polychrome Pass on the park road, while the eerie call of a loon rolls across Wonder Lake. At the same time, a grizzly takes time out to stretch and survey the surroundings while munching berries on Sable Pass, just as the clouds part to reveal the awesome bulk of Mount McKinley for one magical moment. Already the tallest mountain in North America, Mount McKinley—believe it or not—rises a little higher each year above the tundra-covered valleys of Denali National Park.

Preservation First

Yet Denali National Park and Preserve was created to protect not the mountain but its dozens of species of mammals. These range from six types of shrew—cinereus shrew, pygmy shrew, montane shrew, water shrew, tundra shrew, and tiny shrew—to the little brown bat, various coyotes and wolves, the red fox, the Canada lynx, wolverines, North River otters, American martens, various types of ermine and mink, and a world-class collection of red squirrel, northern flying squirrels, the arctic ground squirrel, and its cousin the hoary marmot. There are also eight members of the largest family of mammals, *Muridae,* including muskrats and northern bog lemmings; major populations of snowshoe hares; collared pika; the American beaver; the meadow jumping mouse; and many more.

But these are only the smaller animals. Among larger specimens are Dall sheep, moose, and caribou. And don't forget the bears: *Ursus americanus,* the American black bear, and *Ursus arctos,* the brown

bear, which also includes *Ursus arctos horribilis,* the great grizzly, the undisputed sovereign of this wild terrain. Grizzlies roam the park at will, feeding mainly on roots, berries, and other plants. When they are ravenously hungry—for instance, after a winter's hibernation—the bears may also go after arctic ground squirrels, injured caribou, or moose calves.

Surviving the Difficult Winter

Denali also boasts one tiny amphibian, the wood frog, which measures between four-tenths of an inch and 2.8 inches long, its small size belying its famously loud frog calls. The hardy wood frog survives Alaskan winters in Denali's forests and wetlands. It survives as an extreme example of an ectotherm, a cold-blooded animal, which

means that the little wood frog can adjust its body temperature to at or slightly above the ambient temperature. And in Denali National Park, the temperature is a story all its own.

Wood frogs freeze solid in Denali winters. They survive until spring because of an amazing adaptation called a "cryoprotectant." As winter deepens, a wood frog's toes and eyeballs begin to freeze. Scientists believe this tells the wood frog's brain to convert the glycogen it has stored into sugar, glucose, which acts as frog super-antifreeze, reducing the freezing point of water in the frog's cells and protecting the cells from damage. Its cryoprotectant magic permits the wood frog to endure winter temperatures as low as 10.5 degrees Fahrenheit (−12 degrees Celsius).

Denali National Park and Preserve also hosts birdlife from all over. Migratory birds

The Bears of Denali

Prevalent through all parts of Alaska, one thing is certain: Denali is Bear Country. Home to both brown (including the subspecies grizzly) and American black bears, the backcountry of Denali is known for its sightings of these animals. Bears are often regarded with two distinctive emotions among people: either terror or unguarded curiosity. Certainly, bears are large, have sharp claws and big teeth, and can run very quickly, but they are also mostly just on the lookout for food—and this rarely includes humans.

Bears are, to a large part, carnivores. They search for small rodents, fish, and insects. One might say, however, that they aren't especially picky. Bears often use their long claws to dig through ice, snow, and soil for roots, berries, and nuts. They have a great sense of smell, which will often attract them to campsites where food is left out.

Bears are omnivores, eating meat as well as berries and other plantlife. This bear is feeding on berries in the tundra in preparation for a winter's hibernation.

include ptarmigans, peregrine falcons, trumpeter swans, gyrfalcons, and golden eagles. Migratory avians make up 80 percent of Denali's bird life. These birds return in flocks that can cover the sky in spring, but even winter bird-watching seems spectacular with wintering ptarmigan, pine grosbeaks, northern goshawk, and gyrfalcons. Observers have counted 149 bird species that are regularly found in Denali; 119 species nest there; and 167 species have been observed inside the park.

Mount McKinley is a pluton—igneous rock that crystallized from cooling magma—and it is probably the largest such in the world. The peak remains uplifting, which means it's still growing. The mountain sits atop a major geologic feature called the Denali Fault, where two of the giant plates that make up earth's crust are colliding. The Alaska Range, along with Mount McKinley, is on the northern plate, which geologists believe is over-

riding the southern plate. As the two plates continue on their courses, the landmass below the mountain is pushed down as Mount McKinley itself is pushed up.

The Adventure of Exploration

Mount McKinley has attracted climbers since 1897, when it was announced that "America's rival to Everest" had been discovered. After four miners climbed to the lower north summit in 1909, the south summit was successfully attempted by four Alaskans, one of them a native, in 1913. Today, most climbers try for the summit in May or early June; after that, avalanches threaten. Most climbers take a ski plane to the 7,500-foot level of the Kahiltna Glacier to begin the 10- to 20-day trek.

In a park as vast as this, the opportunities for exploring are practically endless. Most visitors begin by taking the park bus on the 85-mile gravel road that extends deep into the Denali wilderness. From the visitor center on the eastern boundary of the park, the bus climbs out of a stunted spruce forest onto the treeless tundra that rolls through valleys and over gentle ridges to the flanks of Mount McKinley.

Offering stunning vistas of the Alaska Range along the way, the road winds along Primrose Ridge then drops into marshy flats and permafrost where the so-called "drunken forest" of spruce trees lean every which way. The trees slant because of the ground's yearly freezing and thawing cycles.

After crossing three passes, the road finally reaches the Eielson Visitor Center at

mile 66, a rest stop frequented by ground squirrels and even an occasional grizzly. After passing within a mile of the great snout of the Muldrow Glacier, the road comes to its terminus at the Wonder Lake Campground. From here the view is magnificent. If the weather cooperates, visitors can see the sheer Wickersham Wall, McKinley's north face, which rises for more than 14,000 feet and is one of the most awesome mountain walls in the world.

Right: *A solitary canoer experiences Denali National Park and Preserve, vast with innumerable landscapes of soaring mountains and crystalline lakes.* Far left: *Denali's moose grow to 1,200 pounds, making them among the largest of the park's many mammals.* Below left: *A musher urges his dog team forward beneath looming Mount McKinley. The massive mountain towers over 200 miles of Alaskan landscape.*

Bear Safety

As the largest of the bears, grizzlies are the most likely to inspire fear in people. American black bears, however, are often the more curious and bold of the two species. Both can run fast, climb trees, and swim. Black bears, though, are smaller and thus able to do these things better than their larger counterparts.

How worried do visitors need to be about bears? It depends on how well-versed they are in taking care of themselves. Bears in the wild are generally afraid of humans and are not willing to explore too closely—though there are always exceptions to this rule. The most common mistake people make is to think that they are safe. When inside the park boundaries, some people may believe that the bears that come near car trails and picnic areas—bears that are presumably used to humans—are "tame." Such is absolutely not the case, and any attempt to attract or feed bears is likely to land one in trouble.

Thanks to recent studies, wildlife experts have come to believe that the closest one should get to a bear is about 100 feet. Any closer, and curiosity may turn to nervous excitement (on the part of either the human or the bear), and that may lead to danger. Other precautions to take if one sees a bear are to raise both arms above the head and wave them. This makes humans seem much larger than they actually are. Backing away slowly also helps. This is so the person doesn't alarm the bear or make it perceive the person as a threat. The National Park Service says that individuals should make the decision themselves as to whether or not to carry pepper spray. Visitors should keep in mind that many factors—wind and weather, distance to target, and age of the spray itself—can influence for the worse pepper spray's effectiveness.

Overall, bears are an amazing part of the Denali landscape. They should be admired for their beauty and strength rather than feared—they are not out to get people. Very few bear attacks have ever been recorded, and many of those could have been prevented with common sense and calm. With the right knowledge and appreciation for the species, bears can be enjoyed just as much as the park's majestic peaks and valleys.

Dry Tortugas National Park

Dry Tortugas National Park consists of 64,701 acres of land—from time to time. Time to time? Yes, because most of the park's 101 square miles and seven islands are underwater. Even the land portions of the park have been known to sink back into the sea after an especially strong hurricane. Whole islands have vanished or reappeared.

What's in a Name?

There's not much "dry" about the Dry Tortugas, an island group a little less than

Off Florida's Southwestern Coast
Established October 26, 1992
101 square miles

Things to See: *Fort Jefferson; Loggerhead Key; Bush Key; Hospital Key*

Things to Do: *Scuba diving; Snorkeling; Fishing; Camping*

What's Nearby? *Everglades National Park; Biscayne National Park; Big Cypress National Preserve*

70 miles west of Key West, Florida. The area derived the first part of its name from the fact that there are no sources of fresh water on the islands. The *tortugas* part of the name reaches back into history to Spanish explorer Ponce de Leon, who discovered the region in 1513. Despite the hardships of his voyage and the lack of potable water, the adventurer was pleased to be able to keep his ships stocked with sea turtles—in Spanish, *tortugas*. Over time, the islands became known as a sailor's graveyard, a navigation hazard that produced hundreds of shipwrecks.

Dry Tortugas National Park is accessible only by boat, ferry, or seaplane, making it one of the National Park System's most remote and lightly visited parks. Yet the rewards of venturing here are great. Recreational opportunities include world-class swimming, snorkeling, and underwater photography in some of the most beautiful and untouched coral reefs in existence.

Construction of Loggerhead Lighthouse in Dry Tortugas National Park began in 1856. Upon completion, it used a then-new Fresnel lens to scan up to 53 miles out to sea. An earlier lighthouse in this area proved too weak to help seafarers.

Scientists say the shallow waters of the Dry Tortugas are ideal for the development of coral reefs and for the tiny primitive animals called polyps that, over the centuries, accumulate to build the rocklike reefs.

And where there are healthy living reefs, there are innumerable reef fishes flashing stripes, dots, spots, and patterns in reds, yellows, greens, and blues, including predators such as amberjacks, groupers, wahoos, tarpon, sharks, and barracudas. While the worldwide numbers of sea turtles have diminished sharply since Ponce de Leon's era—often hunted to near extinction for leather, meat, and oils—hawksbill, loggerhead, and green sea turtles remain populous in the area. At least twice a season, female turtles clamber onto sand beaches to dig nests and lay their eggs. They then cover the eggs over and return to the sea. When the turtles hatch, the hatchlings crawl seaward by instinct. Few survive to reenter the ocean.

A Birders' Paradise

The islands also are an ideal environment for birds—and bird-watchers. John James Audubon first visited the Dry Tortugas in 1832. The area was designated a wildlife refuge in 1908. Throughout the year, magnificent frigate birds, brown pelicans, double-crested cormorants, and many varieties of land and water birds can be spotted. The Dry Tortugas lie at an ideal crossroads for migratory fowl between the United States, Cuba, and South America. In addition, the islands are a wintering land for terns and gulls. Dry Tortugas National Park officially lists 299 bird species, seven of which—the mourning dove, brown pelican, sooty tern, brown noddy, roseate tern, masked booby,

and magnificent frigate bird—commonly nest within the park. Falcons and cattle egrets are frequent visitors, too.

Most notable is the sooty tern nesting season on Bush Key, when as many as 100,000 sooty terns alight on the island, a spectacular sight that can be viewed from nearby Fort Jefferson. The terns arrive from the Atlantic Ocean and the Caribbean Sea. They spend late January flying at night above the islands and passing their days at sea. When they alight on land in February, the terns immediately begin laying eggs, one per couple, in the

Sooty terns spend their winters at Dry Tortugas, home of the only breeding colony in the continental United States. By June the birds begin to leave, preferring to summer on the high seas.

Piracy and Sunken Ships

The shallow shoals and reefs surrounding Dry Tortugas National Park have been the source of constant headaches for hundreds of years. While they are stunning features of living art that house plentiful sea life, they have been known to cause problems for travelers trying to navigate the waters. The large number of known shipwrecks in the area means a lot of different things. Primarily, the park's proximity to the Gulf of Mexico and the Florida Keys meant that it was the perfect hideout for pirates, waiting to steal the treasures of unwitting passersby. Sea captains were not only in danger of running aground in the shallow waters (and should they do so, attack was almost certain), but they were also subject to pirates who knew the waters far better than they.

One of the most famous pirates to run through the Dry Tortugas was Jean Lafitte, also known as "the Gentleman Pirate." Lafitte's band of criminals stretched all the way through the Gulf of Mexico, attacking Spanish ships in the name of Cartagena (now Columbia) and selling the stolen and smuggled wares at bazaars near New Orleans. The Dry Tortugas were just one of Lafitte's many bases of operation.

These days, visitors can take boat tours of the islands, learning all about the history of piracy in the area. Two of the wrecks in the Dry Tortugas, Windjammer wreck and Bird Key wreck, are featured, but most locations have been kept secret. The Submerged Resource Center of the National Park Service searches out and catalogs the most fascinating underwater sites at all of the parks—whether fantastic sunken ships or delicate reef formations. The center runs projects throughout the Dry Tortugas, cataloging and conducting archaeological research on the wrecks.

The wreck locations are kept secret for several reasons, not the least of which is the fact that many contain unexcavated treasures; the agency fears that visitors will spoil or take them as souvenirs. It is for this reason that there are no metal detectors allowed anywhere near the park. Many of these abandoned vessels were victims of piracy in their past; the park service wishes to keep modern-day pirates at bay!

island's warm sand. Tern parents take turns shading their egg and protecting it from the terns' great enemy, frightening frigate birds with wingspans of up to seven feet. Other rare birding sights include roseate terns, double-crested cormorants, and brown pelicans, a species removed from some U.S. endangered species lists.

Construction of massive Fort Jefferson began in 1846. The fort was designed with the idea of centering a lighthouse within its walls defended by 420 heavy guns facing the sea.

A Past to Be Discovered

The park is also a historic center, which is perhaps surprising in such a remote area. One sign of its historicity is the number of shipwrecks (out of a total of perhaps 300) accessible to divers and snorkelers. There is, for instance, the Bird Key Wreck, a drowned ship thought to have wrecked some time between 1857 and 1861. This vessel was driven onto Bird Key Bank with the engine running, and its bow struck the bank and accordioned, smashing the ship in two. The remains lie in four to six feet of water.

Another favorite shipwreck is the Windjammer, an iron-hulled ship that foundered on January 21, 1907. The Windjammer Wreck, located less than a mile southwest of Loggerhead Key, lies in about 18 to 21 feet of water in two main areas. The bow section, about 110 feet in length, includes the bow, midships, and foremast. The second field, also about 110 feet in length, includes the ship's stern, mizzen, midships, and main mast structures.

The largest island in Dry Tortugas is Loggerhead Key, renowned for its coral reefs and fishes, birds, and wildlife, and named after its many loggerhead sea turtles. About 250 turtle nests produce 15,000 hatchlings each summer on this, the Florida Keys' most significant green and loggerhead sea turtle nesting grounds.

In 1821, the United States completed the purchase of the Dry Tortugas from Spain for $5 million. The U.S. government began planning construction of a lighthouse to protect seafarers from the dangerous reefs. Construction began on Garden Key in 1825. The Garden Key lighthouse's light proved to be too weak to help ships, and in 1856, construction began on a larger, 150-foot-tall lighthouse on Loggerhead

Above: *Michael O'Laughlin, pictured here in manacles, was one of John Wilkes Booth's coconspirators. He and three other confederates were sentenced to the Fort Jefferson penitentiary. O'Laughlin died there of Yellow Fever. Above left: The wide moat and massive walls of Fort Jefferson formed an effective barrier to any amphibious assault. Today the fort is a natural center of recreation in Dry Tortugas.*

Key. The new structure employed a Fresnel lens, which was the state of the art at the time. The lighthouse proved effective up to 53 miles at sea.

Initial inspections of the site rejected the notion of using the Dry Tortugas as a naval station suitable for battling pirates and enemy navies, but a survey in 1829 by Commodore John Rodgers produced a more favorable report. Should an enemy take the Dry Tortugas, Commander Rodgers wrote, shipping would be in danger, but the islands would make a fine advance post for the sea defense of the Gulf Coast. In 1846, construction of Fort Jefferson began. The fort was planned so that Garden Key lighthouse would be within its walls.

Fort Jefferson was designed as a six-sided, three-tiered fortress and prison with 420 heavy guns facing the sea. At one time as many as 2,000 people—machinists,

carpenters, blacksmiths, masons, general laborers, and the resident prisoner population, as well as army and naval personnel—occupied the fort.

At one time, Fort Jefferson held four of the men convicted of conspiracy in the assassination of President Abraham Lincoln: Edmund Spangler, Samuel Arnold, Michael O'Laughlin, and Dr. Samuel Mudd, who set John Wilkes Booth's broken leg. The prison was an effective container, but history notes a couple of lapses. One escapee paddled a homemade raft to Loggerhead Island, stole a boat, and rowed to Cuba. Another swam to Loggerhead Island on a piece of wood with a ball and chain attached to his ankle.

After the Civil War, at the time the Lincoln conspiracy inmates arrived, the fort's population began to decline. In 1888 it was converted to a quarantine station for the Marine Hospital Service. Fort Jefferson's construc-

tion was never entirely finished; nonetheless it is the largest masonry structure in the Western Hemisphere, made up of more than 16 million bricks.

President Franklin D. Roosevelt, who visited by ship in 1935, set the wheels in motion that resulted in the Dry Tortugas becoming a national park. The area was listed on the National Register of Historic Places in 1970, and it was made a national park in 1992. Despite the difficulties of visiting the park, it hosts about 60,000 visitors annually.

Everglades National Park

It's a sunny day. A group of friends walks on a wooden boardwalk a few feet above water. The heavy woods thin out into sawgrass, and the water below deepens and clears. They hear a cuckoo and see a dark anhinga bird with furry-looking feathers and a hooked bill. A cormorant plunges into the water and eats a fish, then settles on the rail just ahead of the friends. They look down into the water and see big, odd-looking gar fish and what looks like bass. An alligator's broad back appears, followed by its head and tail. In the middle distance past a shimmering purple gallinule bird, a coral snake uncoils around a branch. The cormorant flaps its wings and flies away.

Everglades National Park is justly famed for its walkways, which are designed to take visitors through differing ecosystems. The result is a tour of a riotous variety of plant and animal life.

Southern Florida
Established December 6, 1947
2,350 square miles

Things to See: *Shark Valley; Ten Thousand Islands; Flamingo; Wilderness Waterway*

Things to Do: *Boating; Kayaking; Fishing; Diving; Snorkeling; Airboat rides; Canoeing; Camping; Hiking; Bird-watching*

What's Nearby? *Biscayne National Park; Big Cypress National Preserve; Dry Tortugas National Park*

This is south Florida's Everglades, specifically Everglades National Park's Anhinga Trail at the Royal Palm Visitor Center. Just four miles from the park entrance, the trail is surely one of the world's most amazing boardwalks. After a drive from Miami of scarcely more than 90 minutes, visitors might just see gorgeous fish, turtles, otters, lizards, and birds including great blue heron, ibis, wood stork, and the red-cockaded woodpecker—if they are lucky. They'll see plenty of alligators, and—if they are *very* lucky—a Florida panther. But watch for coral snakes coiled overhead!

The Anhinga Trail's walkway is built above Taylor Slough, a representative of one of the park's many ecosystems. The freshwater slough is something like a stream in the middle of a marsh, where the water moves about 100 feet per day. Other Everglades trails take visitors to the park's other mini-worlds: freshwater marl prairie, pinelands, hardwood hammocks, cypress groves, mangrove forests, marine estuaries, and more. Next door to the Anhinga Trail, the Gumbo-Limbo Trail—also a half-mile long and wheelchair accessible—takes

A great egret stands among cypresses growing in an Everglades marsh. Cypresses are a deciduous conifer, related to pine and spruce trees.

travelers through a dense hammock of royal palms and gumbo-limbo trees.

A Long, Long Time Ago

During the Cretaceous period, starting 140 million or so years ago, the Florida peninsula was submerged, and sediments collected undersea over eons became limestone and related rocks. After these limestone platforms had grown large enough, the Everglades emerged. Most of Everglades National Park rests on Miami Limestone, which was formed around 100,000 years ago. As more and more land emerged, plants and birds began to migrate from islands in the Caribbean. Although the Everglades stores immense amounts of fresh water underground, no subterra-

nean springs feed back into the Everglades system.

The National Park Service describes the park as containing eight ecosystems, each and all in constant flux: tropical hardwood hammocks, the park's only dry land; pineland, slash pine in shallow dry sandy loam over limestone; mangrove trees, a nursery for many sea creatures and bird species; cypress, a conifer that has adapted to three different ecological niches; coastal lowlands, or wet prairies, found between mangroves and pine rocklands; marine and estuarine, mainly Florida Bay, the waters between mainland Florida and the Florida Keys; and freshwater marl prairie, which borders the Everglades' deeper sloughs. "The marl allows slow seepage of the water but not

Gators thrive in the soupy sloughs and marshes of the Everglades. ThIs park is the only place in nature where alligators and crocodiles live side by side. Although both creatures tend to live in freshwater, they each can also survive in seawater. Gators prefer not to, however, while crocs are better suited to it.

rapid drainage," explains the park service's literature. "Though the sawgrass is not as tall and the water is not as deep, freshwater marl prairies look a lot like freshwater sloughs." These are the ecosystems most often associated with Everglades National Park—called "River of Grass"—low-lying areas covered in fresh water, flowing, slowly draining at a rate of 100 feet each day.

Less accessible but just as rewarding are some of the lesser environments that

also deserve a visitor's attention. Take mangroves, for instance, which have suffered from the attentions of politicians. In the 1880s, a campaign began to drain the Everglades. Napoleon Bonaparte Broward based his winning 1904 Florida gubernatorial campaign on drainage and how it would enable "The Empire of the Everglades." The success of the campaign triggered a land boom that ended by advancing farming and town building into the area. On the coasts, mangrove trees were uprooted for better views. For the Everglades, a devastating era had begun.

Protecting the Ecosystem

In 1947, a book by Marjory Stoneman Douglas appeared. *The Everglades: River of Grass* was the result of five years of research. "What had been a river of grass and sweet water that had given meaning and life and uniqueness to this enormous geography through centuries in which man had no place here was made, in one chaotic gesture of greed and ignorance and folly, a river of fire," she wrote. The book went on to sell a half-million copies and to provide a platform for those urging the federal government to protect the 'Glades. Included among those people were members of the group Douglas founded, Friends of the Everglades,

which earned her the moniker, "Grandmother of the Everglades." She died at age 108 in 1998.

Floridians had proposed making the

Everglades a national park as early as 1923, but various conflicts delayed that event from coming to pass until 1947 (one month after the publication of Douglas's *The Everglades*), when Everglades National Park was dedicated by President Harry Truman. Yet conflict

Above: *A bird looks for shelter from a gathering storm that prepares to bear down on Everglades National Park.* Left: *President Harry Truman, here pictured with Seminole including shaman Ingram Billie, dedicated Everglades National Park on December 6, 1947.*

over Everglades water continued, and it was not until the early 1970s that the first battles over water diversion were won by the park. The Everglades' victories slowly began to mount: In 1972 measures were taken to hold back South Florida development and supply the park with the water it needed. The park was declared an International Biosphere Reserve in 1976, and in 1978, the vast majority of the park was designated a wilderness area. In 1979, the Everglades was listed as a UNESCO World Heritage Site. In 1990, the Army Corps of Engineers officially changed direction to construct environmental projects.

The Everglades is "one of the unique regions of the earth, remote, never wholly known," wrote Marjory Stoneman Douglas in her influential 1947 book, The Everglades: River of Grass.

All along, more lands were being added to the national park or the protected areas near it, which include Biscayne National Park, Big Cypress National Preserve, Key Largo's John Pennekamp Coral Reef State Park, Ten Thousand Islands National Wildlife Refuge, and the 9,500-acre "Hole in the

Development vs. Conservation: a Never-Ending Struggle

It may be difficult to believe, in today's green-conscious world, that the Everglades were once intended to be paved over. Imagine, instead of alligators, wading birds, and Florida panthers, park visitors could sightsee their way through row upon row of hotels, T-shirt shops, and gas stations!

In the late 1700s, the entire southern tip of Florida looked much the same as the Everglades do today. Shortly after the turn of the 19th century, however, settlers began to complain of the "worthless swamp" that impeded their way to further seaside resorts and greater profits. And so, in the 1880s a great effort to "reclaim" the swamp was underway. Drainage canals proved destructive and ineffectual, with silt erosion overtaking any progress in drying the area out almost as soon as it was made. Instead of giving up, however, industrious developers expanded their dredging efforts and eventually turned the wetlands into usable agricultural areas. This progress brought the South

railroads, industry, and thousands of settlers looking for their piece of land.

It wasn't until the 1930s that conservationist voices began to be heard. In 1934, Congress gave support for the creation of a national park, though it was 13 years before conservationists finally bought up the lands and secured enough funding. The park officially opened in 1947.

Though this was a major conservationist victory, even today it may be only short-lived unless great care is taken. The parklands are only a shadow of their former selves. More than 50 percent of the wetlands have been lost, as have 60 percent of bird species and 90 percent of the population of Florida panthers. Invasive, nonnative plants are spreading throughout the park, taking resources from native plants and killing them off. Even worse, battles still rage with developers.

As development continued in 1948 with the founding of the Central and South Florida Project, cities sprang up where there used to

be lush swampland. This project, however, began to take an interest in the conservation and preservation of the waters that fed into the Everglades, while still setting aside other lands for exploitation.

In 1974, the Big Cypress National Preserve north of the Everglades was inaugurated. Establishing the preserve was considered a compromise with those desiring full national park status, because while building is restricted in Big Cypress, more recreational activities are allowed—which means bigger profits.

While no one can develop areas within any of the parks, everything in southern Florida is connected by waterways and canals. Water pollution from outside the park cannot be controlled from within. To truly save those "worthless swamps" from utter destruction, cooperation is necessary from more than just park rangers and visitors—it will take all of Florida acting to preserve its interconnected waterways.

Donut," an area left out of the original park because of its value as farmland. The crowning addition during this era of ecological givebacks was 1989's Everglades National Park Protection and Expansion Act, which added 109,506 eastern Everglades acres to the park and promised to maintain the park's integrity. Battles over the park, water, agriculture, and development continue to this day, although the park seems to win more of them as time goes by.

Alive in the 'Glades

Many people hope so. Probably the West Indian manatees hope so, as do the other endangered

species who live in Everglades National Park: the Key Largo wood rat and the Key Largo cotton mouse; the green turtle, the Atlantic ridley turtle, the Atlantic hawksbill turtle, and the Atlantic leatherback turtle; the Cape Sable seaside sparrow; the snail kite; the wood stork; and the fearsome Florida panther.

That last magnificent creature makes up the potentially tragic leading edge of the park's magnificent populations of more than 40 mammals, from the short-tailed shrew to the Florida opossum and the exotic nine-banded armadillo to grey and red foxes,

black bear, Everglades mink, long-tailed weasel, bobcat, and white-tailed deer.

The park has five entrances. Most adventurers start from the Ernest F. Coe Visitor Center at the main entrance, which faces toward Miami on the park's eastern flank. The Royal Palm Center is four miles west. The Flamingo Visitor Center, 38 miles from the main entrance, takes travelers deep into the park for hiking and canoeing; some biking and wheelchair access is available, too. The territory around the center is said to be among the park's best for croc-watching, and Eco Pond, one mile past the Flamingo

Saw grass is one iconic inhabitant of the Everglades and of Florida beyond the park. Palm trees, seen here in the background, are another.

Center, is prime gator habitat. The Gulf Coast Visitor Center, 36 miles from Naples in the park's northwest corner, lies across the water from the Ten Thousand Islands. And the Shark Valley Visitor Center, by the Tamiami Trail (Highway 41) on the northern border, hosts a five-mile hike on a path that leads from this center to a two-story observation tower.

Gates of the Arctic National Park and Preserve

America's northernmost national park, Gates of the Arctic National Park and Preserve, has to be the most remote by any measure. It has no roads and no trails in from the outside. "Those seeking a rugged wilderness journey on a limited budget can begin hiking directly off the highway," the National Park Service notes, but approaches from either Anaktuvuk Pass or the Dalton Highway require river crossings. Some visitors approach Gates of the Arctic by driving the Dalton Highway Corridor, a 414-mile gravel road stretch of northern Alaska from Livengood, 84 miles north of Fairbanks, to Deadhorse and the oilfields of Prudhoe Bay. Most visitors, however, come by air from one of the "jump-off communities" on the park's periphery, such as Bettles, Coldfoot, Anaktuvuk Pass, and Kotzebue, where they then can arrange to fly into the park by air taxi. Fewer than 5,000 visitors annually make the trip.

At the Top of the World

The entirety of Gates of the Arctic lies north of the Arctic Circle. The park is the centerpiece of 700 square miles of protected range, with the Noatak Preserve to the west and the Arctic National Wildlife Refuge to the east. Lying within its span is much of the central Brooks Range, a 700-mile-long alpine arctic mountain range linking all of northern Alaska—it is the northernmost range in the world. Gates of the Arctic National Park ranks as the second largest

Northern Alaska
Established December 2, 1980
13,238 square miles

Things to See: *Anaktuvuk Pass; Frigid Crags; Boreal Mountain; Mount Doonarak; Arrigetch Peaks; Mount Igikpak*

Things to Do: *Float plane trips; Camping; Hiking; Rock climbing; Bird-watching; Backpacking*

What's Nearby? *Kobuk Valley National Park; Noatak National Preserve; Inupiat Heritage Center; Cape Krusenstern National Monument; Bering Land Bridge National Preserve*

national park, with 13,238 square miles. That makes it larger than the Netherlands.

Yet it is a paradox of the park and preserve that this is one of the few national parks to contain communities. People have lived in what is now part of the park for about 12,500 years. Nearly all of the Nunamiut people are mountain Inuit who traditionally traveled between the Brooks Range and the Arctic coast, feeding on migrating herds of caribou. In the 1940s, contact with outsiders began to change everything for these Native Americans. Newcomers brought food and guns and, perhaps more importantly, trade for furs.

The Alatna River provides canoeing through the heart of the Brooks Range to the Endicott Mountains past Circle Lake and the jagged spires of the Arrigetch Peaks.

Creeping Modernization

After World War II, a band of five families was convinced to move from distant Chandler Lake to Anaktuvuk Pass. Later, a group of eight families from Killik River joined them to found the village of Anaktuvuk Pass. With increased encroachment on their lands, notably by the "ice road" built to link North Slope oil fields to the south, villagers began to see advantages in joining the system of national parks. When Gates of the Arctic National Park and Preserve was officially established in 1980, the village and the lands around it were included within the park's boundaries. Negotiations between the park service and the native peoples continued until 1996, resulting in a stretch of park that the Nunamiut continue to use to hunt caribou, Dall sheep, and ptarmigan and to fish for trout and grayling, while trading for blubber and meat from whales and seals. Today, the village of Anaktuvuk Pass has a population of about 250, a Nunamiut museum, a village store, a National Park Service ranger station, and air service. It is just one of 11 "resident zone communities" in and around the park that have special hunting

The John River flows through the wide glacial valleys of the central Brooks Range south from Anaktuvuk Pass to the Koyukuk River, providing a major migration route for Arctic caribou.

and fishing privileges inside park boundaries; the others are Nuiqsut, Wiseman, Bettles, Evansville, Allakaket, Alatna, Hughes, Kobuk, Shungnak, and Ambler.

These Inuit cultures certainly were the first to live within the park, but gold brought a stampede of strangers to the area in the

Glacier National Park

Northwestern Montana's Glacier National Park presents the Rocky Mountains as many have always imagined them: granite peaks with glimmering glaciers fitted into their gorges, fields run riot with wildflowers, lakes as deep and blue as the summer sky, cascading waterfalls, grizzly bears, wooded slopes, and miles and miles of wilderness trails.

The park, the southern section of the Waterton-Glacier International Peace Park, which the United States shares with Canada, is adorned with 200 lakes and drained by 936 miles of rivers and streams. Glacier is also graced by two magnificent ranges of the northern Rockies, featuring dozens of the park's namesake glaciers, which seem to flow down every high mountain valley.

Breathtaking Views

The park's nearly 1,600 square miles, which make it about as large as the state of Delaware, offer "the best care-killing scenery on the continent," in the words of naturalist John Muir. The mountains of Glacier are not especially high when compared with those in other national parks in the Rockies, but dramatic contrasts in elevation give the park its own special grandeur.

A stunning example is the abrupt 7,113-foot vertical rise of Mount Cleveland, from the surface of Lake McDonald at 3,153 feet to the snowcapped summit at 10,466 feet. Adding to the distinctive beauty of Glacier are the sheer faces and angular contours of its multicolored peaks, their flanks covered by heavy forests.

Northwestern Montana
Established May 11, 1910
1,583 square miles

Things to See: *Going-to-the-Sun Road; Logan Pass; Mount Logan; McDonald Lake; Sperry Glacier; Saint Mary Lake; West Glacier*

Things to Do: *Hiking; Backpacking; Camping; Horseback riding; Fishing; Cross-country skiing*

What's Nearby? *Grant-Kohrs Ranch National Historic Site; Big Hole National Battlefield; Lewis & Clark National Historic Trail; Nez Perce National Historical Park*

The remnants of dozens of glaciers still cling to the walls of great rock amphitheaters (*cirques*) in the park's mountains, earning them a nickname from the region's Native Americans: "Shining Mountains." At lower elevations, glaciers have carved the awe-inspiring landscape of the park from layer after layer of sedimentary rock, consisting of mudstone, sandstone, and limestone.

Two chief mountain ranges, the Livingston and the Lewis, began forming the backbone of Glacier about 60 million years ago. Erosion, in the form of wind, rain, snow, and flash floods, started reshaping these

With a new panorama around every bend, the trails from Lake Josephine to Grinnell Glacier and Grinnell Point are among the most popular—and most scenic—in all of the Rocky Mountains.

ranges about 50 million years ago, but the prime mountain-carving era started about three million years ago with the Pleistocene epoch, during which four distinct glacial periods occurred. After the last of these ice ages took place only 10,000 years ago, the earth gradually and increasingly warmed over the subsequent millennia.

As the colors of the resident trees change for autumn, morning fog evaporates from Glacier's McDonald Creek as the sun begins to peek over the looming mountains.

During the ice ages, the park's glaciers grew and shrunk time and time again, sculpting the landscape in the process. As the glaciers in the park melted and refroze, they moved boulders, gorged valleys, and otherwise redefined the terrain of the park—in slow motion. The results of the glacial eras are on display all over the modern park, from *arêtes,* or walls separating two glacial valleys, *moraines* of rocks dumped in one spot over the eons, and *hanging valleys* where a smaller glacier above collided with a larger one below.

Warming Up

In 1850, Glacier had about 150 glaciers, and in 1997 there were about 50. As of 2009, only 26 remain. If the current global warming trend continues, scientists have estimated the park's last glacial remnant will melt away in 2030. Park officials say the park's name will remain Glacier National Park no matter what happens.

Two of the remaining glaciers, Grinnell and Sperry, are still easily accessible to hikers. Each is about 200 acres in size—and shrinking—and both are tucked into high

shady hanging valleys where they ever so slowly continue their work of sculpting mountains, valleys, and lakes.

Of the lakes and ponds, many of them are glacial *tarns,* meaning a watery remnant of a departed glacier dammed into a valley by moraines. These lakes and ponds typically lack a fish population, as their only inflow is from snowmelt. Interestingly, Glacier not only straddles the Continental Divide, where water drains into the Atlantic or Pacific oceans depending on which side it drips down, but it also features drainages that send water into Canada's Hudson Bay.

Glacier's modern climate is dominated by cool, wet weather from the Pacific Northwest. The abundance of rainfall makes the forests lush, green, dense, and damp. The park's western slopes catch most of the moisture, meaning the growth is so thick in places that it's literally impassable. The eastern side of the park has far less precipitation and, therefore, far less foliage.

Teeming with Life

The vagaries of elevation and weather combine to produce four distinctive life zones within the park: grassland and prairie; the Canadian zone, with massive lodgepole-pine forests covering hundreds of square miles; the Hudsonian zone, a transition area with whitebark pine, alder, and other trees that are able to withstand long winters; and the Arctic-Alpine zone, with so-called *krummholz,* or "crooked-wood," forests of gnarled and dwarfed fir.

This unusually diverse range of topography supports a remarkable array of plants and wildlife. More than 1,000 plant species—

Fens, Wetlands, and Biodiversity

When one thinks of Glacier National Park, the first word that comes to mind is definitely not *bog.* Bogs, fens, and swamps, however, make up a small but important part of the park's diversity. Glacier's wetlands hold some of the highest concentrations of rare species in the state, including 43 rare plants and the endangered bog lemming.

When talk turns to bogs or fens, people often get a picture of gassy, bubbling mires with crocodiles and other dangerous, meat-eating creatures. This is partially true here, as well, though not in the traditional sense. Bogs and fens are both known for the fact that their water is still—it doesn't wash in and out with an ocean's tides, nor does it run like a stream. The two differ in how they are formed from the bottom up (or the top down): A bog's primary source of water is rain, whereas a fen's source is groundwater. This is significant when it comes to Glacier, where a huge source of water is glacier melt. Bogs are dominated by sphagnum moss, which is highly acidic (and which makes people think of gassy, bubbling mires), while fens tend to be alkaline, having vegetation such as grasses and bladderwort.

While alligators and crocodiles are not to be found far above Florida, some of the *plants* of this park's wetlands have developed carnivorous tastes in response to the lack of minerals in the still waters. This is only dangerous, however, for the insects that call the wetlands home. In fact, the plant worlds of these wetlands are pretty cutthroat places. In the race for nutrients, bog plants such as sphagnum moss render the waters acidic so that few others can survive. On top of that, the mosses put out feelers tipped with what looks like dew, attracting thirsty insects. But the dewlike substance is actually a kind of glue, which traps the insect, pulls it in, and digests its nutrients.

In fens, the bladderwort flower (nearly impossible to find anywhere else) puts out a spectacular floral show for any passersby. It also features an interesting floating root system that not only allows it to gather more oxygen but also carries with it tiny, lethal weapons: small, semi-inflated sacs. When aquatic insects find their way to these sacs, the sacs inflate all the way and slurp up the insects.

The wetlands of Glacier National Park are only one more example of the elegance of nature. Where humans might see a pool of stagnant water, in reality there exists a complex ecosystem that has adapted to harsh conditions and is, in its own right, as beautiful as the snowy peaks.

Glacier Bay National Park and Preserve

At various strategic points around the earth, great tectonic plates crash into each other, moving at an annual rate of perhaps an inch or several centimeters. Glacier Bay National Park and Preserve bestrides the exquisitely slo-mo collision between the North American and Pacific plates, which have been colliding for more than 100 million years. Sometimes pieces of the North American plate break off to form island arcs and pieces of the continental margin and sea floor. These breakaway tectonic plate pieces are called *terranes,* and four of them form the Glacier Bay region in the northwest-southeast pattern that can be seen on a map.

The vast energies of the slow-motion crash are enough to push some rocks up, forming mountain chains, or down, where

Glacier Bay National Park and Preserve's Lituya Bay is remembered for the 1958 mega-tsunami that generated waves higher than 1,700 feet, the highest ever recorded.

they melt into a molten mass that in turn extrudes across the battered landscape via volcanoes. "When it cools," National Parks

Southeastern Alaska
Established December 2, 1980
5,130 square miles

Things to See: *Brady Glacier; Mount Fairweather; Grand Plateau Glacier; Bartlett
Cove; Carroll Glacier; Marble Island*

Things to Do: *Hiking; Boating; Kayaking;
Mountaineering; Rafting; Backpacking; Camping; Fishing*

What's Nearby? *Klondike Gold Rush National
Historic Park; Sitka National Historic Park;
Wrangell–St. Elias National Park and Pre-
serve; Kenai Fjords National Park*

Service literature reports, "it welds together
one of the world's most complex geological
jigsaw puzzles: Glacier Bay."

Clues to a Warming Planet

In his 2006 book, *Geology of Southeast
Alaska: Rock and Ice,* Professor Harold
Hinton Stowell wrote: "Glacier Bay contains
spectacular glaciers, glacial geomorphology
(landform change), and bedrock geology.
The area is currently the only one of three in
Southeast Alaska that has tidewater glaciers
(the other two are the Tracy Arm–Endicott
Arm and LeConte Bay areas). It is also
home to the largest and most active glaciers
in southeast Alaska."

As one might imagine, glaciers are on the
front lines of debates about global warming.
Professor Stowell also described changes
to the area: "These glaciers have retreated
more than 60 miles in the last 200 years,
leaving behind a dense network of fjords,
moraines, and other glacial features. Lateral
moraines and erosional features along the
fjords indicate that the ice was once more

than 3,000 feet thick (900 meters) and that
its volume was about 500 cubic miles."

On a cheerier note, however, the professor adds: "In spite of their dramatic retreat,
many glaciers around Glacier Bay still reach
the ocean." Included in such frozen wonders
are nine tidewater glaciers, four of which
actively calve, or shed, icebergs into the bay.

The closest of Alaska's eight national
parks to western Canada and the lower
48 states, the area around Glacier Bay in
southeastern Alaska was first proclaimed
a U.S. national monument in 1925. Glacier
Bay National Park comprises 5,130 square

miles; 4,164 square miles of it is designated
as a wilderness area.

No roads lead to the park, so it is best
reached by air. In summer, ferries ply the
bay's waters to the community of Gustavus,
Alaska—"Gateway to Glacier Bay Park"—or
directly to the marina at Bartlett Cove. Cruise
ships are also a popular way of taking in
the park. Despite its lack of roads, more
than 300,000 visitors annually come to visit.
Some hardy adventurers brave the mountain
thickets and heavy rain forest by climbing,
hiking, or taking a raft. But a large majority of
guests travel from Alaska's Inside Passage to

*Glacier Bay's sea lions and harbor seals seem innumerable. Visitors also enjoy observing humpback
and gray whales, killer whales, and harbor and Dall's porpoises.*

The park's glaciers have retreated more than 60 miles in the last 200 years, leaving in their wake a complex, picturesque network of moraines and fjords.

the tidewater glaciers through which Glacier Bay is a natural waterway. The cliffs and glaciers, mountain crags and ice fields, islands, lagoons, and sea passages make exploration by sea an unforgettable passage.

Early Exploration

In 1794, when Captain George Vancouver explored the region, he found Icy Strait south of Glacier Bay choked with ice, and Glacier Bay itself was one huge glacier about 20 miles wide, 4,000 feet thick, that extended more than 100 miles to the St. Elias mountain range. Almost 100 years later, however, John Muir became the bay's great early explorer, scientist, and natural-

ist. In 1879, Muir and his Tlingit guides first visited the area. By that time, the glacier had receded 48 miles up the bay. (By 1916, the Grand Pacific Glacier ended 65 miles from the mouth of the bay, making it the fastest glacial retreat recorded anywhere in the world.)

Muir was enthralled by the area. "All . . . day it rained," he wrote on an expedition to Alaska in 1890. "The mountains were smothered in dull-colored mist and fog, the great glacier looming through the gloomy gray fog fringes with wonderful effect. It is bad weather for exploring, but delightful nevertheless, making all the strange, mysterious region yet stranger and more mysterious."

Muir had also long been fascinated by a new science called *glaciology.* In 1891, he and glaciologist Harry Fielding Reid began surveying glacial processes. His 1915 book, *Travels in Alaska,* helped change the region into an attraction for explorers and scientists as well as for more casual visitors. It is symbolic that in past times the park's most famous feature has been the Muir

Gigantic Glacier Bay National Park and Preserve covers a massive amount of wilderness area. No roads lead to the park, which is usually approached by air or, in summer, ferryboats.

A Tlingit Legend

In southeastern Alaska, the aboriginal peoples dominant in the region are the Tlingit, the Hoonah, and the Haida. Southeast Alaska is replete with natural resources: spawning salmon, halibut, and roots and berries nourished these groups just as much as the traditional stories told at potlatches and family gatherings. One such story tells of how Alaska, particularly the Glacier Bay area, came to have its magnificent freshwater rivers.

Raven is the figure in Tlingit myth that resembles other trickster figures from around the world such as Hermes from Greek myth or Anansi from African traditions. Raven is clever, quick-witted, and very lazy, but he can also be cruel and has no qualms about tricking others into doing what he wants. This tale tells of how, long before people can remember, there were no fresh rivers or lakes, just the salty sea. One evening Raven,

who in those days had snow-white feathers, was staying with his brother-in-law Petrel, a blue-gray arctic bird. Petrel had a freshwater stream in his home that dripped into a small pool. When Raven asked about it, Petrel let him drink from the pool but would not let him near the stream.

Raven, of course, could think of nothing but that stream. He kept Petrel awake all night, telling stories of the great adventures he had experienced, until Petrel finally fell asleep, exhausted. Raven flew out of the hut through the hole in the roof for smoke from the fire, collected dog droppings, and put them in Petrel's bed. He then drank from the fresh-water stream until there was almost nothing left. When Petrel woke, he was angry to see the stream almost gone, but he was so distracted by what was in his bed that Raven had a chance to fly away through the smoke hole.

Full to bursting with water, however, Raven was too big for the hole and got stuck. Petrel built up the fire so that Raven might choke and come down, but the only result was to turn Raven's feathers black. He escaped and fled the hut, with Petrel close behind. Flying in such a disarray and so full of water, Raven began to spit the fresh water out all over the ground. Wherever that water hit, large rivers formed. And that, according to Tlingit legend, is how the the fresh water rivers and lakes came to be, even with the great salty Glacier Bay lying in their midst.

Ravens are common in the park, and the fork-tailed storm-petrel can be found in abundance during spring and autumn. The aboriginal tales of southeastern Alaska feed off the land and hold rich and varied meanings. There are still some Tlingit, Haida, and Hoonah living as they ever did—hunting, fishing, and telling stories.

Glacier, which once was nearly 265 feet high and two miles wide. Today, however, it has receded to the point that it no longer reaches the sea. Most visitors favor Lamplugh and Margerie glaciers.

In 1899, Muir paid his last visit to Glacier Bay. He was one of 23 scientists with the grand Harriman Alaska Expedition, mounted by railroad mogul Edward Harriman. More than 5,000 photographs were taken on that trip, which stopped in Glacier Bay, Sitka, Yakutat Bay, Prince William Sound, Kodiak Island, the Shumagin Islands, Unalaska, the Pribilof Islands, Port Clarence, and Cape Fox. "Climbing higher for a still broader outlook, I made notes and sketched, improving

the precious time while sunshine streamed through the luminous fringes of the clouds and fell on the green waters of the fjord, the glittering bergs, the crystal bluffs of the vast glacier, the intensely white, far-spreading fields of ice, and the ineffably chaste and spiritual heights of the Fairweather Range, which were now hidden, now partly revealed, the whole making a picture of icy wildness unspeakably pure and sublime," Muir wrote.

The Harriman expedition concluded in August 1899. In September, a devastating earthquake shattered the Muir Glacier, and for a decade gigantic chunks of floating ice kept ships from nearing it. Tourists and steamship companies vanished, leaving the field open to

a colorful collection of scientists and adventurers, miners, seal hunters, fox farmers, egg gatherers, hermits, and homesteaders, not to mention the salmon cannery at Dundas Bay.

Scientific work, notably that of plant ecologist William S. Cooper, who studied the birth of plant life on the deglaciated terrain, led to calls for protection of the region. The movement succeeded with the creation of Glacier Bay National Monument in 1925, although that park was less than half the size of today's park and preserve.

The Second World War changed the region, largely due to the construction and operation of the Gustavus airfield. Easier park access, combined with postwar enthusiasm for outdoor recreation, led to increased use of Glacier Bay. Yet it took 55 years after achieving national monument status for the Alaska National Interest Lands Conservation Act of 1980 to change the park to Glacier Bay National Park and Preserve. In 1986, the park area was included in an International Biosphere Reserve. Six years later, it became part of a UNESCO World Heritage Site.

The Modern Age

Today's visitors enjoy the sight of marine mammals such as cetaceans: humpback, gray, and killer whales; and harbor and Dall's porpoises. Humpbacks forage through the summer in the less icy fjords, while gray whales can be found during spring and fall

Tarr Inlet's Margerie Glacier is one of Glacier Bay's nine tidewater glaciers. Four of these glaciers calve, or shed, icebergs into the bay in spectacular, explosive splashes.

migrations in waters by the outer coast. Dall's porpoises swim in open waters; harbor porpoises prefer sheltered waters; and killer whales are around all year. Harbor seals seem numberless, but in the early 1990s researchers counted more than 7,000 of them lolling on icebergs in Johns Hopkins Inlet.

Ornithologists and bird-watchers have spotted about 240 species of birds in the park. Seabirds by the thousands nest on rocky shores and cliffs on the outer coast and within the bay. Colonies of puffins, cormorants, gulls, and guillemots scatter along the shores, particularly in the bay's northern section. Flocks of foraging gulls, phalaropes, and molting sea ducks favor summer; murrelets, loons, and gulls prefer winter. Bald eagles can be seen on shorelines throughout the park.

The rain forest of beautiful Bartlett Cove—near both the park's visitor center and the village of Gustavus—displays Sitka spruce and western hemlock trees covered by verdant layers of moss.

Grand Canyon National Park

Arizona's Grand Canyon National Park is a natural, national, and global treasure, unique and unfathomable. It is also a maze and a marvel. The sight of the canyon—especially, of course, one's first sight of it—usually induces speechlessness and a reaction that goes by many names, such as awestruck or amazed. "The wonders of the Grand Canyon cannot be adequately represented in symbols of speech, nor by speech itself," said Major John Wesley Powell, the first to explore the Colorado River through the canyon.

More than a century ago, the sight stunned President Theodore Roosevelt into silence. When he recovered his voice, Roosevelt said, "In the Grand Canyon, Arizona has a natural wonder which, so far as I know, is in kind absolutely unparalleled throughout the rest of the world. . . . Leave it as it is. You cannot improve on it, and man can only mar it. What you can do is to keep it for your children, your children's children, and for all who come after you, as the one great sight which every American should see."

ARIZONA

Grand Canyon

Santa Fe is the only railroad entering this National Park

Northwestern Arizona
Established February 26, 1919
1,900 square miles

Things to See: *South Rim; North Rim; Bright Angel Trail; Phantom Ranch; Desert View; Desert View Watchtower; Tuweep; Toroweap Overlook; Tusayan Ruin and Museum; Point Imperial; Cape Royal*

Things to Do: *Hiking; Whitewater rafting; Mule trips; Camping; Backpacking*

What's Nearby? *Parashant National Monument; Pipe Spring National Monument; Lake Mead National Recreation Area; Sunset Crater National Monument; Wupatki National Monument; Walnut Canyon National Monument; Tuzigoot National Monument; Montezuma Castle National Monument; Zion National Park; Bryce Canyon National Park; Navajo National Monument; Canyon De Chelly National Monument; Hubbell Trading Post National Historic Site; Petrified Forest National Park*

The matchless canyon also brought forth streams of eloquence from Powell, who wrote in his explorer's journal: "We are three-quarters of a mile in the depths of the earth, and the great river shrinks into insignificance, as it dashes its angry waves against the walls and cliffs, that rise to the world above; they are but puny ripples, and we but pygmies, running up and down the sands, or lost among the boulders. We have an unknown distance yet to run, an unknown river yet to explore. What falls there are, we know not; what rocks beset the channel, we know not; what walls rise over the river, we know not."

A Wonder of the Natural World

Although there is no consensus on the Seven Natural Wonders of the World, the Grand Canyon is on virtually every short list—sometimes the only such landmark in the United States. The vast majority of tourists who visit the park see the canyon from the South Rim's Grand Canyon Village Historic District. There the canyon reaches ten miles across and one mile down. Visitors hiking from the rim all the way down to

Right: *A three-day hike follows the course of Deer Creek through the Grand Canyon. The 200-foot-high Deer Creek Falls waits at the end of the journey.* Opposite top: *The railway into Grand Canyon National Park—here romanticized in a famous mid-1950s poster—first journeyed to the canyon in 1901. Passengers since have included both Theodore and Franklin Roosevelt.* Opposite bottom: *The Grand Canyon has been carved by the Colorado River, which came into being with the formation of the Rocky Mountains to the east about 70 million years ago.*

A row of aspen trees shimmering on the less-visited North Rim of Grand Canyon underlines three popular peaks, Deva Temple, Brahma Temple, and Zoroaster Temple.

the river will traverse seven miles. In other parts of the park, however, the Grand Canyon descends another 800 feet farther and stretches eight miles across.

More than four million visitors come to see the canyon every year, seeking its beauty beyond compare. That's more than visit the Lincoln Memorial, even though the Grand Canyon is much farther from most U.S. population centers. Visitors explore the Grand Canyon by boat and raft, horse and mule, car and bus, or helicopter and airplane.

Some of its immensity is indicated by its outsized statistics: The canyon is a chasm 277 miles long and up to 18 miles wide. Its average depth is one mile. The Grand Canyon formed in just three million to six million years, and it continues to change. About 89 mammal species, 56 reptile and amphibian species, and 355 species of bird live in the park.

The 1,450-mile-long Colorado River, the wellspring of the canyon's origin, flows west at approximately four miles per hour. On average the river is 100 feet deep and 300 feet wide. The canyon, of course, is the jewel of the Colorado River, sitting on the borders of the Havasupai, Navajo, and Hualapai reservations. A hike from the rim to the riverbed is an overnight hike from any entrance.

Visitors to the park can choose from four park entrances. Most aim for the South Rim of the canyon, which is easily accessible from Flagstaff, Arizona, the closest city to the park. The popular Mather Point overlook is another common destination. To the north of the South Rim, many enter through the Hualapai Reservation. Other big attractions

The Havasupai People

One of the many aspects of the canyon that has endured for time out of mind is the people. Though only a fraction of what they once were, some native cultures still survive and call the canyon area their home. While not enjoying the same freedoms they once did, they still manage to eke out a living based on the land—though this kind of living is substantially different from what it was in the past.

The Grand Canyon has been home to many different people over the millennia. One of the most enduring groups to call the sheer rock walls home are the Havasupai people. Havasupai means "People of the Blue-Green Water." Havasu Falls—the spectacular blue-green waterfall just outside of the park's boundaries on Havasu Creeks—spills into their reservation and flows through their culture. They consider the falls sacred, and its connection with the land has been a part of their civilization for thousands of years. Visitors to the Grand Canyon are allowed in Havasu Canyon, but they must pay a fee and a tax to be on the land. The Havasupai tribe administers the canyon though some of their lands fall within the boundaries of the park.

in the area include the panoramas seen from Hermit Road and the Grand Canyon Sky-walk, a "glass bridge" built by the Hualapai, which extends 70 feet out over the canyon.

For those coming in to the park's east entrance, the 70-foot-high stone Watchtower at Desert View is a popular sight. Fewer visitors enter the park from its North Rim.

A Spectacular View

Apart from sheer size, one clue to the profound beauty of Grand Canyon was

Grand Canyon's Colorado River ecosystem features sandy beaches and riparian vegetation. The next ecosystem up the canyon wall consists of desert scrub, with cacti predominant.

Scientists today say the Grand Canyon began 17 million years ago as two canyons that, six million years ago, broke through the rocks that separated them and merged into one.

first noted by Powell: its geology displays sequences of Kaibab limestone, thick Coconino sandstone, Hermit shale, and Supai formation shales and sandstones that

create a sense of order on an enormous scale. Extending a mile down, the canyon offers visitors the chance to see millions of years of geologic history, a complete geo-

logical record that can be accessed nowhere else on earth.

History at the canyon begins with a hunting and gathering culture from roughly 2,000 B.C. to 1,000 B.C. Fifteen centuries later, about A.D. 500, another hunting and gathering group, the Anasazi, entered the region. These are the ancient people of the pueblos. They made masonry villages and settled and cultivated more than 2,000 sites in the area. Over time, the Cohonina, the Cerbats, the Sinagua, the Dineh, and the Paiutes moved into the Grand Canyon region. Their descendants—the Hualapai, Havasupai, Navajo, Hopi, and Paiute—live there today.

In 1540, European exploration began when Francisco Vasquez de Coronado explored the Grand Canyon for gold. American mountain men arrived in the late 1820s, but they left little of themselves behind. In the 1850s, Mormon leader Brigham Young sent emissaries to locate sites in the region by which he and his followers could make their way west.

In 1857, Lieutenant Joseph Christmas Ives traveled up the Colorado from the Gulf of California for 350 miles by steamboat. "The region is, of course, altogether value-less," the hapless lieutenant wrote. "It seems intended by nature that the Colorado River, along with the greater portion of its lonely and majestic way, shall be forever unvisited and undisturbed."

Havasu Canyon hosts Mooney Falls and Navajo Falls as well as its self-named Havasu Falls (pictured here), *famed for the blue-green hue of its waters. This coloration is caused by the falls' limestone bed.*

The breakthrough for American exploration came in 1869, when John Wesley Powell explored the Colorado River by boat, gathering scientific information about the Grand Canyon. It was Powell who gave the canyon its name. President Theodore Roosevelt later established the Grand Canyon as a national game reserve in 1906 and as a national monument in 1908. On February 26, 1919, President Woodrow Wilson declared the Grand Canyon a national park.

A Choice of Canyons

For modern travelers, there are actually two Grand Canyons—the South Rim and the North Rim. Although less than a dozen miles apart as the crow flies, the areas are distinctly different. The North Rim, a thousand feet higher than the South Rim and more remote from major interstates and towns, is less crowded. The South Rim, with an elevation of 7,000 feet and direct access from Interstate 40 and Flagstaff, can be a congested place, especially during the tourist season. About nine out of ten park visitors go to the South Rim, partly because of its accessibility, but partly because the views there are thought to be better than those at the North Rim.

The enduring popularity of three great hiking trails down the canyon to the Colorado River stands out from the rest. They

Top: *Mule trekking is a favorite way to see the canyon. Mule trips along the South Rim are booked with the park service more than a year in advance.* Bottom: *Rafting through the canyon on the Colorado River will allow visitors to experience the park in an entirely different manner than is possible from looking down from the rim or even trekking to the bottom.*

are Kaibab Trail, Grandview Trail, and Bright Angel Trail, which leads eight miles from the South Rim to Phantom Ranch, a lodge and campground clustered among a glen of Fremont cottonwoods on the canyon floor.

An alternative to this trek is a ride by muleback through the canyon. Mules leave from the South Rim for day trips as well as for overnight trips to Phantom Ranch, the only place in the canyon itself where visitors are allowed to spend the night, in rustic cabins and dormitories.

Reservations are required long in advance for Colorado River rafting trips, which are another means of getting deep into the Grand Canyon. These expeditions vary in length from about three days by motorized raft to 18 days or more in dories much like those used by John Wesley Powell. Such adventures are only for seasoned outdoor adventurers.

In 1930, the Fred Harvey Company asked architect Mary Colter to design a structure with the most panoramic view of the canyon possible. The result: the Desert View Watchtower.

The Hualapai—Life Ever-Changing

The name of another enduring culture, the Hualapai, means "People of the Tall Pines." They currently live south of the park. One of the great sights on their land is the Skywalk, a glass overhang that thrusts 70 feet over the canyon floor, 4,000 feet below. Though the view from the Skywalk is beautiful, visitors should also make a point to see nearby Guano Point, which some say is the most spectacular sight in the entire park. This spot offers a more peaceful, more colorful view of the Grand Canyon than can be seen at any other point.

The Hualapai make their living from the park in various ways, running tours of the canyon with all-terrain vehicles and guiding kayak tours. They own 108 miles of the park on the South Rim and use the tourism that comes through the area to show off some of the canyon's most heart-soaringly beautiful points. They also offer a nature conservancy and activities such as hiking, camping, and hunting on their reservation, where they issue big-game permits for hunters of bighorn sheep.

The Hualapai people number about 2,300 today. They once stretched from the Grand Canyon to what is now the Bill Williams River in west-central Arizona and from the Black Mountains to the San Francisco Peaks in central Arizona. These volcanic peaks were and remain sacred to the Hualapai.

The Hualapai believe that once, long ago, a great flood covered the world. To save one of their own, a Hualapai couple, according to legend, put their daughter into a log and sealed it with pitch. They set it free in the waters, hoping for a safe landing somewhere. The jagged peaks of the San Francisco rose above the water, and here the girl was able to get out. The waters in the San Francisco peaks were life giving, and she conceived twin sons by them. These boys, it is said, grew to be two warrior deities who roamed that land. From them came the Hualapai.

Named for legendary landscape artist Thomas Moran, Mount Moran, pictured here between a layer of clouds and Oxbow Bend in the Snake River, looms over the adjacent peaks at 12,605 feet.

Many hikers take the trail to Hidden Falls and Inspiration Point, just an uphill mile from the boat docks. More adventurous types continue farther up into the sheer-walled Cascade Canyon, carved by a receding glacier in the last 50,000 years. Today the rushing waters of Cascade Creek—moving considerably faster than the glacier and responsible for this remarkable gorge—fill the air here with sound in springtime. Best of all, Cascade Canyon is just one of many sublime canyons tucked between the phenomenal peaks of the Teton Range.

Flora and Fauna Abound

In the forests and meadows of the Tetons, wildlife enthusiasts will find a diverse population of the original wild animals of the Rockies, including black bears and grizzlies, gray wolves, mountain lions, mule deer, bighorn sheep, pronghorn, water ouzels, and golden eagles. Near Jackson Lake Lodge, Willow Flats is one of the best places in the West to spot the great Shiras moose. Often in the morning, a moose will venture out into the open along the river and creek bottoms

suggesting that the peak was once perched more than 15,000 feet above sea level, which would have made it the valley's tallest mountain.

At the foot of these picturesque peaks are a string of sapphirelike lakes, including Jackson Lake, Leigh Lake, and Jenny Lake. Their crystalline surfaces provide the perfect mirror for the majesty of the summits above. These are the remnants of the glaciers that spilled from the mountains many millennia ago. The largest, Jackson Lake, was dammed and expanded in 1911 to provide more water to Idaho potato farmers—it is popular with boaters today. Farther south and nearly a perfect circle, Jenny Lake is the most popular spot in the park, circum-

navigated by hiking trails. There is a popular campground and a luxury cabin resort on its shores, as well as a water taxi that ferries hikers to a trailhead on the opposite side.

The Colter Stone

Lewis and Clark traveled north of present-day Grand Teton National Park on the Missouri River. It is widely believed that one member of their party, however, a trapper named John

Colter, branched out from the Lewis and Clark expedition and, in 1808, became the first European to reach Jackson Hole. The Colter Stone, which provides potential evidence of his presence, was discovered on the west side of the Tetons in 1933. The stone is carved in the shape of a head. Colter's name is engraved on one side, and *1808*, which may be a reference to the year the stone was created, is carved into the other. The authenticity of the stone has not yet been proved, so it may simply be an elaborate hoax. But if the stone really did come from John Colter, it would prove that he had, indeed, been here before any other European.

in the park's marshlands. On rare occasions, lynx can be spotted in the forests, and on even rarer occasions, the infamous (but quite shy) wolverine makes an appearance.

The park's plant life is equally varied, ranging from open grass and sage communities at the lower elevations to forests of lodgepole pine, Englemann spruce, and Douglas fir up higher. The Tetons are famous for their wildflower displays, which last late into the summer and even early September because of the lingering snowdrifts and near-daily afternoon thun-

derstorms. The park's brilliant wildflowers include wild roses, Indian paintbrushes, blue columbines, and yellow balsamroots.

For about half of the year, the wildflower-clad slopes of the Tetons that can be seen in summer turn a monochromatic white. The extreme winter climate here makes for some pretty unbearable days for most any life form, let alone the wildflowers. The temperature dipped to an all-time low of −66 degrees Fahrenheit in 1933. Regardless of the cold, however, winter has become an increasingly popular season in

the park, with numerous opportunities for snowshoeing, cross-country skiing, and wildlife viewing on the National Elk Wildlife Refuge, sandwiched between the park's southern boundary and the town of Jackson, Wyoming. It also doesn't hurt that Jackson Hole is home to a world-class downhill skiing resort, just south of the park boundary.

The centerpiece of Grand Teton National Park, the Cathedral Range is comprised of three mountains: Teewinot (12,325 feet), Grand Teton (13,770 feet), and Mount Owen (12,928 feet).

The Snake River Overlook provides a breath-taking view of Grand Teton, seen here during a winter sunrise.

balancing of these multiple interests, however, proves as difficult today as it had in the preceding century.

The timeless backdrop of the Tetons provides an unmistakable reminder of the need to conserve the wide-open spaces of the West. As part of the Greater Yellowstone Ecosystem, Grand Teton National Park is part of the largest remaining intact ecosystem in the lower 48 states, and the majestic moose, the beastly grizzly, and the wily wolf pay no mind to park boundaries and other imaginary lines. The need to allow nature to take its own course is as pronounced here as it is anywhere. Serendipitously or not, the need for conservation and the resulting benefit nicely dovetail into one another, keeping safe that dizzyingly beautiful temple of the great outdoors that is the Teton Range, looming over the Snake River in Jackson Hole.

Fur Trappers and the American West

On February 13, 1822, a call went out to the young, enterprising men of Wisconsin. William H. Ashley and his business partner Andrew Henry were looking to reinvent the fur industry. Where once traders had bought furs from native peoples of the areas, these two wanted to brave the wilderness where no white people had ever set foot and establish their own trapping company to corner the market. Applicants from all walks of life answered the call for this adventure, from outlaws to those educated at Harvard alike. From this party would come some of the greatest adventurers in the United States, shaping the history of not just Grand Teton but the entire country.

The trappers of the late 18th century were some of the toughest in the world, not to mention the most educated in the ways of the land. Though very often illiterate, many could speak several languages, enabling them to translate and trade with local cultures and trappers from other countries. Many were skilled in combat—a necessity of the wilderness when trapping in territory that belonged to another. Because of their knowledge of the land, these trappers became some of the first people to chart the unexplored West.

But when more and more trappers were on the move, the Tetons became a thoroughfare. One group of trappers led by adventurer Jedediah Smith, a partner in Henry Ashley's fur company, thoroughly charted the Tetons area and came to know every spring and cranny. Not only was the landscape stunningly beautiful, it was teeming with beaver, bears, fish, eagles, and other wildlife to hunt and trap. The Grand Tetons became one of the trappers' favorite spots to meet.

Every year trappers would leave signs for one another, telling the time and location so that all could come together for the "Rendezvous" in the spring. Traditionally, the meeting location moved with the trappers to a new place each year, but the Tetons were always popular. Visitors can still climb Rendezvous Peak in the southeastern corner of the park.

The high alpine terrain in the park features a number of tarn *lakes—lakes in cirques scoured out by glaciers during ice ages past.*

800 other plant species. Only about ten inches of precipitation falls at Great Basin annually, so plant and animal species are well adapted to the dry climate.

The park's animal population includes 73 mammal species, 18 reptiles, eight fish, and more than 200 varieties of birds. Mammals run the gamut from shrews and voles to bighorn sheep and yellow-bellied marmots. There are a number of animals found only in the Snake Range of Great Basin, including many cave species, as well as springsnails and pygmy rabbits. The latter are in serious decline and are protected under Nevada state law as their old-growth sagebrush habitat falls prey to casinos and subdivisions.

The First Settlers

The Great Basin was first permanently settled about 10,000 years ago, long before John C. Frémont explored the area. Ancestral Puebloan people lived here until about 800 years ago, when the Frémont culture established Baker Village just outside modern park boundaries and occupied it for about a century, cultivating corn, beans, and squash and painting pictographs on rock walls in the area. One of the prime spots to see this artwork in the park today is Upper Pictograph Cave, which has a gallery of ancient paintings of people, animals, and abstract shapes. It's not far from the entrance to Lehman Caves on the slopes of Wheeler Peak.

Basque sheepherders frequented the region in the 1800s, but little else happened until the middle of the 19th century, when a Mormon settlement emerged and gold was discovered at Osceola. Lehman's discovery of the caves that today carry his name kicked off the modern era, as he offered cave tours in the 1880s just as rangers do today. However, Great Basin continues to rank as one of the least-visited national parks in the West—the cave tour is one of the few places for miles and miles where you'll encounter a line of people.

The Lehman Caves

The great marble pillars of the Lehman Caves house more than 300 unique formations not to be found anywhere else, as well as a variety of bats, insects, and other deeply interesting cave dwellers. Formed of marble by the slow carving of springs and inland seas, the caves of Great Basin seem to give off a light unto themselves, reflecting colors and shapes unknown save in one's wildest dreams. It took the perfect combination of salt, acid, and calcium working together over the course of 600 million years to create the fragile system that exists today. The seas that used to wash over the area housed millions of shellfish, which, deeply buried, decayed to provide the lime needed to form marble. The caves really are an example of the cycle of life at its deepest and most complex. Also among their many treasures, Lehman Caves contain excellent examples of cave shields. These large and rare disks grow out of ceiling cracks where seeping mineral-laden water deposits sediments in flat circular shapes.

The cave ecosystems are so fragile and unique that one wrong step can destroy an entire system. Caves are different from, for example, forest ecosystems, because they are so isolated. Each cave-dwelling insect or troglobite species has adapted certain features that allow it to dwell in one area or another of a cave—and nowhere else. Should these creatures' environment become polluted or destabilized, the entire species could die out. What people have learned—often the hard way—is that all ecosystems are interconnected. When one species is affected, the entire system can come crashing down.

Those who seek high adventure on the great peaks should look underfoot when planning their next escape. Rangers lead visitors through approximately one and a half miles of trails. The caverns are filled with latticed columns, undulating draperies, helictites, and stalactites. These formations are so dense that the caves' first explorers took along sledgehammers to clear a trail.

In addition to the Lehman Caves, there are more than 40 different caves in the Great Basin area, but only a very few are open to the public, and those require caving permits. To obtain a permit, one must be able to demonstrate knowledge and competence in horizontal and vertical caving as well as conservation techniques.

Great Sand Dunes National Park and Preserve

In the shadow of the Sangre de Cristo (which means "Blood of Christ") Mountains in southwestern Colorado, Great Sand Dunes National Park and Preserve is home to the tallest dunes in North America, mountains of sand measuring 750 feet in height. Located in the enigmatic San Luis Valley, surrounded on all sides by majestic mountain scenery, the dunes appear as a mirage at the foot of the mountains from afar, only coming into sharp focus as the nation's superlative dunes at close range. The dunes' surprisingly distinct surroundings are nothing like visitors expect. This is the Rocky Mountains, after all, not the Sahara Desert.

Nature at War Against Itself

The park's dunes are a serendipitous by-product of the natural elements battling each other to a standstill. Before the dunes, however, the stage was set by a geological uplift of the Sangre de Cristo Mountains on the east side of the valley and the volcanic genesis of the San Juan Mountains on the west side, forming the San Luis Valley in the last 40 million years. The nascent valley was filled with water—dubbed Lake Alamosa—that scientists believe slowly drained over the eons into the Rio Grande, which cuts across the valley not far from its headwaters.

At 750 feet in height, the Great Sand Dunes rise only about a tenth as high from the floor of the San Luis Valley as the peaks looming to the east.

During the Pleistocene era, which began in earnest about 1.8 million years ago with the advent of one of several ice ages, glaciers pushed ice and rock into the San Luis Valley. As the climate warmed, receding glaciers brought more rock, as well as a good deal of sand and silt, that further catalyzed the phenomenon. In concert with the glacial moraines, the sandy remnant of the lake provided countless building blocks for the

Southern Colorado
Established September 13, 2004
134 square miles

Things to See: *Star Dune; High Dune; Medano Creek; Medano Lake; Mount Herard; Sand Ramp Trail*

Things to Do: *Hiking; Backpacking; Sandboarding, skiing, and sledding; Horseback riding; Camping; Making sand castles*

What's Nearby? *Bent's Old Fort National Historic Site; Capulin Volcano National Monument; Florissant Fossil Beds National Monument; Curecanti National Recreation Area; Sand Creek Massacre National Historic Site; Black Canyon of the Gunnison National Park; Mesa Verde National Park; Aztec Ruins National Monument*

dunes of today. The dunes were born about 440,000 years ago, the product of competing elements—wind and water—circulating and recirculating sand. Because there is no accurate way to date sand, however, the age of the dunes is an educated guess rather than a certainty.

The Great Sand Dunes come in two varieties: reversing dunes, the largest and the product of wind blowing predominately in two opposite directions; and star dunes, shaped by winds blowing in all directions. Often blowing at speeds of more than 13 miles per hour, winds from the southwest and northeast shake loose all available sand, carrying it into one of three deposits in the valley—the cementlike sabkha, the outer sand sheet, and the inner dunefield. The last of the three is the heart of the park and home to the biggest dunes. Medano and Sand creeks also carry sand from the dunefield's north and east borders, trans-

porting it back to where the wind can blow it into the heart of the dunes. All in all, the dunes contain nearly five billion cubic meters of sand.

Thriving Wildlife

The sandy habitats of the park provide refuge for a number of insects found only here. The predatory Great Sand Dunes tiger beetle wanders the sand in search of ants, smaller beetles, and mites. Another insect, the giant sand treader camel cricket, was once thought to be unique to the park but has since been discovered burrowing into other sandy environments in the Four Corners states (Arizona, Colorado, New Mexico, and Utah).

Such insects provide food for a host of other animals in Great Sand Dunes. The park is home to hundreds of different bird species—bald eagles, woodpeckers, hummingbirds, and sparrows—as well as salamanders, frogs, toads, trout, snakes, lizards, and a whole host of mammals. The last group is the most extensive, predominately living on the forested slopes and open meadows around the dunes. Bighorn sheep, skunks, mountain lions,

and several bat species are among this latter category.

Hiking in the dunes is well worth the effort because of the amazing views available, with the summit of High Dune offering one

In stark contrast to the dunes in the background, a stand of cottonwood trees changes hue from green to gold in a meadow in Great Sand Dunes National Park and Preserve.

of the best panoramas in the entire Rocky Mountain region. Although its name suggests otherwise, High Dune is not the tallest point of the dunes—it is actually the second tallest when measuring from the base (650 feet), eclipsed by Star Dune's 750-foot height. Sandcastle building, photography, and camping are all popular activities, and skiing, sledding, and snowboarding are not unheard of on the sandy slopes. There are also plenty of hiking trails in the surrounding wilderness. The Montville Nature Trail

While the Great Sand Dunes themselves appear barren, the park and preserve support a wide range of plant species, including a great variety of grasses, wildflowers, and trees.

Endemic Insects and Biodiversity

Aldo Leopold, one of the great conservationists who lived and worked tirelessly for the forest and park lands of the United States, once said that "the last word in ignorance is the man who says of an animal or plant: 'What good is it?' If the land mechanism as a whole is good, then every part is good, whether we understand it or not." This sentiment applies to those places with little creatures—those things visitors sometimes swat or stomp on while making their way through the park.

To the untrained eye, it might appear as though the sandy desert atmosphere does not contain much diversity of life. In fact, it is one of the most biologically and geologically diverse areas in the country. Most of the park's diversity comes in the form of insects that have specially adapted to life in the barren dunes. More than 1,000 different types of insects and spiders are present in the park,

and those are just the ones known to area ecologists.

But why should anyone care about a bunch of bugs? Seven of these species are endemic, which means that because of the park's unique location, they can be found only in this park. The Great Sand Dunes can be considered an island of sand in a sea of vegetation, making it nearly impossible for sand-loving insects to spread to new areas of the country.

Some of these insects are beautiful, such as the endemic Great Sand Dunes Tiger Beetle *(below)*, which has a head and thorax covered in a rainbow of colors, while its wings

are a maze of brown and cream. These beetles are predators, feeding on sand mites and ants—both things you don't want at your park picnic. Another interesting endemic insect is the circus beetle, which gets its name from the fact that, when threatened, it stands on its head and squirts smelly chemicals at intruders, much like a clown with a bottle of seltzer water. Werner's ant-like flower beetle is another insect endemic to the park. This tiny beetle feeds in an unusual way: Because of its small size, it simply lets the wind blow it wherever the food accumulates!

Each of these insects and others are uniquely suited to the dunes, making the park an unforgettable journey for any insect lover. These creatures play an important role in the goings-on of the dunes, maintaining the balance of life and adding flavor to an already spectacular park.

is a popular day hike that draws its name from a long-abandoned settlement that once consisted of 20 homesteads. More strenuous routes up the mountain passes offer incredible bird's-eye views of the dunes and are popular with backpackers.

Above the dunes, the park and preserve also include a parcel of alpine tundra, complete with a number of lakes and six peaks above 13,000 feet. The forests here, populated by spruce, pine, aspen, and cottonwood, are bordered by grasslands and wetlands, making good habitat for a wide variety of life. The park's animal residents include mule deer, elk, coyotes, and bald eagles; bison graze on the adjacent grassland.

Shifting Dunes, Shifting People

Human history in the Great Sand Dunes area dates back about 11,000 years. The first people in the San Luis Valley hunted bison and mammoth and foraged for edible plants during wet seasons and eras, but they avoided the valley when drought gripped the area. The Ute people have long been familiar with the dunes, dubbing them *sowapophe-uvehe*—"the land that moved back and forth"—as have the Apaches of northern New Mexico, who named them *ei-anyedi*—"it goes up and down."

The first Europeans to see the Great Sand Dunes were likely those in Spanish expeditions of the 17th or 18th century, but the first white explorer to specifically mention them in his writings was U.S. Army Lieutenant Zebulon Pike, the namesake of nearby Pikes Peak, whose party came across

the dunes in 1807. "When we camped, I ascended the largest hills of sand," Pike wrote. "Their appearance was exactly that of a sea in storm, except as to color, not the least sign of vegetation existing thereon."

Later parties explored the Rockies, peak by peak, and more and more people found their way to the San Luis Valley by the mid-1800s as roads and railroads began crisscrossing its floor. A toll road even opened over Mosca Pass, but it was repeatedly flooded and is now a hiking trail. Miners and homesteaders filled the valley for the better part of a century—miners even tried to extract gold dust from the dunes themselves, but the milling process ultimately proved too expensive.

President Herbert Hoover established Great Sand Dunes National Monument in 1932 to protect the dunes from further industrialization or commercialization. In 2004, Congress passed legislation establishing a national park and preserve that is four times the size of the original monument. Most importantly, perhaps, it includes the entire hydrologic and geologic system responsible for these amazing, perpetually shifting sand dunes.

The panoramas from the high points of the park's dunefield are among the best in the state of Colorado, offering bird's-eye views of the ever-changing landscape of sand and of the mountains in all directions.

Great Smoky Mountains National Park

About 10,000 years ago, when glaciers advanced from the north during the last Pleistocene Ice Age, the Great Smoky Mountains were already millions of years old. The glaciers cooled the climate of the Smokies, and northern evergreens and other plants, lured by the cold, extended their range south. The range of the glaciers reached the Smokies and then receded again. The forests they brought with them also withdrew, remaining only on the heights, where conditions were cool and moist.

Throughout Great Smoky Mountains National Park, official signs suggest that visitors can see the world as it once was. Because the great glaciers were stopped in their southward journey by these mountains, which include 25 peaks above 6,000 feet, the Smokies today harbor a unique blend of northern and southern animals and plants. Great Smoky Mountains National Park is a preserve of diversity, with more than 1,660 kinds of flowering plants, for instance, the largest number in any North American national park.

For many good reasons, Great Smoky Mountains park—the most visited park in the National Park Service—seems like a remnant of an ancient time when the world was covered with trees, an epic and mysterious time of showers, fog, and endless mist. The forest floor is thick with spongy green moss and colorful wood sorrel, and everywhere

Eastern Tennessee and western North Carolina
Established June 15, 1934
810 square miles

Things to See: *Cades Cove; Clingmans Dome; Mount LeConte; Newfound Gap; Cataloochee; Fontana Dam; Mountain Farm Museum and Mingus Mill; Balsam Mountain; Chimney Tops*

Things to Do: *Hiking; Backpacking; Horseback riding; Fishing; Bicycling; Camping*

What's Nearby? *Andrew Johnson National Historic Site; Carl Sandburg Home National Historic Site; Obed Wild & Scenic River; Big South Fork National River and Recreation Area; Chickamauga & Chattanooga National Military Park; Cumberland Gap National Historical Park*

waterfalls cascade into nooks of rivers and streams. During the summer, a riot of sound, such as the chatter of red squirrels and the calls of wrens and other birds, seeks a visitor's ears.

A Landscape of Soft Majesty

Great mountains rise, ridge upon rounded ridge, beyond the horizon. Made of ancient rock uplifted from deep below the earth's surface, these behemoths are considerably older than the rough, craggy mountains of

The Great Smoky Mountains have been called "the land of moving water." Part of the reason for this is the 55–85 inches of rain the area receives annually, which feeds dozens of cold, clear creeks and rivers.

the western states. In fact, these ancient mountains are among the oldest on the planet. The Great Smoky Mountains are the quintessential mountains of the eastern United States. Straddling the border of Tennessee and North Carolina, southwest to northeast through the center of the park, they preserve one of the finest deciduous forests left on the earth.

The Smokies are also the highest range east of the Black Hills, and they seem strangely out of place so far south. Yet the Great Smoky Mountains are part of the Blue Ridge Mountains, which are part of the Appalachian Mountain chain. The park,

which covers 810 square miles, or more than 521,000 acres along the high ridges of the mountains, has so many types of forest vegetation that it has been designated an International Biosphere Reserve. About half of this large, lush forest comprises virgin growth that dates back to well before colonial times; the park's cultural heritage is so significant it has also been recognized as a World Heritage Site.

Yet despite all of that, Great Smoky Mountains National Park truly seems like a vestige of an age before human intervention, lost in the mists of time. Northern black bears roam among a profusion of southern

The mists here in the background are responsible for giving the Smoky Mountains their name. The Cherokee called this area Shaconage, *which loosely translates to "Land of the Blue Smoke."*

birds, opossums, and raccoons. In the great forests, rhododendron and mountain laurel grow through narrow openings in the ancient rocks. Many of the park's nearly unbelievable variety of flowers are found only in this place. The vegetation is so dank and dense in some areas that shrubs have taken over altogether, creating jumbled areas called "heath balds" that are too overgrown for trees to survive.

On the southwestern boundary of the park, the Little Tennessee River passes through Tellico Lake, Chilhowee Lake, Calderwood Lake, and Fontana Lake.

Out of the Mists of Time

The Smokies are remarkable for their wild and luxuriant vegetation. More than 100 species of trees grow here, and the tangle of trees and brush throughout the park is responsible for the "smoke" that gives the mountains their name. Water and hydrocarbons are exuded in great profu-

sion by the close-packed array of breathing leaves, producing the filmy haze that never leaves this place during warm weather.

Back in the mists of geological time, the Smoky Mountains more closely resembled the Himalayas than today's rounded mountain range. Water runoff over eons rounded the mighty mountains and carved their steep ridges and V-shape valleys. In 1951, relentless rains caused landslides that created Mount LeConte's large V-slash, just one piece of evidence of how water and weather still shape the land. Today hikers take the

Alum Cave Bluffs trail to the Mount LeConte summit, at 6,593 feet the park's third-highest peak. There they also might overnight at the LeConte Lodge near the summit, renting rooms or cabins except in winter. The lodge is the park's only private accommodation.

The land itself first formed nearly one billion years ago when an ancient sea flooded over an old mountain range, then…slowly… deposited layers of sediment on the ocean floor. This sediment eventually bonded to become rock layers more than nine miles thick. These metamorphic layers were later covered by a limestone layer made of fossilized shells and marine animals.

The Appalachian Mountains themselves arrived with a bang. About 300 million years ago, all land on earth formed one supercontinent called Pangaea. The eastern North American tectonic plate smacked into the African tectonic plate, and one of these epic collisions, grinding on at a rate of two inches per year, energized enough heat and pressure to metamorphose the Great Smokies' sedimentary rocks, crystallizing sandstone into quartzite and shale into slate. The Great

Smoky Mountains represent the highest, most erosion-resistant peaks remaining after Pangaea broke apart into Africa and North America. Ice, wind, and water assailed the ancient ancestors of the Smokies, eroding them over eons. (The vacation beaches of

The Smoky Mountains are the source of rivers including the Little Pigeon River, the Oconaluftee River, and the Little River. This photo shows the middle prong of the Little Pigeon River.

the Gulf of Mexico, as a matter of fact, owe their existence to sediment from the Great Smoky Mountains.) The mountain range formed its highest peaks out of the rock layers that were most resistant to erosion, such as the top of Clingmans Dome, a notable visitors site.

Clingmans Dome is the most visited of the high points in the United States. At 6,643 feet, it is the second-highest point in North America east of the Mississippi River, the highest point of the 2,144-mile Appalachian Trail, the highest point in Great Smoky Mountains National Park, the highest point in Tennessee, and the western terminus of North Carolina's Mountains-to-Sea trail.

Then the People Came

Humans have lived in the area of the Smokies for at least 11,000 years. The earliest inhabitants were the Cherokee people, who were related to the Iroquois. The Cherokee nation controlled the area from the Ohio River into South Carolina, but they considered the Smokies sacred, their ancestral home. The Cherokee lived there in towns of as many as 50 huts made of logs and mud. Organized around the Council House, a domed lodge for religious ceremo-

Appalachian Cherokee and the Trail of Tears

In 1838, the U.S. government forced 13,000 Cherokee to march to Oklahoma along what has come to be known as the tragic Trail of Tears. Not all the Cherokee were removed, however. With the help of William H. Thomas, who had been raised among the Cherokee, the Oconaluftee Cherokee had received permission to opt out of the move west. Other holdouts, however, stayed without permission. A few Cherokee hid between Clingmans Dome and Mount Guyot. One of these was Tsali, a leader and hero among the Cherokee who had used force to resist. In an attempt to cement their favored status, however, the Oconaluftee Cherokee helped U.S. soldiers find Tsali and his band. In the end, it is said that Tsali gave himself up as a sacrifice to help his fellow Cherokee. He was executed, but about 1,000 of his followers and their descendants survived. They were ultimately allowed to remain in the area and join the Oconaluftee Cherokee, who eventually established the 56,000-acre Qualla Indian Reservation, which was chartered in 1889. Today, about 10,500 descendants of the Cherokee live on the reservation along the park's southern boundary.

nies and public meetings, these communities featured their own town square, of sorts. In 1540, Spanish explorer Hernando de Soto led an expedition through Cherokee territory, but large numbers of European settlers held off entering the area until the late 18th century.

Settlement took a sudden upturn when gold was discovered in northern Georgia in 1828, and in 1830 President Andrew Jackson signed the Indian Removal Act. The idea for the establishment of a national park in the Southeast was actually proposed in 1885 by a doctor named Henry O. Mason, who delivered a paper at a Boston conference about "climatic treatment" for diseases. He proposed a plan for a health resort in the North Carolina mountains, further stating that it should be state controlled to "ensure perpetuation of the region's health-giving properties." One person, Dr. Chase P. Ambler from Ohio, was impressed with Dr. Mason's proposal and ran with it.

Ambler first approached Congress with the idea in January 1900 after bringing together teams of passionate mountaineers. Along with the Appalachian National Park Association and the Appalachian Mountain Club, Ambler brought attention to the need for such a park. By this time, nearly everyone had signed on to the cause for different reasons. Gifford Pinchot, a noted conservationist, wanted to use the lands for forestry, instituting sustainable forestry methods. Ambler believed in the idea of using the park for the general health of the visitors. The National Park Association and the Mountain Club

each saw an opportunity to halt logging altogether and begin conservation practices. But the bill to create the park, although it passed the Senate, failed in the House, mostly due to pressures from the businesses that wanted to continue operations in the mountains.

By the early 20th century railroad and steam-powered logging tools had sped the pace of logging in the mountains to the point of near-destruction of southern Appalachia's forests. And while the idea for the Southern park was gone for a while, it was not forgotten. In 1911, the Weeks Act, authorizing the development of a park in the East, was passed. Unfortunately, the law didn't say precisely where in the East a park should be established. Almost immediately, the Forest Service optioned 61,350 acres from the Little River Lumber Company in the Smoky Mountains for the establishment of a national forest. It brought together money and hired people to begin the organization of the park, its trails, and its fire practices. Over the next couple of years, however, there were land disputes over deeds that dated back to Cherokee times. The Forest Service could never quite get the necessary paperwork organized. Once World War I hit, however, the opportunity passed. The price of lumber rose and, in the crisis, the lumber company canceled the Forest Service's option for the land.

After this setback, the assistant to the secretary of the interior in charge of national

parks, Stephen T. Mather, believed that the Smoky Mountains were lost for the time being. Instead, he launched an investigation into other potential Eastern parks. Mammoth Cave was named as a possibility, as were Niagara Falls, Shenandoah, and a multitude of others, leaving explorers to set out into the Southern states to find land that would befit a national park. Virginians were adamant that Shenandoah be named the first eastern park, though the Smoky Mountains made a resurgence in the voting system. While Shenandoah's peaks and views were unmatched, the Smoky Mountains' cascade of rare wildflow-

Part of the Appalachian system, Great Smoky Mountains National Park is famed for its rolling, misty mountains, glaciated rocks and boulders, and 800 miles of hiking trails.

ers in its iconic beauty has been likened to the explosive geysers of Yellowstone.

In the end, the committee chose Smoky Mountain as the first eastern park, and in 1923 another attempt was made to establish it, this one led by Willis P. Davis. Fortunately, although it still took a few more years to come to fruition, this effort was successful. The park was authorized by Congress in 1926, but the story wasn't finished yet. Congress mandated that 427,000 acres of parklands be set aside for adequate use by the public, but because almost the entire park would be on land owned by private residences or logging companies, much of it would have to be bought—and the government refused to provide the money.

This prompted an enormous outpouring of support for the park. Booster clubs were formed to collect money from every part of the region. Schoolchildren donated pen-

nies and held essay contests to answer the question, "Why I Want a Smoky Mountain National Park." Families of all socioeconomic backgrounds pitched in with as much money as possible. Some of the landowners even donated their properties. All in all, 6,000 personal residences would need to be bought out at the cost of nearly ten million dollars. For all the enthusiasm and fundraising efforts, however, the endeavor fell short.

Fortunately, the philanthropy of John D. Rockefeller Jr. came to the rescue. In 1928,

in memory of his mother, Laura Spelman Rockefeller, the younger Rockefeller made the final monetary contributions needed for the remaining purchases of privately owned lands, which totaled about $50 million. Yet more work was necessary: There were still the logging companies to tackle. Purchase of the land owned by large lumber companies proved difficult, as the economic crash that began the Great Depression ate into land-purchasing funds. In addition, in the hardscrabble 1930s, more than half of the

area's residents accepted cash from loggers to clear-cut their land. Thus, all but the most inaccessible regions came to be logged.

The Endgame

On February 6, 1930, the governors of the states of Tennessee and North Carolina presented 158,876 acres of state land to the secretary of the interior. This put the park on fairly solid footing, having gained enough land to warrant protection. And in spite of the original park bill's mandate that no federal funds be used to purchase park land, in 1933 President Franklin D. Roosevelt issued

The 2,015-mile Appalachian Trail stretches from Maine to Georgia. A 69-mile section of the trail winds through Great Smoky Mountains National Park.

an order to allocate the necessary money to complete the land acquisition. He defended this action by asserting that the completion of the park would benefit the Civilian Conservation Corps in western North Carolina and eastern Tennessee, creating jobs in poverty-stricken areas.

With this piece of the puzzle in place, Congress changed the minimum acreage necessary from 427,000 to 400,000, paving the way for the final establishment of

the park in 1934. But the victory was bittersweet. Many residents of the town of Cades Cove fought the park movement all the way to Tennessee's supreme court. There, a compromise allowed the townspeople lifetime leases to remain in their homes. One family remains to this day. The Great Smoky Mountains National Park is home to the largest group of historic log buildings in the East. Today, Cades Cove is the most-visited attraction in the most-visited national

The view from 6,643-foot-high Clingmans Dome—the high point of the Appalachian Trail—shows the rolling eastern ridges of the Great Smoky Mountains.

park—a glorious mountain valley dotted with buildings dating back to the19th century. And on September 2, 1940, six years after Congress had acted, President Roosevelt formally dedicated the Great Smoky Mountains National Park to public use.

Guadalupe Mountains National Park

The dry flatlands of the Chihuahan Desert, a vast, mostly barren stretch of cactus and greasewood that extends for hundreds of miles across West Texas and south into Mexico, seem an unlikely place to find an ocean reef. But here, hundreds of miles from the nearest saltwater, an immense escarpment of orange and red limestone that was once at the bottom of a sea glistens in the bright sunlight: Guadalupe Mountains National Park in far northwest Texas.

The Guadalupe Mountains, a V-shape range with its northern arm extending into New Mexico and its southern arm pointing toward Mexico, rise more than a mile above the desert. Visible for nearly 50 miles, a great monolithic rock called El Capitan, Spanish for "the chief," rises audaciously

With El Capitan looming on the horizon, these balanced rocks sit on the long-buried floor of a dry sea that once covered much of West Texas.

at the point of the V. For centuries it has been a landmark for travelers crossing this immense and arid desert.

Commanding the Desert

At more than a mile and a half above sea level, El Capitan (8,085 feet) and adjacent Guadalupe Peak (8,751 feet) are the two tallest mountains in Texas, earning the area its nickname, "The Top of Texas." These mountains have their origins not as volcanic or sedimentary rock but as an ancient undersea reef created by the accumulation of countless plant and animal skeletons over millions of years, eventually forming a massive limestone ridge.

More than 200 million years ago, this immense fossilized reef was submerged under about 10,000 square miles of a shallow inland sea, populated by ancient cephalopods (related to squid and octopi), sea urchins, and other forms of marine life. Gradually the climate of the region changed, and the sea dried up, leaving much of

Western Texas
Established October 15, 1966
135 square miles

Things to See: *El Capitan; Guadalupe Peak; Bush Mountain; Shumard Peak; Bartlett Peak; Dog Canyon; McKittrick Canyon; Frijole Ranch History Museum; Salt Basin Dunes; Williams Ranch*

Things to Do: *Hiking, Camping, Backpacking, Horseback riding; Bird-watching*

What's Nearby? *Carlsbad Caverns National Park; Chamizal National Memorial; Fort Davis National Historic Site; Rio Grande Wild & Scenic River; Big Bend National Park*

the reef exposed and leading to a mass extinction of the sea's endemic plants and animals.

As the millennia passed, the seabed and the reef were buried beneath a vast plain of sediment, where they remained for millions of years. But about 26 million years ago, faulting processes deep beneath the earth's surface raised and tilted the ancient seabed and reef, leaving the 40-mile section now known as the Guadalupe Mountains exposed to the elements.

In the process of buckling, the reef was fractured in several places. Wind and water

The vibrant fall colors sported by the foliage in Guadalupe Mountains National Park's McKittrick Canyon attract leaf-peepers from all over the Lone Star State and beyond.

subsequently wore deep cracks into lovely canyons that slice into the mountains and can be seen today, including McKittrick Canyon, Dog Canyon, and many others. The shade of these chasms' walls has kept alive small pockets of an ancient woodland environment that thrived here in wetter times. Even today, a number of springs and seeps provide water for an array of plants and animals incapable of surviving in other parts of the park. In these riparian woodlands, mule deer are common, along with skunks and raccoons. In McKittrick Canyon, the stream even provides habitat for sunfish, nonnative rainbow trout, and an occasional Rio Grande leopard frog.

The abundant water and shade in the park's canyons allow for a diverse range of trees that are not found in other parts of the park, such as oak, maple, walnut, madrone, and pine. The deciduous trees in the canyons turn colors brilliantly in the fall and make McKittrick Canyon a popular annual destination for tree-peepers.

The Desert Floor

Outside of the relative sanctuary of the canyons, a much harsher climate makes for a completely different ecosystem. The desert offers great habitat for nocturnal foxes, coyotes, mountain lions, and three kinds of horned lizards, as well as 16 species of bats. In all, the park sees almost 300 species of birds. Desert plants include agave, sotol, ocotillo, yucca, and cacti common throughout the Southwest, as well as a number of plants found only in the park. There are 50 species of cacti rooted in the park, including delicate claret cup cacti, cholla, and prickly pear. Many of these and other desert flora bloom in quite colorful ways in spring or after the

rare desert rainstorm, attracting pollinators such as bees, moths, and hummingbirds.

Archaeological remnants, such as spear tips, knife blades, bits of basket work, and pottery shards, attest to a human presence in the Guadalupe Mountains that goes back

Shadows from the setting sun dance on the face of El Capitan, the southern tip of the ancient reef that is now the Guadalupe Mountain Range in West Texas.

about 12,000 years. When people first came to the area, during the decline of the last Pleistocene Ice Age, the climate was wet and humid. The first people who lived here probably foraged for various edible plants and hunted such animals as camels and mammoths.

By the time Spanish explorers appeared in the middle of the 16th century, wandering Mescalero Apaches often made their camps at springs near the base of the range, foraging for agave and hunting deer, elk, and bighorn sheep. Apache and Spanish legends about great treasures of gold and silver hidden in the mountains eventually drew American prospectors to this desert. With the end of the Mexican-American War in 1848, Mexico ceded the land that is now West Texas to the United States. In the years after the Civil War, farmers, ranchers, and African American "Buffalo Soldiers" of the U.S. Cavalry came to the area. The springs—and who controlled them—remained constant points of contention among various factions. Toward the end of the 1860s, a "salt war" broke out when corporations tried to stake claim on the historically communal salt flats east of today's park.

The violence continued until the end of the century. The Mescalero Apaches made their last stand in the Guadalupe Mountains, but by 1890 virtually every Apache in the country had been killed or forced onto a reservation. Initially, this territory was taken over by private ranching and mining interests that left their mark on the modern park in the form of a number of surviving structures at Frijole Ranch and other locations.

A Legacy of Giving

In the 1920s, Wallace Pratt, a geologist with the oil and gas industry, came to the Guadalupe Mountains. Working for the company that would later become Exxon, Pratt fell in love with McKittrick Canyon at first sight and began buying land in the area for a pair of summer homes. He eventually owned about 6,000 acres in McKittrick Canyon, which he donated to the federal government in the 1960s as the heart of the park to come. Pratt's donation was coordinated with local ranching scion J. C. Hunter Jr., who sold the government an additional 80,000 acres of his land around the canyon. After these two deals were completed, Congress passed the necessary legislation to establish Guadalupe Mountains National Park in 1966.

Visitors to the park today take to its 80 miles of trails on foot and horseback, often with a pack on their back. Birding and wildlife watching are popular pursuits, as is stargazing. The remoteness of the park pays off in terms of the night sky, a jeweled tapestry with 10,000 points of light and the shroud of the Milky Way clearly visible—all of which help make this spectacular mountain range a magnet for backpackers: Guadalupe Mountains National Park is one of the best places in the country to get away from it all—in very a big way.

The Salt Flats and the El Paso Salt War

Among the most precious resources of the El Paso area are the Salt Flats of the Guadalupe Mountains. Salt has been a valuable resource to nearly every culture. The Apache and Tigua tribes living in the area considered salt sacred, using it not merely as a condiment and preservative but as a curative for animal hides, as well. They guarded the flats jealously, but as explorers infiltrated the region, there were two minerals they sought above all others: gold and salt. Despite the legends, there weren't large stores of gold here, but salt was in abundance, in both salt flats and salt basin pools *(below)*. Diego de Vargas was the first European settler to find the salt flats at Guadalupe, and he inspired other Spanish explorers to visit the area. From that time forward, many settlers in the area depended on collecting salt to sell further south—even if it meant fending off attack by the Apaches.

Until the late 1860s, local residents saw this land as a common-use area. It belonged to everyone, and no one had a right to claim it. None of the long-time residents, Apache or former Mexican, thought to file a land claim with the U.S. government. What was to follow was a short-lived but complex and violent war, one that nearly led the United States into a second major conflict with Mexico.

The El Paso Salt War began in the late 1860s when several businesses attempted to put in land claims for the salt flats. Not only did people representing these firms clash with one another, but they also came up against the Mexican and Mexican American residents who had been collecting free salt for years and were now facing salt-collecting fees on what they considered public land. Over the next decade, divisive factions would vie for control over the area, spawning mob riots and murder. Charles Howard, a chief instigator of the wars, along with a troop of Texas Rangers, was accosted by an angry mob of Mexican citizens. As a result, Howard and two others were shot by a firing squad. Americans retaliated by sending in troops who killed and ransacked their way through the town of San Elizario.

This was enough, however, to end the salt wars. Mexican citizens were driven from the area, and Americans claimed control of the salt flats. Business concerns made others pay for the salt that had once been a natural resource, free to all residents.

Haleakala National Park

A mighty volcano named Haleakala sleeps within the domain of Haleakala National Park on the Hawaiian island of Maui. This huge, dormant volcano—a wild moonscape that extends for 33 miles in one direction and 24 miles in the other—is capped by a circular crater of 19 square miles. The volcano's floor, 2,720 feet below the summit, is a starkly beautiful and forbidding landscape of cinder cones and sculp-tured lava colored with startling shades of red and yellow. Haleakala is a volcano that has grown cold, at least for now, but its enormous crater is filled with unearthly shapes and profiles that are vivid reminders of its fiery past.

The House of the Sun

Light from the sun comes early to the rim of the vast crater, and it remains here long

Mount Haleakala's name is a linguistic tribute to the demigod Maui's victory over the sun, which brought longer days to the island.

after darkness has fallen on the lower slopes of the mountain. Haleakala means "house of the sun," and according to legend, the mischievous demigod Maui tamed the sun in the great mountain's summit basin.

Hawaiian island of Maui
Established July 1, 1961
45 square miles

Things to See: *Haleakala summit area; Kipahulu valley; Haleakala Wilderness*

Things to Do: *Hiking; Backpacking; Star-gazing; Bird-watching; Camping*

What's Nearby? *Ala Kahakai National Historic Trail; Kalaupapa National Historical Park; Puukohola Heiau National Historic Site; Kaloko-Honokohau National Historical Park; Hawai'i Volcanoes National Park; Pu'uhonua o Honaunau National Historical Park, USS* Arizona *Memorial*

Long ago, so the stories say, there were only a few hours of light each day because the sun was so lazy that it hurried home to rest. The demigod's mother, Hina, was unable to dry her fine bark cloth, her kapa, during the few hours of sunshine. Maui reasoned that the problem was that the sun moved too swiftly across the sky, and he swore to force the star to slow. Hina tried to reason with him but finally gave up. "At least take along your magic club and paddle," she warned him. "You will surely need all the power you have." Maui climbed to the summit of Haleakala, where he caught the sun by trapping its first rays as they crept over the crater's rim at dawn, releasing the sun only after it promised to move more slowly across the sky.

The Quiet Volcano

Haleakala has not had a major eruption since about 1790, according to Hawaiian legend and records kept by Europeans. Maps and charts made by early European explorers show significant changes in the island's topography that probably resulted from the flow of lava. But even though Haleakala has been dormant, earthquakes on Maui indicate to geologists that the great volcano still rumbles far below the surface. Islanders adamantly believe the sleeping mountain will wake up and breathe fire again within a century.

Haleakala National Park, along with the Mauna Loa and Kilauea volcanoes, made up the original Hawaii National Park in 1916. Later, in 1961, Haleakala was split off from Hawai'i Volcanoes National Park and made into a separate national park. It was designated an International Biosphere Reserve in 1980. Of its 30,183 acres of parkland, 24,719 acres are designated wilderness. The park has continued to grow over the years. It originally included the dormant Haleakala (East Maui) Volcano; Kipahulu, on the coast, was added in 1969. The adjacent coastal area of Puhilele was a further addition in 1998, and the 1,500-acre Ka'apahu rain forest was incorporated in February 1999. The name Ka'apahu means "rolling drum," and legends say that on still nights one can hear the drums of Hawaiian warrior ghosts within Ka'apahu. The popular park draws about 1.5 million visitors per year.

Haleakala Crater today appears littered with volcanic cones, streaked gray, red, black, and yellow by flows of cinder, ash, and lava. This gigantic crater—seven and a half miles across by two and a half miles wide by 2,600 feet deep—was not created by the kind of explosion that blew the top off Mount St. Helens in 1980. The Hawaiian Islands are near the middle of the Pacific Plate, a tectonic structure moving to the northwest by a couple of inches per year. Like all volcanic islands, Maui was caused by magma swell-

The caldera at Mount Haleakala, which is also known as the East Maui Volcano, is filled with caves just as dormant as the volcano itself.

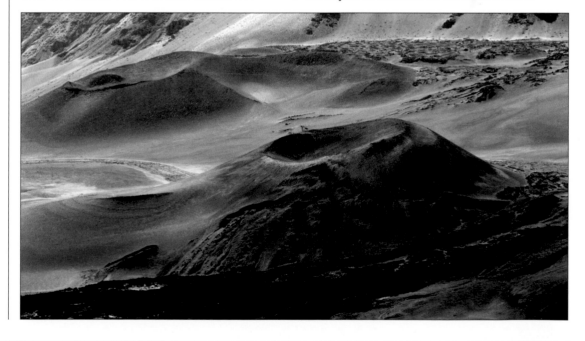

ing upward in plumes through a rupture in the earth's crust; these plumes became volcanoes and volcanic islands. Maui formed after eons of eruptions by two separate volcanoes on the ocean floor, slowly spreading lava until their volcanic peaks emerged above the surface of the ocean. The two eventually joined when an isthmus valley formed between them through an accumulation of ash, alluvium, and lava. Maui has come to be known as "The Valley Isle." At its peak, the larger volcano, Haleakala, stood at an altitude of 12,000 feet, which would make it 30,000 feet from its base on the ocean floor.

Once all this accumulation had created a towering masterpiece, erosion began tear-

The same parking area that leads to the Seven Sacred Pools brings hikers to Pipiwai Trail, a two-mile round-trip hike leading through bamboo groves and waterfalls to 600-foot Waimoku Falls.

Pele's Children

In the world of conservation and in every national park, there is a popular motto: "Take only pictures, leave only footprints." This slogan reminds parkgoers that the unspoiled natural beauty is unspoiled and natural only because people keep it that way. Everyone wants the parks to be pristine, beautiful, and blossoming—and they want them to continue so. To try not to litter or dump garbage has always been the most obvious intention of "leave only footprints." Sometimes, however, when guests are hiking or otherwise visiting these special places, the beautiful rocks, shells, flowers, and other naturally occurring objects that make up the parks seem to call out to them. Surely no one will notice one

missing pebble? That's where the "take only pictures" part comes in. Viewing rocks, shells, and artifacts are all part of the national parks experience. People picking and choosing to take what they want ruins it for those who follow. Pictures can provide memories enough.

What happens, though, when the gods step in? In the national parks of Hawaii, this might be entirely possible. The legend goes that anyone who takes lava rocks from the parks (or anywhere else on the islands) will suffer a curse levied by the volcano goddess Pele—unless, of course, the offender returns what has been taken. Pele views each of these rocks as her children, and taking them away will incur her wrath.

Some say that this was simply a ploy by the islanders to get *haloe* (tourists) to stop taking material from the island—that the legend has no actual basis in Hawaiian myth. But this isn't always how the tourists feel, however. Every year hundreds of lava rocks are returned to the parks by mail or messenger service from around the globe. Many of these packages contain actual letters to Pele, asking her forgiveness and telling of horrific runs of bad luck suffered after the rock was taken. Island priestesses have even offered to take these rocks (for a small fee), pray over them, and return them to a sacred place in the park—for extra forgiveness.

ing it down. The mountain caught the trade winds, bringing rain and streams that carved the park's characteristic slopes, ridges, and channels. Ultimately the two volcanoes' valleys joined to create a long "crater" in which, time and again, lava has poured through vents, spewing multihued cones and "volcanic bombs," cinders and ash, altering a valley hewn by water into a volcanic crater.

Geologists today say Haleakala is on the path to extinction. The mountain's crater—which they quickly point out is not really a crater, but a canyon—is a dry, desolate terrain where the temperature can be unbearably hot during the day and frosty cold at night. The bowl is pocked with small craters and studded with cones formed of cinder and ash, the highest of which, Pu'u O Maui, rises 600 feet. Two main trails lead into the crater from the summit area: the Halemau'u and Sliding Sands trails. Hikers in the crater can stay in one of three cabins, which can be reserved through the park offices. Haleakala lures visitors each morning to its summit to watch the sunrise and then again in the afternoon to see the sunset.

The volcanic islands are barren at birth, and native plants are rare. But Haleakala features Hosmer Grove, a forest of trees whose forebears migrated across the ocean: sugi from Japan; eucalyptus from Australia; deodar from the Himalayas; and pine, spruce, cypress, and fir from North America.

The People of Haleakala

Humans arrived in the area of what we today call Haleakala National Park about 1,500 years ago. Polynesians sailed large double-hulled canoes on arduous 2,500-mile voyages across the South Pacific using the currents, winds, stars, birds, and tides, and eating dogs, pigs, chickens, and vegetarian courses of *uhi* (yams), *'uala* (sweet potato), *'ulu* (breadfruit), and *ko* (sugar cane).

When Captain Cook voyaged to the Hawaiian Islands in 1778 for the first time, he encountered a population of some hundreds of thousands of people busy making crafts, farming, and fishing according to the principle of *malama 'aina,* "caring for the land," and its tenets, *lokahi,* "working together," and *laulima,* "many hands."

Haleakala represents one portion of its self-named park. The other is Kipahulu. From the summit of Haleakala, travelers to Kipahulu must drive a winding coastal road that is sometimes closed by landslides. The lower Kipahulu Valley is separated from the summit area of the park by the upper valley, but it is well worth seeking. This section of the park features more than two dozen pools of rare native freshwater fish along Palikea Stream in the gulch called 'Ohe'o. Visitors may swim in the pools or hike a trail that takes them up to the base of Waimoku Falls.

The contrast between the Haleakala and Kipahulu sections of the park could not be greater. Haleakala is dominated by volcanic vents and towering cinders. Kipahulu Valley—where rain forests receive as much as 250 inches of annual rainfall—is all lush pools, cascading waterfalls, and plunging, swirling streams. Around the sylvan pools flow forested valleys of mango, guava, kukui, and bamboo, while ancient pictographs can still be found on Kipahulu's stones. So can long-abandoned farms, where sweet potatoes and the starchy taro still grow.

The road to the Hana Coast takes breathless visitors past the Seven Sacred Pools, a series of many more than seven pools and waterfalls that thread through 'Ohe'o Gulch.

Hawai'i Volcanoes National Park

Roughly 1.6 million visitors arrive annually to see Hawai'i Volcanoes National Park, which is 30 miles from Hilo, Hawaii. The area was made a national park in 1916, and it included the Mauna Loa and Kilauea volcanoes along with what today is Haleakala National Park on the island of Maui. The parks became independent of each other in 1961. Hawai'i Volcanoes National Park comprises 330,000 acres, or 505 square miles.

Protecting the Volcanoes

In the early 20th century, Lorrin Thurston was publisher of the *Honolulu Pacific Commercial Advertiser,* although today he is better remembered as the man who discovered the Thurston Lava Tube, or *Nahuku,* which is now a major attraction on Crater Rim Drive. Today the lava tube is a drive of a bit more than a mile from the Pu'u Pua'i Overlook, followed by a 20-minute walk through

a tree fern forest to arrive at the well-lighted lava tube. Lava tubes are created by nature as channels to drain lava from its source. They can become tourist attractions if the volcanoes become extinct—or at least if the lava stops flowing, cools, and leaves a long, round, cavelike channel. In 1906, Thurston began campaigning to preserve this area as a park. In 1912, Dr. Thomas Jaggar, the new director of the Hawaiian Volcano Observa-

Right: *Visitors marvel at the park's amazing flora. The sight of seedlings sprouting and life persisting through a field of hardened lava adds to the mystery of Hawai'i Volcanoes National Park. Opposite: Kilauea and Mauna Loa volcanoes produce awesome fiery fountains and flowing rivers of lava that visitors can watch safely from a distance. In this picture, Kilauea's Pu'u O'o Crater hurls molten lava skyward.*

tory, joined Thurston, and their campaign really took off. Four years later President Woodrow Wilson signed the 13th U.S. national park into existence.

On the island of Hawaii, the original Hawaii National Park included only the summits of Kilauea and Mauna Loa. Over time, however, Kilauea Caldera was added, as were the forests of Mauna Loa, the Ka'u Desert, the rain forest of Ola'a, and the Kalapana archaeological area.

Hawaiian island of Hawai'i
Established September 22, 1961
505 square miles

Things to See: *Kilauea; Crater Rim Drive; Chain of Craters Road; Jaggar Museum; Thurston Lava Tube*

Things to Do: *Hiking; Lava viewing; Camping; Biking*

What's Nearby? *Ala Kahakai National Historic Trail; Pu'uhonua o Honaunau National Historical Park; Kaloko-Honokohau National Historical Park; Pu'ukohola Heiau National Historic Site; Haleakala National Park; Kalaupapa National Historical Park; USS Arizona Memorial*

Hawaiian Myths

For centuries, Hawaiian legends have explained the way volcanic islands form. It was all the doing of Pele, the goddess of fire. Pele was (or is) a cranky goddess who from time to time would lose patience with her brothers and sisters. According to 1916's *Hawaiian Legends of Volcanoes*, in which W. D. Westervelt collected and translated local tales, Pele "would destroy their pleasure resorts in the valleys. She would send a flood of lava in her anger and burn everything up.... Earthquakes came when Pele stamped the floor of the fire-pit in anger. Flames thrusting themselves through cracks in a breaking lava crust were the fire spears of Pele's household of *au-makuas* or ghost-gods." When Pele became angry,

her very voice became *pu,* or explosive. *Pu* is the word in the Hawaiian language that was later given to "gun," but it was originally reserved to describe the explosions of gas in volcanic eruptions. Pele liked to move around the islands, and when she stamped her foot, she could make the earth tremble and form new islands.

Perhaps surprisingly, geologists recognize some amount of truth in this legend. The spot where an island was likely to appear did seem to move from place to place. Scientists explain this with a theory of "hot spots" and plate tectonics. For some unknown reason, there are approximately 100 hot spots beneath the earth's surface. These places produce more molten rock, or magma, than is produced anywhere else.

Lorrin Thurston, namesake of the Thurston Lava Tube (above), *launched the campaign that brought this national park into existence.*

The Hawaiian hot spot, it turns out, is one of the largest.

Eruption!

The amazing phenomenon featured in this national park begins as a deep rumble, more felt than heard. Sometimes this reverberation is coupled with an ominous, slow hiss that sounds like a disturbed snake. A series of temblors may follow: slow rumbling quakes or great cracking snaps in the ground. These early warnings may last for hours or days.

Suddenly a fissure opens, and as it rapidly lengthens, it emits a blast of steam followed by a fiery fountain of white-hot lava that shoots hundreds of feet into the sky. More and more spouts of lava burst from fresh cracks, and at night they light up the sky for miles around. The frightening roar builds to an overwhelming cascade of sound, and the acrid smell of burning sulfur is everywhere.

It is impossible to witness such a spectacle and not realize that the most colossal raw powers of nature are on display. Scientists who study volcanoes know that there are few better places to see this grandest of all sound-and-light shows than at Hawai'i Volcanoes National Park. They tell us that Kilauea and Mauna Loa produce awesome fiery fountains and flowing rivers of lava that visitors can watch safely, from a distance, because—as opposed to explosive continental volcanoes—eruptions at Kilauea and Mauna Loa expend more lava and less gas. Yet Kilauea produces enough lava and cinders each day to cover a football field more than 500 feet high. The island of Hawai'i contains five volcanoes. Kilauea stands more than 4,000 feet above sea level and is still growing. Most active of all, it rises from the southeastern flank of the older and much larger Mauna Loa, which is at an altitude of 13,677 feet. The world's most massive mountain when measured from its base on the sea floor to its peak, Mauna Loa rises more than 30,000 feet.

In 1823, English missionary and author William Ellis and a few American friends were the first Westerners to see Kilauea in action. "A spectacle, sublime and even appalling, presented itself before us," Ellis wrote. "We stopped and trembled. Astonishment and awe for some moments rendered us mute, and, like statues, we stood fixed to the spot, with our eyes riveted on the abyss below."

Park activities include driving, bicycling, camping, hiking, and volcano viewing. In June 2007, Kilauea began to rumble with activity and started a new eruption. On March 19, 2008, the crater issued an explosion signaling new eruptions, the first of this kind since 1924. At this writing, Kilauea's

Halema'uma'u Crater was still rocking with earthquakes, and lava has continued to flow into the ocean from a vent outside park boundaries, about 12 miles from Kilauea's summit caldera. The vent is in a remote, inaccessible area east of the park, but the state of Hawaii has closed off access, just in case.

Scientists know there are few better, and safer, places to see an erupting volcano than on the Big Island of Hawai'i at Hawai'i Volcanoes National Park.

The Night Marchers

One myth that pervades the Hawaiian islands and many specific trails in Hawai'i Volcanoes National Park is that of the Night Marchers. The Night Marchers are said to be many different people. Some claim that they are processions of gods who come back down to earth on sacred nights. Other marchers are chiefs and warriors who are helping their ancestors to the next realm. Still others are spirits who cannot find their way and are searching for the entrance to the next life. Many among the Hawaiian Islands claim to have seen these marchers, and most firmly believe in them.

There are rules for dealing with the Night Marchers in Hawaii. The most important thing is to know how to recognize them. On dark nights, many times on sacred holidays, they will appear as apparitions floating side by side or in single-file lines. When the marchers are gods, they will float five abreast and carry red torches between them, with no sound other than a low chanting. Chieftains and warriors play the flute and drums and sing; often a heavy wind or fog will rise up as they pass. It is most important that any visitor who sees a spirit procession does not disturb it. Instead, observers should lie down and hide their eyes, for it is said that to see a Night March can be deadly. If the spirits notice one who is not honoring the death of an ancestor, they will attack with their spears, killing the watcher.

Legends like this abound in Hawaii, and many of the natives take them very seriously. Should visitors be interested in more legends, ghost tours are common forms of entertainment. The luau is not the only ritual that native Hawaiians celebrate. Many would be happy to share their beliefs, stories, and folklore with visitors around a campfire. Just be careful should an unexpected wind rise, carrying the soft beat of a drum.

Hot Springs National Park

I n many ways Hot Springs National Park is the most unusual national park in the federal system. It has stood out from the rest almost since the area was first acquired by the United States as a part of the Louisiana Purchase in 1803. Hot Springs National Park has existed in some sort of park form since 1832, when Andrew Jackson was president. It is the smallest national park, the only one surrounded by a city, and surely the only national park in which the focus of interest is its bathhouses. Much of Hot Springs National Park is a National Historic Landmark District located in downtown Hot Springs, Arkansas.

The Real Draw

The popularity of the 5,550-acre park has been on the rise ever since settlers first noticed the area and its unique characteristics, with attendance bubbling to about 1.4 million visitors each year. From the veteran insider's point of view, the most important aspect of the park is that it is a

Southern Arkansas
Established March 4, 1921
9 square miles

Things to See: *Bathhouse Row; Fordyce Bathhouse; Hot Springs Mountain Tower; Sugarloaf Mountain; Music Mountain; North Mountain; West Mountain*

Things to Do: *Hiking; Horseback riding; Bird-watching; Soaking and bathing*

What's Nearby? *Central High School National Historic Site; Arkansas Post National Memorial; Trail of Tears National Historic Trail; Fort Smith National Historic Site, Buffalo National River; Pea Ridge National Military Park*

terrific soak, containing what enthusiasts call the world's best hot springs water, about 850,000 gallons of it per day, percolating up at 143 degrees Fahrenheit from 47 hot springs on the side of Hot Springs Mountain.

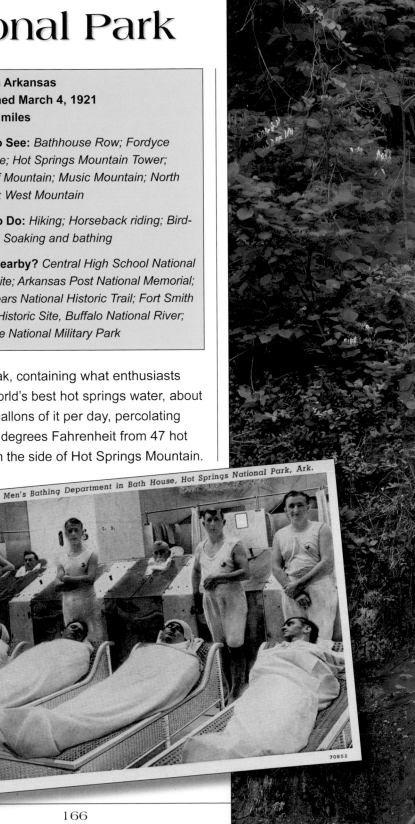

Right: *A postcard from the second decade of the 20th century shows Hot Springs bathers relaxing and soaking in steam compartments under the capable guidance of Men's Bathing Department staff.* Far right: *Visitors to Hot Springs National Park still can soak their feet in the water flowing from the Hot Spring Cascade, adjacent to Arlington Lawn, a favorite picnic area.*

The spring water has been studied closely for decades, of course: It is widely known to contain bicarbonate (130 parts per million), silica (53 ppm), calcium (47 ppm), sodium (4 ppm), chloride (2.2 ppm), potassium (1.4 ppm), fluoride (0.26 ppm), and more.

Somehow these chemical ingredients have combined to create the park's distinctive waters, drawing visitors from presidents Herbert Hoover, Franklin Roosevelt, Harry Truman, and John Kennedy, to Western law officers Wyatt Earp and Bat Masterson, outlaws Frank and Jesse James, ballplayers Cy Young and Babe Ruth (and manager Connie Mack with the Pittsburgh Pirates of 1896), reformer Carrie Nation, preacher Billy Sunday, Helen Keller, boxer Jack Dempsey, Sam Houston, and, perhaps most famously, gangsters Owney Madden and Al Capone. When Chicago became infested with gangsters in the Prohibition era, Capone and other mobsters sometimes fled their mob rivalries and the Chicago summer heat to Hot Springs. On at least one occasion, Capone and his arch Chicago rival Bugs Moran vacationed here at the same time in peace. Capone also cut deals with Hot Springs bootleggers who supplied his Chicago nightclubs with illegal brew. One story says Capone shipped the moonshine from Arkansas by rail tankers labeled "Mountain Valley Water."

The importance of preserving these Hot Springs waters was evident to early Americans, and the main mission of the National Park Service today is to maintain them. The Bathhouse Row historic district displays how early visitors enjoyed the park, and the many matchless examples of Gilded Age architecture show how the resort early on earned the title "The American Spa." This name was also earned in recognition of how Hot Springs served the indigent as well as the well-off.

The Zigzag Mountains, a small, geologically complex range within the Ouachita Mountains, provide the springs, which begin to come to life when rainwater percolates through the ground. As the water reacts with carbon

Hot Springs National Park features a National Historic Landmark District located in downtown Hot Springs, Arkansas. Here is seen the fabled Fordyce Bathhouse.

dioxide in the earth, it forms carbonic acid. As that acid solution sinks, it filters through layers of novaculite and broken chert, dissolving calcium carbonate, iron oxides, and other minerals. Continuing deep into the earth, the acidic water's temperature rises. After about 4,000 years of seeping, the water gathers 6,000 to 8,000 feet below the surface near downtown Hot Springs, where fractures in the earth allow underground pressure to force the water to the surface on the west side of Hot Springs Mountain.

From Out of the Past

The early human history of the area is a bit of a mystery. Archaeologists have failed to find evidence of Native American use of the waters, despite signs that the first people arrived in what today is Arkansas by 9,500 B.C. Peoples associated with the Caddo Confederation dominated the area from about A.D. 800 through the colonial period until they were decimated by imported diseases. Native cultures forced westward by American expansion, especially the Choctaw and the Quapaw, sometimes occupied the Hot Springs area, but they never settled in what they called the Valley of the Vapors. Spanish explorer Hernando de Soto discovered the springs in 1541.

When the United States and France concluded the 828,800-square-mile, $15-million transfer of the Louisiana Purchase in 1803, Hot Springs came along with the deal. In 1804, President Thomas Jefferson commissioned an expedition to the Ouachita River's well-known springs. The expedition reached the springs in December 1804 and stayed for a month, studying the water, the mountains,

and the area's unique plant and animal life. The explorers also found deserted cabins, which had perhaps been built by settlers who used the springs in warmer months. John Percifull, a Revolutionary War veteran who

arrived in about 1807, appears to have been the first permanent settler. He worked the land, built a cabin, and soon had set up a business offering room and board for summer tourists.

Civil Rights in Bathhouse Row

In the late 19th century, the waters were considered medical necessities in the area. Doctors prescribed time in the baths for all manner of ailments. They believed that bathing at certain times (the most beneficial being from 10 A.M. to noon) and places was more healthful than others. In 1878, the city of Hot Springs built a wooden house over what was called the "Mud Hole," opening a free bath to indigent folk of the area. This included men, women, and children of all races and incomes. The waters of the Mud Hole, however, were believed to be more healthful than those of the paying bathhouses, and people lined up for hours to take advantage of the free facilities. In 1898, the indigent bath house was restructured, segregating rooms by race and gender. While the baths were still free for all, they were no longer together.

In terms of pay bathhouses, African Americans had been able to buy tickets to certain local houses from the early 1880s. These houses, however, restricted the hours that black patrons were allowed to use them—usually only very early in the morning or at night, times that were not considered as good for the health. This prompted the building in 1904 of the first bathhouse run by African Americans. Called The Crystal, it provided a great service and a huge boost in morale for black residents and visitors.

The Crystal operated successfully until 1913, when a great fire burned it down along with 50 city blocks. The Pythian, a bathhouse built and owned by W. T. Bailey, the head of the Tuskegee Institute's architectural department, was built on top of it. It was named after its proprietors, an architectural organization called the Knights of Pythia, and it provided half-price bathing to those who belonged to the order. Many of the bathhouses soon expanded their services, becoming sanitariums, as well. They provided sickrooms and doctor services, as well as healthful spa treatments such as massage therapy and chiropodiatry—hand and foot care.

Other African American bathhouses soon sprang up all over, including such famous examples as the Woodmen of the Union building and the National Baptist Hotel and Sanitarium. These became the primary health and entertainment spots for African Americans in the Hot Springs area for everyone from blue-collar workers to famous entertainers. These segregated bathhouses endured until, and sometimes even beyond, desegregation in 1965. Some of the buildings stand today as a reminder of the service they provided in a time of difficulty for a large, and often marginalized, segment of the population.

In 1818 the United States and the Quapaw nation concluded a treaty that ended competing claims over the springs, effectively opening the area to claims on its territory. In 1832, responding to years of pleading to preserve the springs, Congress agreed to fund, build, maintain, and manage a hospital at the springs and to reserve 2,529 acres in and around the hot springs as the preserve of the government. (The hospital wasn't actually built until the 1880s.) President Andrew Jackson signed this act to create Hot Springs Reservation in 1832, arguably making Hot Springs the oldest national park, predating Yellowstone.

Congress finally got serious about Hot Springs in 1887, when it established a commission to tax the spring water, set new boundaries, sell excess land, and appoint an administrator. The first overseer, General Benjamin F. Kelly, harnessed the energies of entrepreneurs eager to build up the area, as well as federal funding for engineering and landscaping projects. By the end of the century, Hot Springs had been transformed from a rough-and-tumble country town to a sophisticated little city built around a Bathhouse Row of attractive Victorian-style bathhouses, the last ones completed in 1888.

This era climaxed in 1913, when an associate of General Kelly, railroad tycoon Colonel Samuel W. Fordyce, announced plans for a "veritable temple of health and beauty as a monument and grateful trib-

Gulpha Creek cascades through Gulpha Gorge, a popular camping and hiking area. In high water, the creek turns into a boiling rapids.

Not surprisingly, the Hot Springs National Park area is home to a variety of reptiles—here, an American chameleon—and an impressive list of amphibians, from the three-toed amphiuma eel to the four-toed salamander.

ute of the fact that his life had been saved by the use of the life-giving waters." The Fordyce Bathhouse opened in March 1915, offering all of the day's medical therapies, comforts, and amenities. The bathhouse's extravagant Spanish Renaissance Revival style paid tribute to the de Soto expedition that first brought Europeans to the area.

In 1916, Congress established the National Park Service. In 1921, Hot Springs Reservation became Hot Springs National Park, and by the end of the decade the Victorian structures had been replaced by more durable brick and stucco bathhouses.

By the 1950s, however, a long decline had begun. The Fordyce Bathhouse closed in 1962, and more closings followed in the 1970s. Bathhouse Row and its environs were placed on the National Register of Historic Places on November 13, 1974, but

that did not stanch the drain on business. In 1984, further bathhouses closed, and when the Lamar Bathhouse shut its doors the next year, the Buckstaff stood as the last survivor of Bathhouse Row.

But just a few years later in 1989, the deluxe Fordyce Bathhouse reopened. It had been adapted for use as the park museum and visitor center, its original furnishings restored or replaced with replicas. In the Fordyce Bathhouse today, tourists can see stained-glass windows, assorted statuary, and gleaming pipes, as well as luxurious tubs like the ones in which the aficionados of another age undertook three-week therapy courses of daily hot baths and massages.

Not Just for Soaking

Yet there's much more to Hot Springs National Park than great bathing. Favorite

recreations include hiking, crystal prospecting, camping in Gulpha Gorge Campground, and driving or hiking up Hot Springs Mountain to the 140-mile view from Hot Springs Mountain Tower. Today, Central Avenue is the heart of the national park. Hot Springs Mountain rises above the street. The mountain's lower slopes were once covered by an unusual, white porous rock called tufa, which was formed of minerals deposited by the hot water. But the slopes were altered more than a century ago when the rock was covered with tons of dirt and professional landscapers planted shrubs, trees, and grass.

Park officials cleared away all that landscaping in 1982 to restore part of the park to something similar to its natural condition. The cascade of natural hot springs flows onto new tufa rock, which is building at the rate of one inch every eight years. The bright blue-green color on the rock is algae, the only plant species that can survive in such hot water. Several concealed natural springs are located along the Tufa Terrace Trail, which is on the opposite side of the Grand Promenade from the hot spring cascade. Today you can still enjoy a traditional hot spring water bath at the Buckstaff, the only bathhouse on Bathhouse Row in continuous operation since the early 20th century. The Quapaw Bathhouse has recently been renovated and reopened as a spa with pools and hot tubs filled with hot spring water.

Isle Royale National Park

Isle Royale, the largest island in the world's largest freshwater lake, has no roads, but it has 165 miles of hiking trails. It can be reached only by boat, seaplane, or ferry. Together with hundreds of small islands, it makes up Isle Royale National Park in the waters of Lake Superior, north of Michigan's Upper Peninsula. Isle Royale is far closer to Canada, about 20 miles away, than it is to any part of Michigan. All of this explains why fewer than 20,000 visitors each year take advantage of the park, making it the least-visited national park in the lower 48 states. Yet it also explains why, when visitors do arrive, they spend more than three days there, on average.

Isle Royale has long been recognized as a special place: It was made a national park in 1940, a wilderness area in 1976, and a UNESCO International Biosphere Reserve in 1980. The park contains 893 square miles, all but 209 of that consisting of water.

Northern Michigan
Established April 3, 1940
893 square miles

Things to See: *Rock Harbor; Siskiwit Bay; Windigo Area*

Things to Do: *Kayaking and canoeing; Hiking; Camping; Scuba diving; Berry picking*

What's Nearby? *Keweenaw National Historical Park; Grand Portage National Monument; Apostle Islands National Lakeshore; Pictured Rocks National Lakeshore; Sleeping Bear Dunes National Lakeshore; Voyageurs National Park*

This park exists in splendid ecological isolation. For instance, it hosts 20 species of mammals, while the mainland around it has more than 40. Scientists speculate that the island's moose and wolf populations were imported. Ten major shipwrecks rest in its waters and are a favorite source of underwater recreation.

Amidst the Wilderness

This unusual national park consists of Isle Royale and another 400 smaller islands that rise out of the vastness of Lake Superior and surround it. Isle Royale National Park is actually an archipelago whose spine is Greenstone Ridge, which runs for more than 40 miles and tops out at 1,394 feet. The island itself is 45 miles long and nine miles wide. Several large lakes were gouged out by the last ice sheet that moved through here, as well as a 20-square-mile lowland swamp. Hikes lead through spruce and fir to sugar maple forests ablaze with wildflowers, the white blooms and bright red fruit of bunchberry, three types of calypso orchids, baneberry, bearberry, naked miterwort, early saxifrage, eastern paintbrush, gay wings, Douglas honeysuckle, pink moccasin, bastard toadflax, wild comfrey, and ram's head ladyslippers.

Although seaplane flights are available from Houghton, Michigan, most visitors reach Isle Royale on boats operated by the National Park Service. The ride takes two and a half hours from Grand Portage, Minnesota, or approximately six hours from either Houghton or Copper Harbor, Michigan.

Isle Royale bedrock is basalt or sandstone and conglomerates on the Midcontinent Rift, which itself is 1.1 billion years old. A thin layer of glacial material covers most of the island. In recent geological time, Isle Royale was shaped by molten lava that seeped through cracks in the floor of Lake Superior. The lava hardened and formed the island, but it was carved and compressed by glaciers as ice withdrew during the last Pleistocene Ice Age 10,000 years ago. The

Below: *Seen here is the eastern edge of 45-mile-long, nine-mile-wide Isle Royale, the largest island in Lake Superior, the largest Great Lake. The national park actually is an archipelago.* Opposite: *Isle Royale National Park contains 893 square miles, all but 209 of them water, including Isle Royale and about 400 smaller islands. The island complex exists in ecological isolation.*

glaciers cut enormous grooves in the island, visible today as the park's cliffs, ridges, and valleys. The rich deposits of mud, silt, and water left when the ice melted created ideal soil for vegetable life, while the gouges and depressions on the island filled with water to form its numberless lakes and swamps. A long ridge extends along the length of the island; its landscape has been complicated by eons of geological upheaval and

Left: The rocky coasts of Isle Royale, such as this exposed area east of Davidson Island, provide an ideal habitat for a rich array of birdlife, including loons, osprey, and golden eagles. Above: Not far south from Isle Royale National Park headquarters is Rock Harbor Lighthouse, built in 1855, which today features exhibits and a nearby beach.

sculpting. A 40-mile lava seam, it is tinted green by copper.

A Natural Ecosystem

Separated from mainland Michigan, which claims it, by 56 miles of rough water (and from the shores of Minnesota by only 20 miles), Isle Royale is pure wilderness, with no roads and almost no development. The island's isolation has helped to keep it pristine, looking much as it did more than two centuries ago when Europeans first stepped on its shores.

Isle Royale is the only place in the United States south of Alaska where wolves roam free and still play a useful role in the local ecology by preying on weaker members of other species. Moose, the wolves' main prey, also inhabit the island in large numbers. While the wolves are elusive, moose can frequently be seen in the meadows alongside woodland trails. Isle Royale's wolf population grew famous largely thanks to Durward Allen, a conservation biologist of the last century who authored *Our Wildlife*

Legacy and who recognized isolated Isle Royale as the perfect natural laboratory for his work. In 1958, Allen, then a Purdue University professor of wildlife ecology, began the longest-running study of wolves, or any large predator, and its favorite prey.

At the time the three Lake Superior states still paid bounties on wolves, which were nearing extermination in many areas in and around the park. In spring 2008, by contrast, observers counted 23 wolves and approximately 650 moose.

Moose and Wolf, an Experiment in Wildlife Conservation

The remote island park of Isle Royale has provided a great lesson into how nature can spring back from disaster and regulate itself. In fact, the island has become its own isolated wildlife experiment.

Near the end of the 19th century, the island was all but dead. Copper miners had stripped the land of forest cover, and loggers took over where the miners had left off. Hunters and trappers across the island had claimed most of the beaver population. The island's resources depleted, humans left, and the land began to heal itself.

No one knows exactly when the first moose came to the island. Wildlife experts think that they probably swam from Canada's mainland, somewhere toward the beginning of the 20th century. Like the humans, the moose saw a land of plenty. They went to work eating the newly grown plants, thriving, and having lots of babies. Within 20 years, the population had exploded into the thousands, and the food supply was once

again devastated. In the 1930s, the island was hit by a series of seemingly unfortunate events: The food ran out, a catastrophic drought hit the region, and a fire ravaged the area. The moose population declined from a few thousand to a few hundred.

The 1940s, however, saw resurgence. With plenty of rain, the fire-scorched land again produced bountiful vegetation, and with this new source of food, the moose population began to rise, healthy and once again ready to eat its way to destruction. In the winter of 1948–49, this all changed. A pack of breeding wolves crossed a frozen bridge of ice to the island. Thus began the longest-recorded wildlife research project in history.

The wolf pack was carefully watched from the time it first arrived on the island. Biologists were afraid that the pack would kill off the moose and a new cycle of destruction would begin. What actually happened, however, was that, while the wolf population did grow and expand, it merely kept the moose population in check. Moose are large and boisterous animals, more than able to care for themselves. Wolves are able to take out only the slow, aged, and diseased of the moose population, leaving the healthy to reproduce. Because of this, moose populations are, in the long run, healthier than they ever were in the periods of lush vegetation and rampant overcrowding.

Since the late 1940s, the wildlife world has watched the interaction between the wolves and moose of Isle Royale and will continue to do so. Observational data has helped scientists understand more about the balance of nature and the interaction between predators and prey worldwide.

The half-century-long Ecological Study of Wolves on Isle Royale has produced surprises on both sides of the moose-wolf equation. It turns out that all the members of Isle Royale's wolf population descended from a single female on the island in the late 1940s. And it also transpires that the island's moose population is most closely related to the moose of northwestern Minnesota. But how did the moose get there? No one knows.

The Making of a Park

The island's Stall Trail near Scoville Point shows three small pits in the rock, signs of Native American copper mines dating from perhaps 2000 B.C. American Indians mined the island steadily for 1,000 years. Royale- and Superior-area copper made its way by trade as far as modern-day Illinois, Indiana, and New York, most actively, it appears, from A.D. 800 to 1600. Native peoples never lived full-time on the island, however, and by the 1840s, only two native camps remained on Isle Royale, a fishing camp and a maple sugar camp.

Michigan gained control of the island in 1837, the same year it became the first Lake Superior territory to be admitted as a state to the Union. Also in 1837, the American Fur Company built several fishing camps on Isle Royale, but a recession swiftly shut them down in 1841. Miners arrived on the island

as early as 1843, failed, and left again by 1855. Mine pits from the time remain visible today, one only a few yards off the Rock Harbor Trail. Improved mining techniques led to renewed interest in Isle Royale mining by the time of the Civil War. By 1875 two mine sites boasted houses, stores, docks, roads, and schools, and that year Isle Royale County was formed. The last mining activity in Isle Royale shut down in the early 1890s.

As this mining era drew to an end, entrepreneurs discovered the island's attractions for steamship tourism, which lasted until the 1920s. Around that time a *Detroit News* reporter named Albert Stoll wrote a series of stories about the island, raising interest in

A study showed that the island's moose population is most closely related to moose in northwestern Minnesota. A popular theory holds that moose swam Lake Superior to Isle Royale.

making it a national park. In 1931, Congress agreed.

The park has two developed areas: Windigo, at the island's southwest end, where ferries from Minnesota dock; and Rock Harbor on the south side of the island's northeast end. Sleeping at the park means staying at the lodge at Rock Harbor or at one of 36 wilderness campgrounds, some accessible only by private boat, others only by trail or by canoe or kayak from the island lakes.

Joshua Tree National Park

While traveling through the Mojave Desert in 1844, Western explorer John C. Frémont encountered an odd-looking plant. He didn't care much for its appearance and called it "the most repulsive tree in the vegetable kingdom."

But beauty, of course, is in the eye of the beholder. A few years after Frémont's negative review, a party of Mormon pioneers passed through a grove of these unusual plants, and their reaction was considerably

A threatened species that makes its home in the park, the iconic desert tortoise lives up to 100 years, spending 95 percent of its long life underground and moving at a top speed of one-fifth of a mile per hour.

different. In contrast to Frémont's reaction, they thought the uplifted branches evoked the arms of the Hebrew leader Joshua reaching skyward toward the heavens. Thus the name Joshua tree was born.

The early reviews about the Joshua tree's aesthetic appeal obviously vary, but one thing is certain: The plant is ideally adapted to the harsh desert environment of south-central California. An average of about four inches of precipitation falls annually in this parched country, although much less has appeared in recent years. Temperatures soar to more than 110 degrees Fahrenheit in summer and dip well below freezing in winter. Strong winds are common in all seasons. In spite of these extreme conditions,

Southern California
Established October 31, 1994
1,235 square miles

Things to See: *Lost Palms Oasis; Black Rock Canyon; Skull Rock; Indian Cove; Cottonwood Springs; Covington Flats; Berdoo Canyon Road; Black Eagle Mine Road; Eureka Peak*

Things to Do: *Wildflower viewing; Hiking; Spring birding; Rock climbing; Backpacking; Camping; Horseback riding, Mountain biking; Stargazing*

What's Nearby? *Mojave National Preserve; Cabrillo National Monument; Death Valley National Park; Lake Mead National Recreation Area; Sunset Crater Volcano National Monument; Tuzigoot National Monument; Grand Canyon National Park*

the Joshua tree thrives in the highlands of Joshua Tree National Park in Southern California.

This Astonishing Yucca

Like other desert plants, the Joshua tree, a yucca and also a member of the lily family, survives these arid conditions by soaking up moisture during infrequent showers and minimizing evaporation during long periods of drought. Once a year, usually after a heavy spring rain, it sends forth a spectacular, if somewhat bizarre-looking, blossom that resembles an artichoke with creamy yellow petals. Other flowering plants come alive, too, putting on a dazzling display of spring color that includes ocotillo, lupine, blazing star, golden coreopsis, Mojave aster, scarlet locoweed, and desert mallow.

The Joshua tree, of course, is only one element in a complex web of life that makes up the park's fragile desert ecosystem. There are at least three distinct ecological zones within the park. The Joshua tree forest is found in the Mojave Desert in the western half of the park, where one also finds the jumbled granite formations that have become so popular for rock climbing and bouldering.

The eastern half of the park is in the Colorado Desert—essentially the northwestern arm of the larger Sonoran Desert—occupied by the low-lying Pinto Basin and surrounded by mountains. The Pinto Basin's northern and western boundaries mark the line between the two different ecosystems. The Mojave, defined by its cold winters, is in fact a transition desert of sorts between the lower-lying, warmer Sonoran to the south

The Joshua Tree appears throughout the park, both singly and in groves. It can grow to heights of 40 feet.

and the even colder Great Basin Desert to the north. The transition zone is a thriving place where the native plants and animals of both distinct ecosystems are found.

Joshua trees only flower as adults. After blooming, the brightly colored blossoms dry and fall off, leaving a stalk that subsequently becomes a new branch on the tree.

The desert landscape also includes fertile oases, those rare year-round water supplies that can be found in this harsh desert environment. Shaded by dense stands of fan palms and enlivened by the sounds of birds singing, these oases are islands of life where green plants flourish and animals such as coyotes and the occasional bighorn sheep come to slake their thirst. The oases owe their constant supply of water to fault lines in the otherwise impermeable rock below the earth's surface that allow underground aquifers to percolate up from below ground.

As Joshua Tree is located just north of the San Andreas Fault, the seismic activity that helps keep the oases wet has also shaped the undulating landscape. Six mountain ranges lie within park boundaries, and most of the park lies at elevations above 4,000 feet—in fact, the Little San Bernadino Mountains provide the park's third ecosystem. Several of the ranges are simultaneously in sight from the sublime lookout known as Keys View, accessible via a highly recommended detour off the main road. In between the mountain ranges are valleys caused by erosion and faulting. Temporary lakes—also known as *playas*—appear in many of these valleys after the rare rainfall in the park.

But when it rains, it pours: The Mojave Desert is a rain shadow desert. The mountains west of the park block most of the storms from the Pacific coast, creating an arid "shadow" to the east. But the tropical storms that move in from the south in August and September avoid the barrier and are known to dump 10 inches of rain on the park in just a few hours, creating potentially deadly flash floods and catalyzing brilliant wildflower displays in the ensuing days.

Life Endures

The surprising diversity of animal life in the park includes 250 kinds of birds, 52 species of desert mammals (primarily rodents), three amphibians (the tree frog and two types of toads), and 44 species of reptiles. Many lizards in the park are so well-adapted to the desert that they never urinate during their entire lives or need to take a drink—they get all of their water from food. This is not to mention the thousands of insect and arachnid species that live in Joshua Tree, including scorpions, tarantulas, and unusual honeypot ants.

The plant life is also clearly well-adapted to the park's feast-or-famine precipitation pattern. The initial name proposed for the park involved not just one of the 700 plant species found here, but all of them: Desert Plants National Park. These plants include not only the iconic Joshua trees, but also desert willow, cottonwood, and mesquite trees; yucca, cholla cactus, and creosote bushes; as well as the numerous species that comprise the park's grasslands.

In fact, the desert soil itself is alive. Topped by a layer of cryptobiotic crust—*cryptobiotic* means "hidden life"—this living soil is dominated by blue-green algae that somehow thrives in the arid climate, as well as other algae, fungi, mosses, and bacteria.

Poking out of the soil all over the park are monzogranite monoliths and boulders. These unearthly-looking formations that often dominate the landscape bubbled toward the surface but never saw the light

Just a few of the wildflowers commonly seen in the Joshua Tree area, clusters of purple sand verbena and white dune evening primrose bloom every spring at Cottonwood Springs.

The Lost Horse Gold Mine Corruption

Full of life, history, and outlaws, Joshua Tree had more than its share of hard-riding, gun-toting homesteaders and cattle herders looking for that great gold nugget to help them strike it rich. In the days of prospectors, many mines sprung up in southern California. The only truly profitable one, however, was the Lost Horse gold mine, with Johnny Lang as proprietor. As local legend tells the tale, its founding goes back to 1890, when Lang was driving cattle into the Lost Horse Valley with his father. While the Langs were camping overnight, their horses disappeared.

Tracking the horses, the Langs were eventually led to Keys Ranch, where the McHaney gang of cattle rustlers, a notoriously violent group, had set up camp. Johnny Lang approached them about his horses, but, not surprisingly, they denied

having anything to do with the disappearance. And when the McHaney gang denied something, it was best not to push the issue.

Having found out the hard way that there were gangs nearby who would steal without a second thought, Lang didn't want to take any chances. He approached a man named Dutch Frank, who had also had problems with the gang of rustlers and was in no mood to be threatened again. Together they armed themselves and recruited other men by distributing shares of the mine that Lang wished to open.

Staking their claim for gold, they named their mine Lost Horse, in tribute to the horses that had been stolen and Lang's resolve to not be taken in again.

As the mine virtually exploded with gold, a wealthy man by the name of J. D. Ryan

bought out Lang's partners. Giant gold bricks left the mine by day and night, though for some reason, more often by day than by night. Lang was in charge of the night production of the gold, and apparently, he had learned the idea of thieving pretty quickly. Every night, only half of the processed gold would leave the mine for the bank—the other half went straight into Lang's pocket. Ryan threatened Lang with legal action if he didn't sell his share of the mine and leave the area. This he did, considerably richer than the day he drove his cattle into the canyon.

The mine continued to produce until 1905, when instead of striking gold, the prospectors struck a fault line. The entire vein of ore was lost. Though the mine is abandoned today, visitors to Joshua Tree can still see it during a hike from Keys View Lodge.

and then view the bears from specially constructed bear observation facilities right on the river.

Ice on the Move

Several glaciers near the Valley of Ten Thousand Smokes continue to advance because of the thick layers of ash left by the 1912 eruptions insulating their ice. One glacier, formed after the eruption on the inside wall of Mount Katmai caldera (the concave cauldron-shaped top of an erupted volcano), is said to be the world's only glacier whose date of origin is known. Today it reaches to the caldera lake.

The Ukak River winds through the Valley of the Ten Thousand Smokes, eroding new channels through the up-to-700 feet of ash and pumice buried there.

Archaeology and the Prehistoric Traditions

One of the amazing things about the National Park Service is that it protects not only the environment but the rich cultural resources from past civilizations. At any given time in any given park, archaeologists and paleontologists work to uncover that park's deep past.

This past is especially fascinating in Alaska, which has been inhabited for 11,000 years. In Katmai, however, the land maintains its secrets. Though humans came here 9,000 years ago, their remains are scattered and elusive. Not only did they create mostly perishable items (such as weaving and basketry), but Katmai soil is highly acidic, destroying much of what was buried.

What is known about the people of Katmai is that they originally came across the Bering Strait, or the Land Bridge, from Russia. Their technology was fairly advanced for the time, with intricate netting and basket-weaving techniques that helped them catch, store, and transport food. They had complex spiritual beliefs and political processes. While several traditions emerged through the years, the two oldest and most mysterious are the Paleo-arctic tradition and the Northern Archaic.

The Paleoarctic people first arrived at Katmai 9,000 years ago and lingered for about 2,000 years. This was during the glacial age, either while glaciers still ruled much of the planet or just as they were beginning to retreat. It is partly because of this activity that the tradition is so skewed and difficult to follow. There are, however, many known and

suspected sites that are methodically uncovered by archaeologists each day.

The Northern Archaic tradition, which existed from 5,000 to 3,850 years ago, is easier to track because those peoples used stone arrowheads that survive more easily than other artifacts. Many scientists believe that these people were nomadic and lived in forests, hunting most of their food instead of subsisting on fish.

As the ages and technology progress, from basketry to pottery and from clay to stone and metal, more is known about the different, rich traditions of Alaska. Because these lands are open to visitors, it's possible that park guests might be the ones to make the next ground-breaking archaeological discovery.

The highest peaks of the vast Alaska peninsula's Aleutian Range rise within the boundaries of Katmai National Park, formed for the most part by volcanic action, rising to altitudes above 7,000 feet from the Shelikof Strait coastline across from Kodiak Island. At 7,606 feet, Mount Dennison is the tallest.

On either side of the Aleutian divide, the mountains' highest slopes and valleys also contain glaciers, the largest of which measure three to four miles wide and ten to twelve miles long. The divide between the Aleutians' east coast and west coast has created two wildly differing regions. Katmai's eastern coast is separated from the remainder of the park by the mountains. It is a wilderness with wild landscapes ranging from coastal flats to narrow fjords. The 497-mile coastline extends from Cape Kubugakli in Shelikof Strait to the mouth of the Kamishak River in Kamishak Bay, all of it carved by glaciation, its low points occupied by salt marshes, sedges, salmonberry bushes, mud flats, beaches, rocky shorelines, and alder thickets. The park's only stand of Sitka spruce also lives on its east coast.

Katmai's western side is open terrain sloping down to the Bristol Bay coastal plain with its streams, low ridges, and sand dunes, most of it underlain by permafrost. Northwestern and north-central Katmai

The jagged, forbidding mountains of Katmai National Park march from the massive Aleutian Range, including volcanic Mount Katmai, to Shelikof Strait across from Kodiak Island.

is known as the park's lake region, with Naknek Lake dominating an intricate web of marshes, streams, rivers, and ponds. Lakes sometimes are bordered by mountains rising 3,000 feet above their waters.

Apart from its volcanoes, glaciers, and overall otherworldliness, Katmai National Park and Preserve is most appreciated for its wildlife. The area provides habitat for wolves, foxes, puffins, cormorants, kittiwakes, moose, caribou, red foxes, wolves, lynxes, wolverines, river otters, minks, martens, weasels, porcupines, snowshoe hare, red squirrels, and beavers. Along the coastline are sea lions, sea otters, and hail seals, with beluga, killer, and gray whales swimming the nearby sea.

Don't Feed the Bears

But the stars of the show are Katmai's brown bears, North America's largest land predators, to be found in the greatest numbers along the Katmai coast. In early summer they forage on the sedge flats at Chiniak, Swikshak, Kukak Bay, and Hallo Bay. Once salmon begin running on the coast, the bears move to streams and rivers for the catch, although they also are ardent tidal-flats clammers. Katmai contains the world's largest protected brown bear population. *Largest* in this case can mean most—in

Top: *Although steam rarely escapes anymore, mists can still settle into the Valley of the Ten Thousand Smokes, which is 40 square miles of volcanic ash.* Bottom: *In the northeastern reaches of the park, Mount Kaguyak rises almost 3,000 feet from near sea level to a 1.5-mile-wide volcanic caldera filled by a lake 600 feet deep.*

some years the park hosts more than 2,000 bruins. But it can also mean largest in size: The salmon-fed bears are huge, bigger than grizzlies, with males weighing up to 900 pounds. The Katmai bears also appear to be unique because, while bears are normally solitary creatures, the Katmai bears tend to stay in groups. To see the bears, one shouldn't arrive between November and April, when the browns are hibernating.

But come midsummer, when the sockeye salmon are spawning, viewers and photographers are given an unparalleled chance to see these giants in action.

If viewers find brown bears blasé and volcanoes wearisome, plenty of other recreational opportunities exist at Katmai National Park, including hiking, backpacking, camping, cross-country skiing, fishing, kayaking, boat tours, and interpretive programs. Also

Crowds of Alaskan brown bears gather each summer to feed on salmon in Katmai National Park, where bear observation stations on the river keep both bears and visitors safe.

attractive are the park's many archaeological sites, which reveal much about the prehistoric peoples of the Paleoarctic tradition up to the Thule tradition, exploring the ancestors of today's Inuit population.

Kenai Fjords National Park

Close to 300,000 visitors each year head for Kenai Fjords National Park at the tip of Alaska's Kenai Peninsula, and it's not hard to figure out why. One easy answer is that Kenai Fjords is, as Alaska's eight national parks go, fairly accessible. It's found within Alaska's Anchorage area, and it's not far from Juneau.

Another answer is that the park contains the Harding Icefield, occupying more than 300 square miles while being as much as a mile thick. The Harding Icefield crowns the mountains of Kenai Fjords National Park in south-central Alaska, a raw, ragged land that has yet to recover from the great Pleistocene ice sheets that flowed over most of Alaska 12,000 years ago.

Yet a third answer is that the rocks of the Kenai Fjords' coast are so jagged, sharp, and free from erosion that land and sea seem to be locked in a fearsome, primal struggle for dominance. The sea challenges the land with majestic deep fjords and hundreds of inlets and coves, while the coast abuts the Gulf of Alaska with great, rocky headlands and clawlike peninsulas.

An Arctic Wonderland

The mammoth park covers almost 1,050 square miles, or 669,983 acres, of Alaska's wildest coast. The park's dynamic geology includes spectacular mountains with great glaciers flowing down between them to the sea, as well as awesome fjords that provide

Southeastern Alaska
Established December 2, 1980
1,050 square miles

Things to See: *Harding Icefield; Exit Glacier; Holgate Glacier; Three Hole Point*

Things to Do: *Hiking; Sea kayaking; Backpacking; Camping; Mountaineering; Sled dog touring, Sport-fishing; Cross-country skiing; Ice climbing*

What's Nearby? *Lake Clark National Park and Preserve; Denali National Park and Preserve; Katmai National Park; Alagnak Wild River; Aniakchak National Monument and Preserve; Wrangell–St. Elias National Park and Preserve*

a habitat for thousands of nesting seabirds and seafaring mammals.

Kenai Fjords National Park sits at the edge of the North Pacific Ocean, where storm patterns develop and feed a land of ice. The Harding Icefield crowns the park and is the source of 38 named glaciers that sculpt and scour the land, huge rivers of ice that shaped the terrain and are now receding to reveal their art.

The land has a rough, unfinished appearance. A vast sea of whiteness, the glistening Harding Icefield is covered here and there by great dunes of snow that move constantly with the vagaries of the wind. In places, the

Humpback whales are just one of the whale families liable to show off for observers in Kenai Fjords National Park. Others include gray, killer, and minke whales.

The peaks of Kenai Fjords' coast are little touched by erosion. The coast abuts the Gulf of Alaska with rocky headlands and claw-shaped peninsulas.

peaks of mountains buried by ice since the Pleistocene Epoch rise above the frozen plain. In stormy weather, these peaks, called *nunataks,* seem to float like castles on a sea of white. They are awesome reminders of an age not so long ago, when vast sections of the world were cold and frozen.

As massive as it seems today, the Harding Icefield is a relatively small remnant of the much larger ice cap that covered the entire region 10,000 years ago during the Pleistocene Epoch. An expansive ice sheet covered south-central Alaska at that time. As the ancient ice advanced, then retreated, then advanced again over the centuries, it carved out the rugged coastline of the Kenai peninsula and gouged out the fjords. Finally, as the earth's climate warmed, the ice began to melt, leaving in its wake a spectacular landscape and habitats for throngs of wildlife. The ice-

Harding Icefield covers more than 300 square miles and acts as the source of more than 40 named and unnamed glaciers, including Exit Glacier, McCarty Glacier, and Tustumena Glacier.

field could also be a vestige of the massive Truuli Icefield (recorded by naturalist Ilia G. Wosnesenski in 1842), which once contained both the Sargent and Harding icefields.

Kenai Fjords National Park's icefields continue to grow as moist air from the warm Gulf of Alaska winds temper the winter weather, creating a maritime climate, while snow settling above the mountains feeds

high-altitude glaciers. Snowfall occurs primarily in the winter months, but in summer, too, storms are common, and the icefield accumulates as much as 400 inches of snow annually. Meantime, glacial runoff feeds the park's streams and lakes, which drain into the peninsula's milder lowland terrain, while glacial till and vegetation-covered moraines make up most of the lowlands.

In the Ice, Diversity

"The line of coast is broken by bays and coves, but none offering good anchorage; there being very close to shore not more than thirty to fifty fathoms of water. The coast is very rocky, steep and mountainous, yet covered with wood, while the ravines and gorges between the mountains contain in many places, glaciers which stretch back from the heads of the bays even to the gorges descending towards Cooks inlet." These are observations of scientist George Davidson, who was commissioned by Congress in 1867 to supervise the first major American survey of Alaska's coast.

The park's biological, geographic, and geological diversity makes it a prime wildlife viewing site. The barren Chiswell Islands, serviced by ferry boat, are an excellent place to see giant Steller sea lions. Females grow to about eight feet in length and weigh in at around 660 pounds; males can grow 11 feet long and weigh 1,300 to 2,500 pounds. They boast wide chests and darker tufted hair around their large necks that gives them a leonine mane. Steller sea lions' Latin name, *Eumetopias jubatus,* can be translated as, "maned one with broad forehead."

On the park's southern end, McCarty Fjord cuts 23 miles into the mainland, its huge cliffs rising nearly a mile above the water. Nearby Nuka Bay includes a 900-foot waterfall and historic gold-mining camps. Visitors often spy martens and river otters, moose and black bears, while icy inlets might reveal a humpback whale jumping almost completely out of the water, flashing in the sun. Three types of orca whale swim the waters around Kenai Fjords National Park: fish-eating residents; marine mammal-eating migratory orcas; and more rarely observed offshore orca whales that remain in open water eating fish of all sizes and varieties, up to and including sharks.

People who climb the mountain cliffs of Kenai Fjords are liable to see mountain goats and Dall sheep. More than 200 bird species call the peninsula environments home, including the double-crested cormo-

Holgate Glacier is retreating rapidly and may soon cease to be a tidewater glacier—a glacier whose ice actually fronts on the saltwater. Like most of the large glaciers in Kenai Fjords National Park, Holgate is part of the immense Harding Icefield, a roughly 300-square-mile mass.

Viewing Exit Glacier requires an unchallenging walk from a convenient road—it is the only part of the park accessible by road (a fact irrelevant to mountain goats). Easy trails take visitors around the glacier.

rant, the trumpeter swan, the greater white-fronted goose, the red-breasted merganser, the harlequin duck, the great blue heron, the northern harrier, the peregrine falcon, the sharp-shinned hawk, the red-tailed hawk, the rough-legged hawk, the bald eagle, the golden eagle, and more than two dozen kinds of sandpiper. Kenai Fjords birds are often better at swimming with their wings than flying. From the lowly ice worm that dwells in glacial ice to mighty black bears sledding steep snow chutes, the variety of life in the park is dazzling.

Human Hunters

Ancient people hunted the Kenai peninsula for millennia. The arrival of European settlers in the 1880s, disease, commercial fishing, and prodding by the Russian Orthodox clergy combined to produce a tragic synergy that brought about the end of permanent Native American settlements. Instead, natives from the peninsula's communities of Port Graham and English Bay traveled east to hunt and trap game. Nuka Island, which is now part of the park, became a center for autumn hunting camps, and winter and spring hunting camps sprung up at Nuka, Yalik, and Aialik bays.

The native hunters eventually moved on, but they left plenty of evidence behind. "When we first came here we found all sorts of old contraptions set up in the trails and close to dens, their purpose having been to catch land otters," observed Josephine Tuerck, who settled on Nuka Island in 1921. "We found little box-like houses built with sticks, in which to set steel traps for minks; all manner of spring poles; plenty of other evidence of the ingenuity of man in his effort to outwit every living thing that walked on legs.... Everything pointed to the cleverness of our predecessors on Nuka Island."

The park has no hotels or resorts, and most visitors stay in Seward, Alaska, about 70 miles distant. But many visitors enjoy three rustic public-use cabins: Aialik, Holgate, and North Arm, available from late May through mid-September. Willow Cabin at Exit Glacier can be used from about late autumn to early April, when the glacier road is covered with snow.

The rock formation called roche moutonnée, *or sheepback rock, is formed by glacial action that produces a steep drop on its down-glacier side and a smooth slope on its up-glacier side.*

Orca: The Whale with a Porpoise

Some of the biggest attractions in Kenai Fjords, in both size and grace, are the killer whales. Orcas, another name for the whales, can be found all over the world and in every ocean, though the largest populations are found in the far north or south, near Norway, Japan, Iceland, Alaska, and Antarctica. Killer whales are carnivorous mammals, with sharp, pronounced teeth. Living in groups called pods, orcas in different parts of the ocean and with different migration patterns eat different foods. Residential pods around Kenai eat mainly salmon, whereas transient pods that migrate constantly eat marine mammals. Orcas can feed on everything from fish and squid to dolphins and other porpoises, seals, and even small whales. Though this might make some people nervous, orcas have never been known to feed on humans. In fact, they are very gentle and interact well with humans.

There is a Tlingit legend about the creation of the killer whale. After being betrayed and almost killed by his brothers-in-law, a Tlingit hero named Natsilane carved a great black fish from the wood of the yellow cedar tree. He sang the songs of his ancestors to it, and it came to life. Natsilane gave orders that it should take revenge on the treacherous brothers-in-law, who were out fishing. The killer whale destroyed the boat of the evil brothers-in-law, but at the request of Natsilane, it spared his kind youngest brother-in-law. After this, Natsilane told the whale never to hurt another human and that it should instead bring good luck. More than one Alaskan people uses the great black fish as a symbol of peace, luck, and prosperity.

Other groups of cetaceans live in the waters around the Kenai Fjords, as well. Cetacea is the order to which all marine mammals such as dolphins, whales, and porpoises belong. Dall's porpoise is another sea mammal that lives alongside killer whales off the coast of Alaska and is said to be the fastest cetacean in the world. Visitors can watch for these porpoises as they scan the seas for wildlife, but they should know how to differentiate them from orcas. While both are black with white spots, only orcas have white pandalike spots around their eyes. Orcas also have bigger heads and smaller tails, while the Dall's porpoise has a small head with a thick body. Both are important to the beauty and biodiversity of the park and remain a treat for every visitor who catches a glimpse.

Kobuk Valley National Park

Less than 40 miles west of Gates of the Arctic National Park, Kobuk Valley is pure Arctic terrain. Its wide bowl is filled with great boreal forests and a tundra that creeps up the lower slopes of the mountains.

The Lazy River

Flowing from its headwaters in the Brooks Range on the east and draining into the Hotham Inlet, the Kobuk River glides across the heart of the valley. Its floor is so flat that the river drops only about two or three inches every mile. The river's barely detectable current makes it look like a lake in places where it is especially broad.

The river is the main artery for transportation in Kobuk Valley National Park, which lies entirely above the Arctic Circle. A paddle or motor trip on the river usually begins from the little settlement of Ambler on the east side of the park and ends in Kiana, a village outside the park's western boundary.

In late August and early September, a herd of 400,000 or more barren ground caribou crosses the Kobuk River, foraging for lichen, reindeer moss, dwarfed ground willows, saxifrage, and lupines.

Floating on the river provides solitude in the wilderness. The Inupiaq people still hunt the great herds of caribou that migrate through this remote natural realm each summer.

Placid and pleasant, the Kobuk River flows through land belonging to the Inupiaq. In some places, steep banks rise above the water, while elsewhere great boreal forests line both shores, interrupted by lakes and tundra. In late August and early September, visitors can sit above the river and watch huge herds of caribou swim across it, the great antlers of the males bobbing and swaying with the motion of the water. In a stream that meanders through a grassy meadow down to a confluence with the river, they may see a grizzly bear fishing for dinner, its enormous paws slashing through the water with lightning speed.

Kobuk Valley forests grow along the better-drained stream courses and on higher ground, forming a pattern of alternating tundra and forest across the valley. Spruce and balsam poplar grow in the lower and middle reaches of the river valleys that extend into the Baird and Waring mountains. Willow and

Northern Alaska
Established December 2, 1980
2,750 square miles

Things to See: *Great Kobuk Sand Dunes; Onion Portage Archeological District; Kobuk River; Mount Angayukaqsraq*

Things to Do: *Hiking; Backpacking; Camping; Boating; Fishing; Wildlife watching*

What's Nearby? *Gates of the Arctic National Park & Reserve; Noatak National Preserve; Bering Land Bridge National Preserve; Cape Krusenstern National Monument*

alder thickets and isolated cottonwood grow to the headwaters of the rivers and streams. Alpine tundra covers the higher slopes and ridges. Tussock tundra and low vegetation cover most of the valley floor. Although Kobuk Valley National Park gets less than 20 inches of rain and snow each year, much of its lowland tundra is soggy because permafrost well beneath the soil surface won't allow the water to drain.

Like its fellow Alaskan national parks, Kobuk Valley is enormous, encompassing 1,669,813 acres. It was designated a U.S. National Park in 1980, signed into law by President Jimmy Carter in the last full month of his presidency. There are no trails or roads in the park, which is about as big as the state of Delaware. Kobuk Valley can

About 40 miles above the Arctic Circle, the Little Kobuk Sand Dunes, the Hunt River Dunes, and the Great Kobuk Sand Dunes provide surprising glimpses of a Sahara-like landscape.

be reached only by foot, dogsled, snow-mobile, and chartered air taxis from Nome and Kotzebue, Alaska. The park is one of the least visited in the National Park Service, ranking at the bottom of the national park list in 2008 with just 1,565 visitors (which was actually a step up from the 847 who came to the park in 2007).

Vast Arctic Wilderness

Kobuk Valley National Park is also part of the vast Northwest Alaska Areas, along with Cape Krusenstern National Monument and Noatak National Preserve. These three National Park Service units preserve more than nine million acres of subarctic and arctic wildlands east from the Chukchi Sea to the

upper Noatak River. The parks complex encompasses the Brooks Range, the north-ernmost portion of the Rocky Mountains, tracing the northern limit of tree growth, as the boreal forest yields to tundra. Counting Gates of the Arctic National Park, the north-west Alaska protected lands include 16.8 mil-lion acres extending 360 miles inland. The Northwest Alaska Areas also protect the archaeologically significant beach ridges of Cape Krusenstern, the Great Kobuk Sand Dunes, most of the vast Noatak River water-shed, and a population of about 400,000 bar-ren ground caribou, who migrate through the Arctic foraging for lichen, reindeer moss, dwarfed ground willows, saxifrage, and lupines. The great herd crosses the Kobuk

River each year, a huge migration central to the Inupiaq people's subsistence.

South of a bend in the river on the eastern side of the park, great yellow and beige sand dunes appear suddenly. This is an Arctic Sahara in a strange and unlikely setting. Today, the Great Kobuk Sand Dunes, the Little Kobuk Sand Dunes, and the Hunt River Sand Dunes lie on the south side of the Kobuk River, while older dunes covered with vegetation blanket much of the southern val-ley. Visitors reach the dunes by boat and can then take a short walk through the sand.

Evidence of Humans

East of the dunes is Onion Portage, prob-ably the park's most famous site. In 1961, archaeologist J. Louis Gid-dings crowned his distin-guished Arctic career with discoveries here of evidence of flint-working technology by seven different cultures dating back at least 10,000 years. "The deep, stratified Onion Portage site on the middle Kobuk, discovered by Gid-dings in 1961, is without doubt the most important archaeo-logical site within the Arctic," said an obituary of Giddings

Kobuk Valley National Park's forests grow along the better-drained stream courses and on higher ground, forming a pattern of alternating tundra and forest across the valley.

by Smithsonian Institution ethnographer Dr. H. B. Collins. "Covering some 20 acres and reaching a depth of 18 feet, it has over 30 distinct occupation levels containing in vertical sequence the hearths and artifacts of most of the cultures represented on the Krusenstern beaches, as well as others."

So many Arctic people from so many cultures across so many millennia worked flint at the Onion Portage site because the place has been a major caribou herd crossing for at least 10,000 years. Local cultures still intensively hunt Onion Portage, which they continue to own even though it is inside the park. Just off the Kobuk River near the park's eastern border, visitors often set up camp and then hike or paddle to the site.

Mammals range in size and power from moose to Alaska pygmy shrews and also include gray wolves, American black bears, American mink, grizzly bears, Canada lynx, Dall sheep, and the ever-present arctic ground squirrels. But it is the vast, magisterial herds of barren-ground caribou that reign. The herd, numbering hundreds of thousands, migrates through the park twice a year: northbound in March from their winter range in the Selawik Hills-Buckland River area, and southbound in August from their summer range north of the Brooks Range and the DeLong Mountains.

Amigaiksivik, meaning "the time the velvet is lost from antlers," is the local word for *August,* a month often considered the best time to see Kobuk Valley. The paramount reason is the sight of the caribou, 300,000 to 500,000 of them, crossing the Kobuk River, accompanying their newborns south to wait out winter.

The Arctic Sand Dunes

Trudging through the vast, majestic, seemingly unending peaks of ice and snow that characterize most of Alaska, the last thing one expects to see is an expanse of sand dunes cresting to 100 feet. Visitors might stop in puzzlement and wonder when, exactly, they had been teleported to the Mojave Desert. This confusion would last only until a bitterly chill wind rushed through with a reminder that they were, indeed, above the Arctic Circle.

As some of the only sand dunes above the Arctic Circle, these majestic anomalies are thought to be the remnants of a day long ago, when glacial melt rushed into the sandy bottoms of lakes and rivers. The dunes are vast and active, moving quickly and reaching summertime temperatures that top 100 degrees Fahrenheit. The Great Kobuk Sand Dunes today cover 23.5 square miles, but are believed at one time to have covered an area of perhaps 300 square miles. Some dunes rise to a height of more than 150 feet. Geologists believe the dunes to be perhaps 24,000 years old, existing long before the last ice age of about 10,000 years ago. At that time, the Kobuk Valley would have been free of ice; rather,

it was covered with grassy tundra similar to today's Siberia. In those days, sand created by the grinding action of glaciers was carried to the valley by wind and water. Today there are only three active Kobuk dune areas that move quickly with the wind in the shapes of crescents.

The rest of the dune area is covered in plant life, though these dunes move too, albeit at a slower pace. Plant life in the dunes is more diverse than one might think. Despite its appearance as an arctic desert, the Kobuk region receives plenty of water. In fact, the dunes are less than two miles from the Kobuk River! Birch, pine, and alder trees are common, as are a plethora of nonwoody vegetation. And even the inhospitable dune area is rife with flowers in the spring.

Lake Clark National Park and Preserve

Take one pristine 42-mile-long lake, so clear that the salmon spawning in it can even be seen from an airplane. For wildlife, add grizzlies and huge brown bears, beluga whales and snowshoe hares. Include active volcanoes, major river systems, the collision of two major mountain ranges, tundra foothills, glacial valleys, river gravel bars, and old-growth forests, and what you have is "Essence of Alaska," a favorite nickname for Lake Clark National Park and Preserve.

Pure Alaska

Lake Clark park is a four-million-acre slice of the Last Frontier that is 100 miles north of Anchorage, accessible only on foot through glaciated passes or by air. To its south and west lay the park's foothills, rivers and lakes, and tundra plains. The park's southeast is bounded by Cook Inlet, from Chinitna Bay to Tuxedni Bay, where the mountains plunge into the inlet, its glacial valleys giving way to coves and fjords. Lake Clark is 50 miles long and five miles wide, and its color is a sparkling blue. On its southeastern shore, the little community of Port Alsworth is the site of the park's field headquarters and the place where most visitors settle in for a good, long look at some of North America's most outstanding and varied scenery. All of Alaska seems to converge here. In fact, Lake Clark National Park and Preserve is considered a special jewel among the cluster of its neighboring parks: Katmai National Park and Preserve,

Southwestern Alaska
Established December 2, 1980
6,300 square miles

Things to See: *Redoubt volcano; Lake Clark; Ilamna volcano; Telaquana Lake; Port Alsworth; Tanalian Trail; Richard Proenneke Historic Site*

Things to Do: *Camping and backpacking; Kayaking and canoeing; Mountaineering; Hiking; Dog mushing; Fishing; Hunting; Backcountry skiing; Bird-watching; Rafting, Wildlife viewing, Rock climbing; Snowshoeing*

What's Nearby? *Katmai National Park and Preserve; Alagnak Wild River; Kenai Fjords National Park; Denali National Park and Preserve; Aniakchak National Monument and Preserve*

Alagnak Wild River, Aniakchak National Monument and Preserve, Becharof National Wildlife Refuge, and the State of Alaska's McNeil River State Game Sanctuary.

The park also includes almost all the Chigmit Mountains, jagged mountains once described as a "frenzy of peaks." Where the Aleutian and Alaska mountain ranges come together, the peaks of the rugged, challenging Chigmits arose, divided by plunging river canyons. Inside the park stand two immense active volcanoes: the 10,016-foot Mount Iliamna and the 10,197-foot Mount Redoubt, which erupted in 2009. A third active volcano, Mount Spurr, 11,070 feet, rises just to the north, while Mount St. Augustine to the southwest erupted as recently as 2006.

Alongside the fire, Lake Clark National Park has also seen its share of ice: The

Azure, translucent Lake Crescent, in southeast Lake Clark National Park, plunges more than 600 icy feet deep in a mountain valley carved by retreating glaciers.

park was born out of three or more major glacial advances and recessions. During the Pleistocene Epoch, or Great Ice Age, half of Alaska was covered by glaciers, snow packs built up and into ice sheets. As the glaciers receded from the western foothills, their ice melt filled the rents in the landscape they left behind. This left the necklace of Two Lakes, Telaquana Lake, Turquoise Lake, Twin Lakes, Lachbuna Lake, Lake Clark, Kontrashibuna Lake, and the Tazimina lakes.

A Pristine Natural World

Wilderness reigns supreme around Lake Clark. This is a land of glaciers, volcanoes, alpine peaks, and costal inlets with countless seabirds, herds of caribou, and great roving bears. It is a dazzling place to explore. Access to most areas of the park is by water—air taxi, boat, or kayak. Taking a kayak out on Lake Clark itself is an open invitation to wander where you will, exploring countless inlets and miles of coastline. The smaller lakes in the park also offer excellent kayaking, while some of the rivers give experienced kayakers or rafters fine white-water experiences.

Surprisingly, the only maintained hiking trail is just two and a half miles long, although adventurous hikers are welcome to explore other existing trails. The 50-mile-long Telaquana Trail is a historic Dena'ina

Lovely Tanalian Mountain is reflected in this shallow moose pond. It typifies the pristine grandeur of the Lake Clark region.

Athabascan route along Lake Clark that should be undertaken by serious hikers only. The Inland Dena'ina were famed hikers, and their trails connected all the area's major villages and seasonal camps. The Telaquana Trail, from Telaquana Lake to Kijik Village on Lake Clark, is just one tributary of that network. The trail has been designated both a Historic District and a Cultural Landscape.

Visitors also are drawn to Tanalian Point, an abandoned settlement on Lake Clark's

southeastern shore where the Tanalian River flows into Lake Clark itself. For the first half of the 20th century, Tanalian Point was a prospectors' and trappers' hub that became settled due to its fish, game, fur, firewood, and rich soil, not to mention its proximity to prospecting sites on Portage Lake, on Kontrashibuna Lake, and in the Bonanza Hills.

A Salmon Homecoming

The salmon of Lake Clark National Park and Preserve provide feed for some of the

Tuxedni Bay contains the island Tuxedni Wildlife Refuge. The area comprises famed bird-watching grounds, including nests of the once-endangered peregrine falcon along the bay's coastline.

Starring: A Russian Orthodox Christmas Tradition

It is guessed that the first humans came to North America across the frozen Bering Strait. In truth, Alaska is much closer to Russia than any of the continental United States. It is no surprise, then, that there is a large concentration of Russian Orthodox residents in the area, a legacy of the Russian traders and explorers who came to Alaska in the 18th century.

These traders first appeared in the Aleutian Islands in 1741, as explorers set off to find more places to trap and trade fur. Accounts suggest that the early relations between the explorers and the native people were not at all stable, with skirmishes and retaliation over property pervading many accounts.

The Russian Orthodox missionary boom began in 1794 in response to the natives

they felt needed to be "saved." Traveling priests roamed the Alaskan wilderness, looking for anyone who would listen to their message. The difference between the Orthodox religion and many other Christian denominations was that conversion by force was not condoned. Some locals converted and set up churches. Lake Clark is one of those locations. In fact, Russian Orthodox traditions survive there.

One of the more popular traditions is practiced at Christmas (which in the Russian Orthodox Church is in early January). It is called *Selaviq,* or "Starring." During this exuberant and highly social occasion, neighbors walk from door to door singing carols, eating, and spinning large, colorful, elaborate stars. The tradition comes from the journey of the Magi, who followed the Star of Bethlehem to

the birth of Jesus. The stars are often family heirlooms, made of wood or glass. Most importantly, they have no nails holding them together—a sign of respect for Christ, nailed to the cross.

This practice, as well as others within the faith, came to the Lake Clark area in 1889 along with a Russian Orthodox Church built in Kijik, an ancient village in the eastern part of the park. In a relatively short amount of time, the miners and explorers who moved into the village spread foreign diseases that ravaged the native population. Eventually, natives and settlers alike drifted away, leaving Kijik in ruins in the early 1900s. The tradition was kept alive, however, in Nondalton and Tanalian Point—as well as other lands within the Lake Clark National Park's southeastern boundaries.

world's mightiest bears. The park contains two major watersheds. Some lakes and rivers in the northern part of the park are part of the Kuskokwim watershed, the conjunction of the Necons and Telaquana, which flow into the Stony River, which in turns flows to join the Kuskokwim River. Yet it is the Kvichak/Lake Clark watershed that claims dominion over the park's water, from the mountain lakes and streams that flow into Lake Clark, and then on to the Newhalen River, Iliamna Lake, and the Kvichak River, which flows into Bristol Bay. This chain represents the globe's most productive sockeye salmon habitat. One-third of all U.S. salmon—one-sixth of all the salmon in the world—are caught in Bristol Bay after spawning in the Kvichak watershed. "One of the primary reasons Lake Clark National Park and Preserve was established was to protect a portion of the Bristol Bay watershed for the perpetuation of the sockeye salmon fishery," the National Park Service explained.

Connecting the southwestern end of Lake Clark to Iliamna Lake, the Newhalen River is an excellent place to watch the annual migration of salmon heading upriver to spawn. During the spawning season, which begins in late June, the fish arrive at the Alaska coast after traveling thousands of miles through the Pacific. In peak years the migrating salmon color the river red. As many as nine million fish fight their way upstream to Lake Clark and its shallow tributaries where they themselves were spawned.

The park has three rivers—Mulchatna, Tlikakila, and Chilikadrotna—that have been officially designated "wild and scenic" by the National Park Service. In this strictly fly-in park with no roads, canoeing or kayaking is the only way to get close to this magnificent wilderness. The park's rivers and lakes also offer some of the finest fishing in the world, with Dolly Varden trout, northern pike, and five kinds of salmon (chum, king, coho, humpback, and sockeye).

Lake Clark National Park is beautiful and lonely, hosting about 4,000 to 6,000 visitors annually. This could be ironic because, as the subject of the best-selling book *One Man's Wilderness: An Alaskan Odyssey,* Lake Clark is as famous as an Alaskan national park possibly can be. *One Man's Wilderness* became a classic soon after its 1973 publication. Written by Sam Keith, the book was based on the journals and photography of Richard Proenneke, who built his own cabin in the park's Upper Twin Lakes. Dick Proenneke lived there for 31 years, and the book was made into a favorite documentary played frequently on PBS. Today, Proenneke's cabin—made with hand tools that were themselves handmade—remains preserved for visitors.

"The glacial river below is now flowing in a northerly direction through a dense forest of spruce, dividing now and then past slender islands of silt, and merging again in its rush to Lake Clark," Proenneke wrote about landing at Lake Clark ready to build his cabin. "There was a great silvery area in the darkness of the spruce—Lake Clark. We came in low over the water, heading for Tanalian Point."

There is no trail to the summit of Tanalian Mountain. At lower elevations, however, day hikers have a myriad of trails to choose from, including the Tanalian Falls Trail.

Lassen Volcanic National Park

About an hour's drive east of Redding in northeastern California, the seismically active area now known as Lassen Volcanic National Park was first protected in 1907 when President Theodore Roosevelt designated two national monuments, Cinder Cone and Lassen Peak. Much would transpire before they were merged into one national park nine years later.

In May 1914, Lassen Peak, the largest plug dome volcano in the world, belched lava, steam, and ash, beginning a period of sustained eruptions that continued for a full seven years. The coup de grace was the blast on May 22, 1915, that resulted in a massive mushroom cloud, a 30,000-foot-tall apparition from the thermal underworld that could be seen hundreds of miles away.

These eruptions irrevocably altered the sibling monuments, and in 1916 a section of more than 106,000 acres of the decimated

As seen from Bumpass Mountain, Crumbaugh Lake is a popular day-hiking destination in Northern California's Lassen Volcanic National Park. The area is an excellent place for watching wildlife.

landscape was unified into Lassen Volcanic National Park. The western part of the park has been shaped by volcanic cataclysm from both this most recent spate of eruptions and those of eons past—with hardened lava, vanquished forests, and expansive craters. And some of the park's landscape is still geologically active, with boiling water, hot streams, fumaroles, sulfur vents, and steam holes.

The Heart of the Park

A craggy massif that rises to the considerable height of 10,457 feet, Lassen Peak is the park's centerpiece. Lassen is the southernmost peak of the Cascade Mountain Range, which contains a number of other notable volcanic peaks, including Mount Shasta in California and Mount Rainier and Mount St. Helens in Washington State. The subterranean heat that underpins all of its volcanic activity stems from the slow-motion but super-powered collision of the North American Plate and the Gorda Plate off the Northern California coast. Plunging under

Northeastern California
Established August 9, 1916
165 square miles

Things to See: *Lassen Peak; Manzanita Lake; Bumpass Hell; Boiling Springs Lake; Loomis Museum*

Things to Do: *Hiking; Camping; Boating and kayaking; Swimming; Horseback riding; Birdwatching; Snowshoeing and cross-country skiing in winter*

What's Nearby? *Whiskeytown National Recreational Area; Lava Beds National Monument; Redwood National and State Parks; California National Historic Trail*

the continent's primary plate, the Gorda Plate is the source of the geothermal heat associated with Lassen Peak as well as Mount Shasta to the northwest.

Since Lassen Peak's last eruption in 1921, the volcano has been dormant. Most of the park has been reclaimed by nature and presents a familiar northern California scene—aspen, firs, pines, willows, alders, poplar, shrubs, and wildflowers. Not to say that the eruptions over the eons have not left a lasting mark. Throughout the park, cinder crags and magma canyons offer proof of former violence, while gurgling thermal features and sulfur fumes suggest the possibility of a fiery future. In the appropriately named Devastated Zone, scorched and fallen trees dot the landscape amid such signs of renewal as saplings, grass, and

An entire mountainside has been altered by a hydrothermal basin on its flank off of Bumpass Hell Trail, en route to Cold Boiling Lake.

stubborn new bushes. At Bumpass Hell, powerful-smelling vapors drift over boiling hot springs with golden flakes floating on their surface. The flakes are crystals of iron pyrite, or fool's gold, that have been carried along by superheated steam.

Cinder Cone, a cylindrical mountain of hardened lava in the park's northeastern corner, is yet another Lassen landmark. Topped with a 230-foot crater, this 750-foot-tall cone of loose igneous rock was responsible for spewing ash on 20 square miles of surrounding land, creating what are today known as the Fantastic Lava Beds. These former lava flows that were red-hot and

Like Yellowstone, Lassen Volcanic National Park is dotted with bubbling and steaming thermal features, powered by the interaction between the magma underground and the snowmelt that seeps through the cracks.

molten in the 17th century are now forever frozen in time amidst evergreen forests and crystalline lakes and streams of this remote and alien wilderness.

In the northwest corner of the park, Manzanita Lake also adds to the drama of the park's furious landscape. Geologists believe that the lake was formed when a volcanic dome on the Chaos Crags suddenly collapsed, possibly as the result of an earthquake, as recently as 300 years ago. Riding a gigantic cushion of trapped air, millions of tons of rock and debris flew across about two miles of flat terrain. The horizontal

landslide—which geologists believe hit speeds exceeding 100 miles an hour—slammed into a mountain and came to a stop, in the process creating a dam of debris on Manzanita Creek that formed the lake.

Abundant Wildlife
Surprisingly, the park's volcanism has not scared away the wildlife. Lassen's resident fauna includes about 300 species of verte-

The lush and green Dersch Meadows in Lassen Volcanic National Park were named for Fred Dersch, a sheep rancher who was later killed in an 1884 skirmish with hostile Native Americans.

brates that live at the park's far-flung elevations. At lower reaches of the park—around 5,000 to 8,000 feet above sea level—the conifer forest supports a diverse animal population that includes black bear, mule deer, and long-toed salamanders. Higher up in the hemlock forest are deer mice, chipmunks, and several bird species. Above timberline, the hardy inhabitants include pikas and ground squirrels.

The park also provides habitat to a remarkably varied collection of plants, about 750 distinct species in all. This biodiversity stems from Lassen's position at the intersection of three distinct ecosystems: the Cascades to the north, the Sierras to the south, and the Basin Range to the east.

As is the case with most of the high country in the Cascades, Lassen Volcanic National Park is covered with deep snow for much of the year. Its upper elevations can get overwhelmed by frozen precipitation. The road near Lake Helen is sometimes buried under 40 feet of powder. It should be no surprise that the park is a favorite with snowshoers and cross-country skiers. The park once competed with the posh resorts ringing Lake Tahoe, but the downhill ski slopes in Lassen shut down for good in 1992.

Some years, park-goers will see the Main Park Road—the highest in all of the Cascades, cresting at over 8,000 feet—still closed on Independence Day because of late blizzards that dump as much as ten feet

Mammoth Cave National Park

Mammoth Cave is the longest known cave system in the world by far. Hidden beneath the forests of southern Kentucky, this cave system has been explored for about 4,000 years. More than 360 miles of its underground passages have been explored—so far.

New passages in the inconceivable labyrinth are constantly being found. It took explorers until 1972 to find a passageway joining Mammoth Cave with the Flint Ridge cave system, but they did that through Hanson's Lost River, one of a series of underground streams such as Echo River, River Styx, and Lake Lethe.

A Hidden World

Vast and overwhelming, Mammoth Cave is part of the South Central Kentucky karst, a system of underground drainage basins pouring through 400 square miles. Looked at one way, the cave is an imposingly complex, diverse ecosystem linked to the above-ground world. The region in 1990 was named an International Biosphere Reserve; at the heart of the reserve is Mammoth Cave National Park. The total surveyed extent of Mammoth Cave today is 360 miles, although scientists say the cave system could be as large as 1,000 miles. Another 200 caves inside the park appear to be disconnected fragments of the larger system.

Mammoth Cave was formed, and is still being formed, by calcium carbonate, or limestone, which dissolves in water and seeps through the ground. Observed from the top down, then, Mammoth Cave consists of an upper layer of sandstone as thick as 50 feet

---

Southern Kentucky
Established July 1, 1941
83 square miles

Things to See: *Natural entrance; Broadway Avenue; Bottomless Pit; Fat Man's Misery; Frozen Niagara; Drapery Room; Giant's Coffin; Tuberculosis huts; Star Chamber*

Things to Do: *Touring cave; Hiking; Canoeing; Horseback riding; Camping*

What's Nearby? *Abraham Lincoln Birthplace National Historic Site; Big South Fork National River and Recreation Area; Cumberland Gap National Historical Park; Trail of Tears National Historic Trail; Obed Wild & Scenic River; Fort Donelson National Battlefield; Lincoln Boyhood National Memorial*

---

in places, beneath which lies a series of limestone ridges. Sinkholes permit surface water to penetrate the upper sandstone, eroding the limestone as it seeps downward and forming stalagmites, stalactites, and columns at a rate of about one cubic inch every 200 years.

What became Mammoth Cave began perhaps 325 million years ago when Mississippian limestones formed at the bottom of a shallow saltwater sea. This sea, now called the Mississippian Sea, left behind an intricate fossil record in the limestone layers, including long-ago creatures such as crinoids, blastoids, and gastropods. The teeth of fossil sharks have also been found in the cave. The karst, or carbonate bedrock, spreads through a region that reaches west to the Ozarks, south to Georgia, north

Spelunkers stand in Mammoth Cave New Discovery Bore Hole, first explored in 1939. Many bore holes, both manmade and natural, are found in the cave.

to Indiana, and east to the Cumberland Plateau.

The Green River flows east to west and divides the park in two, separating its geology, hydrology, physiography, and ecology into two distinct areas. South of the Green River, Mammoth Cave is preserved by insoluble sandstone and shale caprock, which provide an umbrella over the limestone. North of the river, limestones and insoluble rocks alternate with exposed limestone, a rugged land where streams flow and then vanish underground only to emerge in springs. Within the cave, the eons have created a vast array of features including a family of gypsum formations called "gypsum flowers," and stalactites, stalagmites, helictites, and travertine dams.

Of course, the 52,800-acre national park includes the above-ground world, as well, providing visitors with opportunities for boating, canoeing, fishing, and camping. But whether above- or below-ground, the park allows views of a fascinating world within a

Mammoth Cave has been forming for millions and millions of years. Stalactites such as those seen here are only a few of the geological formations that have taken shape over that time.

world, starting with six miles of trail near the visitor center, four short trails and a motor trail on the south side of the Green River, and more than 60 miles of trail on the north side of the river. Then there's the Sloan's Crossing Pond Nature Trail and nearby Cedar Sink, a huge sinkhole formed by a

Mesa Verde National Park

More than 700 years ago, the people now called the Ancient Ones lived in communities clinging to the cliffsides of the American Southwest. These ancient people, the ancestors of today's Pueblo nation—24 tribes including the Hopi and Zuni—left their most remarkable traces in what is now Mesa Verde National Park: more than 4,000 archaeological sites, more than 600 of which are cliff dwellings.

A handful of the most spectacular of these uncanny communities today are open to visitors on tours led by park rangers. Some tourists balk at the regimentation of the guided tours, although a score of trails to mesa tops and panoramas are open to hikers and walkers. But regulation is the price today's travelers pay for the damage done by visitors who came before them.

Still, Mesa Verde casts a spell. An anonymous architect put it well: "Timeless forms and abiding mystery."

Author Evan S. Connell wrote of bringing a jaded visitor from back East to Mesa Verde: "Near the park's museum we sat on a bench and looked down at a creamy ruin called Spruce Tree House. There were slowly moving shadows, sunlight on disintegrating walls, and the mysterious aura of people seven centuries gone. My Eastern friend did not move or speak for half an hour. Now he wants to come back."

Here at Balcony House is a kiva, the keyhole-shaped depression at center. Puebloans today use kivas for religious rituals, as the Ancient Ones are believed to have done before them.

The Cliff Dwellers

About 1,400 years ago, the Ancient Pueblos, living in the Four Corners region, migrated to Mesa Verde, where they resided for more than 700 years. Also called the Basketmakers, the Ancestral Puebloans settled Mesa Verde about A.D. 550. They had abandoned hunting and gathering, settling in pit-houses—which later evolved into kivas—in small villages. Most often these subterranean homes were built on mesa tops, although they were sometimes built into cliffs. Only in later years did the Basketmakers begin building above-ground houses made of mud and poles, designed to fit one beside the other in long rows. The

Southwestern Colorado
Established June 29, 1906
80 square miles

Things to See: *Cliff Palace; Balcony House; Long House; Spruce Tree House; Chapin Mesa Archeological Museum; Step House*

Things to Do: *Touring cliff dwellings; Hiking; Bird-watching; Cross-country skiing; Stargazing*

What's Nearby? *Yucca House National Monument; Hovenweep National Monument; Rainbow Bridge National Monument; Black Canyon of the Gunnison National Park; Curecanti National Recreation Area; Natural Bridges National Monument; Aztec Ruins National Monument; Navajo National Monument*

A shaft of sunlight pierces the interior of Spruce Tree House, Mesa Verde National Park's third-largest cliff dwelling, built in the 1200s by the ancestors of today's Puebloan Indians.

recorded the ranchers' discovery: "The edge of the deep canyon in the opposite cliff sheltered by a huge, massive vault of rock . . . laid before their astonished eyes a whole town with towers and walls, rising out of a heap of ruins . . . ruins so magnificent that they surpass anything of the kind known in the United States."

Looting began and went on almost unchecked for 20 years. However, one ranching family, the Wetherills, acted as unofficial custodians of the cliff houses, selling artifacts to the Historical Society of Colorado and becoming amateur experts on the dwellings.

Today, however, Swedish archaeologist Gustaf Nordenskiöld is considered to be Mesa Verde's great early champion. Nordenskiöld wrote *Cliff Dwellers of the Mesa Verde* and was the son of a Finnish-Swedish polar explorer from a family of scientists and adventurers. Working with the Wetherills, Nordenskiöld made the first serious studies of the ruins. But when locals discovered some artifacts were to be sent to museums in Sweden, opposition erupted, and Nordenskiöld was arrested for "devastating the ruins." He was finally freed with the aid of several federal cabinet secretaries.

"Judged by the everyday life that is familiar to us it seems incredible that houses should ever have been built or homes established in such hazardous places, or that any people should have ever lived there," Nordenskiöld wrote. "But that they did is an established fact as there stand the houses which were built and occupied by human beings in the midst of surroundings that might appall the stoutest heart. Children played and men and women wrought on the brink of frightful precipices in a space so limited and dangerous that a single misstep made it fatal."

"I shudder to think what Mesa Verde would be today had there been no Gustaf Nordenskiöld," said former Mesa Verde National Park superintendent Robert Heyder. "It is through his book that the cliff dwellings of Mesa Verde became known and his volume might well be called the harbinger of Mesa Verde National Park as we know it today."

Today's Cliffs

Despite modern amenities, visitors should make no mistake that the park is part of the rugged American West: It rises up to 8,400 feet in altitude and has next to no humidity. A guest's passport to enjoying Mesa Verde includes lots of water, sunblock, and good boots. Today's urban dwellers should also be prepared to travel unaccustomed distances: The visitor center is 15 miles from the park entrance, and the park's most popular area, Chapin Mesa, is another six miles beyond that. Three Chapin Mesa cliff dwellings are open to the public.

Cliff Palace and Balcony House are open except in winter; visitors may tour them only on ranger-guided tours. Spruce Tree House is open all year, weather permitting.

Most Mesa Verde visitors stay in nearby Cortez or Mancos, Colorado, or in Durango, about 20 miles farther but the site of the historic Strater, Rochester, and General Palmer hotels. Some visitors hold out for reservations at the only hotel inside the park, the Far View Lodge, nearer to the heart of the mysteries of the Ancient Ones.

Balcony House, the second-largest cliff dwelling, is probably the most dramatic. Accessible only by ranger-led tour, visitors enter the way the Ancient Ones did—by ladders and stone steps.

North Cascades National Park Service Complex

An astonishing variety of ecosystems comprises Washington State's North Cascades National Park, with 9,000 feet worth of elevation change in the park complex and radically different climates on either side of the divide. The varied life zones of this remote and vast wilderness combine into a greater whole that is one of the largest uninterrupted ecosystems in North America.

In the high country, the park is a land of perpetual snow and ice. More than 300 glaciers are concentrated in North Cascades' boundaries, with another 400 in the general vicinity in Washington and Canada—many more than can be found anywhere else in the United States outside of Alaska. There are also numerous snowfields, which are areas of permanent snow cover, as the park

is in the center of one of the snowiest regions on the planet. While a shrinking trend has been going on for more than a

One of the loveliest views in the North Cascades is that of towering Mount Shuksan, reflected in peaceful Picture Lake.

century, most of the park's glaciers have been receding at a faster rate in recent years.

Peaks atop the Park

In addition to glaciers and snowfields, the looming presence of mountains defines the park, topping out at the 9,206-foot summit of Goode Mountain—which makes a precipitous 6,000-foot vertical rise over the course of 8,500 horizontal feet. But the park is an alpine wonderland of many mountains: There are soaring, glacier-scoured peaks, spires that pierce the clouds, ragged ridges, alpine tarns, and flower-bedazzled meadows in cirques below the mountain summits. On the flanks of the mountains, forests of fir and pine surround tranquil lakes and deep glacial valleys that dip down to elevations of just 400 feet above sea level.

The peaks of the North Cascades are so ragged and vertical that they are some-

Northern Washington
Established October 2, 1968
1,075 square miles

Things to See: *Diablo Lake; Mount Logan; Mount Shuksan; Ross Lake; Forbidden Peak; Mount Redoubt; Gorge Lake; Gorge Creek Falls*

Things to Do: *Hiking; Climbing; Camping; Boating; Fishing; Backpacking; Bird and wildlife viewing; Horseback riding; Rafting*

What's Nearby? *Ross Lake National Recreation Area; Lake Chelan National Recreation Area; Ebey's Landing National Historical Reserve; San Juan Island National Historical Park; Klondike Gold Rush National Historical Park; Olympic National Park; Lake Roosevelt National Recreational Area; Mount Rainier National Park*

times called the American Alps. Like the European Alps, they attract scores of mountaineers, hikers, and backpackers. In 1814, fur trapper Alexander Ross wrote of this rugged terrain, "A more difficult route to travel never fell to man's lot." The names of some of the mountains in the region attest to the hardships the peaks imposed on early trappers and prospectors: Damnation Peak, Mount Despair, Mount Fury, Forbidden Peak, and Desolation Peak, among them.

These mountains have their geological origins some 90 million years ago, when oceanic land masses collided with the North American tectonic plate and pushed upward in the form of the sheer mountains seen today. In more recent millennia, volcanism has further shaped the park's mountains, as has erosion from the many glaciers, a tiny remnant of a former landscape that was at one time encased entirely in ice.

North Cascades is also a land of unearthly sounds. On warm days, you can hear the booming crack of sloughing ice and the thunderous roar of avalanches. When the weather is bad, thunder blasts up the valleys and circles around the peaks, while the wind rushes between the mountains

The Diablo Lake Overlook near Ruby Mountain provides a view that might cause guests to wonder why this mountain lake was given such a foreboding name.

and ridges and down the slopes of glaciers. And always, in this mountain range that was named for its innumerable cascading waterfalls, there is the sound of falling water. Several rivers have headwaters inside the boundaries of North Cascades, including the Skagit, the Stehekin, and the Nooksack rivers.

Parks on Fire: Prescribed and Accidental Burning

While fire is an obvious force of destruction, it can, surprisingly, also be helpful in some national parks. An agent of change, fire is an essential component to many ecosystems. In forests, it reduces leaf litter, which allows foraging animals to easily find seeds to eat. It clears out underbrush (such as grasses, weeds, and small, weak, or diseased trees) that keeps certain species from growing and is dangerous for another reason—it poses its own threat of fire.

One way nature takes care of itself is by letting fire burn at certain times. Lightning strikes are the usual cause of such conflagrations. In a natural ecosystem, such fires burn for a while, take out some underbrush, put essential minerals back into the soil that are stripped out by plant growth, activate some heat-loving seeds, and then burn out naturally. When humans began taking care of the parklands, they viewed all fire as a threat and immediately fought any burning—natural or otherwise. This worked for a while, but foresters found that such actions had an unforeseen consequence: All of the underbrush that had been left made for an even bigger threat. When park visitors came and were careless, a single dropped cigarette or unwatched camp fire could set off an uncontrollable forest fire that fed on easily burned weeds and grasses.

The Northern Cascades are a spectacular example of how disturbances can affect the park and how fire can make or break the system. The Cascades are notable for having the most native plant species in America—substantially more than 1,600. A huge threat to these native species, however, has been the influx of aggressive nonnative plants, such as Reed canary grass and knapweed. These fast-growing plants not only steal nutrients from the soil and take over where native plants used to thrive, but they also provide fodder for uncontrollable fires. Where the native plant species were once resilient to natural fires, invasive species made them vulnerable.

Today the North Cascades have their very own fire teams, which walk the forests and areas consumed by knapweed and Reed canary grass, setting controlled fires. The teams help maintain the balance between fire that is helpful and fire that is destructive, and are available in case an accidental, careless fire is started. Fire is a powerful force that can help or hurt an ecosystem. It's important not just to embrace these resources but to also treat them with respect.

Many Parks Form the Whole

North Cascades is a topographic jumble, consisting of two national park units (North and South), as well as two national recreation areas (Ross Lake, named for the early trapper, and Lake Chelan). All four are administered by the National Park Service and are jointly called the North Cascades National Park Service Complex. A road through the Ross Lake area, which was completed in 1972, divides the North and South units and makes the alpine wonderland of the park readily accessible. In all, the complex includes nearly 700,000 acres of land, with habitats ranging from alpine environments to wetlands to lakes, rivers, and streams.

The mountains themselves create another kind of division within the park. Moist prevailing winds blow in from Puget Sound and the Strait of Juan de Fuca. Flowing up the western slopes and cooling as they rise, the moist winds condense into rain and snow. The west side of the park is covered by lush green forests of Douglas fir, western red cedar, and hemlock, which grow to towering heights because the trees receive more than 100 inches of precipitation a year.

By contrast, the eastern slope of the mountains, lying in the rain shadow of the great peaks, receives only a little more than 30 inches of precipitation a year on average. Douglas firs on the east side of the mountains reach only half the height of firs on the western slope. Moisture-loving hemlocks do not grow here at all; instead, the eastern slopes foster trees that tolerate dryness, such as ponderosa and other pine trees. North Cascades' flora is remarkably diverse: In all, the park is home to 1,600 different species of plants.

The park is also renowned for its diverse animal population. From wolverines to grizzly bears to banana slugs to bald eagles, the park's wide-ranging ecosystems offer habitats for 75 mammal species, 21 reptile and amphibian varieties, and some 200 bird species, not to mention 28 fish species and 750 invertebrates. Each habitat has its own specially adapted residents: The alpine zone's hardy residents include ice worms and red algae growing on snow. Among the park's endangered and threatened denizens are gray wolves, Harlequin ducks, and North American lynx.

An Active Human History

The park has been inhabited and explored by people as far back as 8,500 years ago, as native groups used Cascade Pass to traverse the mountains, dubbing the pass Stehekin—or "the way through"—now an often-used name in these parts. Along with

numerous sites in the lowlands, archaeologists have identified obsidian worked by prehistoric people in what is today the park's high country.

More recent historic sites in the park include mines and mills, sheepherder camps, sawmills, homesteads, and even a ghost hotel. Miners and loggers were in the area by the middle of the 19th century. The miners came and went without much success, but the loggers made plenty of money—and left a lasting mark on the local landscape. In the 20th century, several major dams were built, including the 389-

foot Diablo Dam in 1930 and the 540-foot Ross Dam in 1949. While the national park was established by Congress in 1968, the North Cascades highway wasn't completed until 1972, finally opening up the wilderness to the general public.

Today, the park complex attracts a wide range of visitors and recreation seekers. Popular outdoor pursuits in the short summer season include hiking and backpacking, as well as boating, fishing, horseback riding, and rock climbing. One of the most popular tours is aboard the Lady of the Lake, which ferries passengers across Lake Chelan to the historic village of Stehekin, complete with many active lodgings.

There are nearly 400 miles of trails in the park complex, through both the valley bottoms and the summits of these glorious snow-capped peaks. Backpackers often venture into the two million acres of wilderness that surround the park, one of the largest such areas in the continental United States. Not only is the park bordered by a trio of national forests that encompass five wilderness areas, there are other provincial parks just across the border in British Columbia, Canada.

Up here on the northern frontier, there are certainly more than enough peaks and wild mountain scenery to keep a person occupied for a lifetime, give or take.

Liberty Bell Mountain and the Early Winter Spires offer stark reminders of how barren the landscape of the American Northwest can become, particularly when winter sets in.

Olympic National Park

On the Olympic Peninsula in far northwestern Washington State, visitors to Olympic National Park behold a rain forest as green and dense as any found on earth. In some years, the rainfall that sustains this extraordinary productivity exceeds 160 inches, making it the wettest spot in all of the lower 48 states.

Three Parks in One

Park visitors walking in the Hoh Rain Forest on the western side of the park near the Pacific Coast find a cool northern woodland where everything is literally covered with moss. Western hemlock, Sitka spruce, Douglas fir, and western red cedars, some with diameters of 30 to 60 feet and ages in the hundreds of years, tower 250 feet above. The climate also proves habitable to a few deciduous trees, namely maples and cottonwoods. Underfoot, the perpetually wet sword ferns overlap densely on the forest floor, as new trees grow from the trunks of fallen trees, from clumps of sphagnum moss, and even from masses of flowered greenery.

This abundant rainfall is only part of the picture. Olympic is arguably the most diverse national park in the system. Along with the Hoh and three other rain forests (Quinault, Queets, and Bogachiel), the park contains a rugged wilderness seacoast, with headlands and beaches covered with drift-wood, and the Olympic Mountains, a rugged range of high alpine meadows, great jagged ridges, and glaciers.

Because of this remarkably varied land-scape, climatic changes within the park are unbelievably abrupt. The western side of the park has the wettest weather in the United States, averaging nearly 12 feet of precipita-tion each year. The eastern side of the park, however, which lies in the rain shadow of the mountains, is the driest area on the Pacific Coast north of Los Angeles.

Olympic's rain forests, with trees and veg-etation as lush as an Amazon jungle, may be the most fascinating ecosystems in the

Northwestern Washington
Established June 29, 1938
1,450 square miles

Things to See: *Mount Olympus; Hoh Rain Forest; Lake Crescent; Hurricane Ridge; Rialto Beach; Elwah Valley; Deer Park; Dose-wallips; Sol Duc Valley*

Things to Do: *Hiking; Backpacking; Fishing; Skiing; Snowshoeing; Bird-watching*

What's Nearby? *Ebey's Landing National Historical Reserve; San Juan Island National Historical Park; Klondike Gold Rush National Historical Park; North Cascades National Park; Lake Chelan National Recreation Area; Ross Lake National Recreation Area; Mount Rainier National Park*

Above: *The term* rain forest *often conjurs images of dense, tropical wilderness. But a rain forest does not need to be hot. The Hoh Rain Forest is quite temperate, with cool summers and mild winters. It is the 12 feet of annual rainfall that nurtures such lush landscapes.* Opposite: *The core of Olympic National Park is its mountains, seen here reflected in a tranquil lake.*

park. The richness of these forests exists only because certain conditions are met: Moisture is incredibly plentiful, and even when it is not raining, the air is humid and misty and the temperature is mild. The steep

The dense greenery that characterizes Olympic National Park could at one time be found all along the Pacific coast of North America.

rise of the inland mountains forces Pacific storm clouds to ascend and release their moisture as heavy rainfall.

This unique combination of weather and topographical conditions perpetuates the life cycle of these forests. After a tree falls, it can become a nurse log for new seedlings. Bacteria and fungi slowly break down the fibers of the fallen log, which becomes covered by mosses, lichens, and other epiphytes—

plants that grow on other plants. This surface is rich in nutrients and allows seeds to germinate and sprout. After a seedling takes root, a young sapling grows. Over time, the nurse log rots completely away, leaving a tree standing tall on its stilt-like roots.

These vivid green landscapes once lined the coast from Oregon to Alaska, but logging and development have destroyed the vast majority of North American rain forests. The

Reintroduction of the Fishers

It is a story that's heard throughout many of the parks: Over-trapping, poaching, and depletion of the natural habitats and resources cause the destruction of native species, bringing them to the brink of extinction. It happened with the gray wolf in Yellowstone and the beaver in Voyageurs. In Olympic, it was the fishers that disappeared. The native weasel, about the size of a house cat, was once plentiful in the park. A relative of the mink, the marten, and the polecat, it was known less for its grace in hunting small animals and more for its soft, downy pelts.

These animals became victims of the fur-trapping craze that gripped the nation in the mid-1800s. From that time on, their numbers dwindled. Though the frenzy of fur trading diminished, the habitat changed under human influence. Fishers disappeared completely from the park after the 1940s. Thought to be heavily endangered—or possibly even extinct—the fishers became another cautionary tale of the consequences of greed and the squandering of natural resources, something to be taught to visitors in natural history museums.

In 2007, however, Olympic National Park sought to bring them back. Fishers were found to be living in the Canadian province of British Columbia, north of Washington. Though there have been many accounts of disastrous attempts to introduce animals into parks—the elks of Yellowstone being, possibly, the most significant *(see page 299)*—area biologists and ecologists began their bid to reintroduce the weasels by conducting impact studies to decide the feasibility of the project. Instead of shepherding in large quantities of animals, they decided to release the fishers in small quantities over a period of three years. A total of 100 animals, all outfitted with radio collars and GPS devices to track movements and mating habits, were slotted for reintroduction.

On January 28, 2008, the first 11 fishers were reintroduced to Olympic National Park near the Elwha Valley. One can only hope that these once-native critters will again become widespread inhabitants of the area—in a safe, noninvasive manner.

temperate rain forests in Olympic are among the few that remain in the world, let alone the country. Their only true peers are rooted in Chile, Australia, and New Zealand.

But the rain forests are just one of several spectacular varieties of forest that are on display in Olympic. There are also montane and subalpine forests, featuring silver fir along with Douglas fir, mountain hemlock, and Alaska yellow cedar (including a world-record tree); coastal forests, with similar species as the rain forests interspersed with beaches and boggy coastal prairies; and lowland forests, primarily populated by western hemlock and Douglas fir.

Peaks and Oceans

In the center of the park are the Olympic Mountains, a wilderness range that is nearly circular. Thirteen rivers radiate from the Olympics' center like the spokes of a wheel. The highlands are up-and-down country, where deep valleys separate the peaks and ridges. Geologists believe that the rock of the mountains developed beneath the sea, because marine fossils are found near the summits.

Around 35 million years ago, the great tectonic plate carrying the floor of the Pacific Ocean collided with the North American plate. The upper levels of the seabed plate rose up and crumpled into the Olympic Mountains. Later, glaciers, wind, and water

The melt-off of snow keeps Sol Duc River flowing. In late summer, Chinook and coho salmon return here, fighting their way upstream to their natal streams to spawn.

Rocky Mounain goats can be found traversing the precarious heights of Olympic National Park's peaks. Their ability to maneuver on the craggy landscape is truly remarkable.

shaped the mountains into what we see today: breathtaking vistas of deep canyons, towering mountain ridges, and meadows dense with wildflowers. The high mountains have some of the best alpine lily displays in the Pacific Northwest, with entire meadows covered by mid-July in most years.

Olympic is also renowned for its wild beaches, which include rock cliffs and sea stacks, and its glaciers, of which there are more than 50, constantly fed by the moisture that comes in from the Pacific Ocean just to the west. The wild animals that roam the park range from Roosevelt elk, often seen along park trails and roads at dawn and dusk, to the great white sharks that haunt the intertidal zones of the beaches in search of seals and sea lions. In fact, the Olympic peninsula is home to the largest populations of the majestic Roosevelt elk in the entire country. On the other end of the size spectrum, banana slugs patrol the floor of the rain forest, acting as important biological recyclers in this intricate ecosystem.

But because of its climactic and topographical variety, the park has many specialized animals that find refuge in all of its diverse habitats. During the winter, for example, the high country of the park is covered with a blanket of snow, 10 feet deep in some places; the park's endemic snow moles carve tunnels in this white mantle and are keenly adapted to the frosty environment. There are also a number of species of fish that migrate from the sea and freshwater rivers to inland streams in the park to spawn every year, including several kinds of salmon, steelhead, and bull trout.

The Human Touch

Like the wildlife, the human history of the Olympic peninsula is rich. Native people have lived in the region for at least 12,000 years, long before the first Europeans laid eyes on the area in the 16th century. As time went on, nomadic hunters shifted to a more stationary lifestyle in villages near lowland rivers and lakes with easy access to the sea and the forest, which were bounteous sources of food and wood.

The first European to see what is now the park was perhaps Juan de Fuca, a Greek explorer sailing under the Spanish flag in the late 16th century in search of the fabled Northwest Passage. In 1788, an English sea captain named John Meares sighted the peninsula's tallest mountain, dramatically rising 7,965 feet into the sky, and named it Mount Olympus after the mythological home of the Greek gods. Soon thereafter, Captain George Vancouver explored the region's waters from Puget Sound to Mount Rainier. However, the foreboding and rugged interior of the modern park proved difficult to conquer. Lieutenant Joseph P. O'Neil led the first official expedition into the northern Olympic Mountains in 1885. After the mountains were first successfully crossed by a party four years later, O'Neil led a second expedition in 1890 into the eastern and southern Olympics and began pushing politicians to establish a national park.

As homesteaders began arriving on the Olympic peninsula in the 1890s, the nation's leaders in Washington, D.C., took note of the alarming rate at which the forests of the Pacific Northwest were disappearing. President Grover Cleveland designated most of the peninsula's forests as the Olympic Forest Reserve in 1897, effectively banning logging, but subsequent overhunting of the Roosevelt elk demonstrated that additional protection was necessary. To protect the elk and other wildlife, President Theodore Roosevelt established Mount Olympus National Monument in 1909. This also proved too weak of a status, as large tracts of the forest again became available to loggers in the following decade, thanks to local proindustry sentiment.

But with the support of President Franklin D. Roosevelt, a national movement favoring conservation of the peninsula prevailed over the loggers, and Olympic National Park was established in 1938. (An additional strip of wild coast was added in 1953.) The original legislation sought "to preserve . . . the finest sample of primeval forests of Sitka spruce, western hemlock, Douglas fir, and western red-cedar in the entire United States"; that language holds true to this day.

Nonetheless, the scars of industry past surround the park. When you enter from the southwest, a checkerboard pattern on the surrounding lands is easily seen from the highway: forest, then clear cut, then forest, then clear cut. The views of the clear-cut forest can be disheartening, because the land is so strikingly devastated, a near void where a remarkable ecosystem once thrived.

Upon entering the park, however, the spectacular old-growth forest is uninterrupted by the hands—and saws—of humanity. Here in Olympic National Park, the fertile forests continue to grow unfettered and wild.

Olympic National Park protects 57 miles of Washington's wild coast. The rocky shore, tiny islets, and sea stacks provide a rich habitat for a variety of seabirds and marine mammals.

Petrified Forest National Park

In eastern Arizona, the blistering sun scorches a mysterious stretch of bleached badlands. This landscape of tortured contours has been eaten away by endless erosion. The forces of nature have carved a high plateau into a jumble of buttes, mesas, gullies, and cones, all tilted at unlikely angles. Much of this spectacularly eroded landscape—resplendent in hues of red, pink, yellow, bluish gray, purple, brown, and black—is contained within Petrified Forest National Park.

Another dimension is added to the mystery of this otherworldly scene by great hulking logs of stone clustered randomly on the ground, and scattered across the desert. Many of the logs are broken into segments so perfectly cut that they look like cordwood felled by a prehistoric giant. A closer look reveals that the logs' cross sections have glasslike surfaces that, just like the surrounding landscape itself, come in a rainbow of colors.

These columns of petrified wood date from around 200 million years ago. Floods and lava flows originally uprooted the trees, washing them down from the surrounding highlands and burying them in silt and vol-

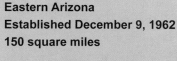

Eastern Arizona
Established December 9, 1962
150 square miles

Things to See: *Kachina Point; Rainbow Forest Museum; Puerco Pueblo Trail; Giant Logs Trail; Painted Desert Rim; Blue Mesa; Crystal Forest; Long Logs; Agate House*

Things to Do: *Hiking; Camping; Backpacking; Horseback riding*

What's Nearby? *Hubble Trading Post National Historic Site; Canyon De Chelly National Monument; Walnut Canyon National Monument; Wupatki National Monument; Sunset Crater Volcano National Monument; El Morro National Monument; El Malpais National Monument; Chaco Culture National Historical Park*

canic ash. Water seeped through the wood and replaced decaying organic material, cell by cell, with multicolored silica, ultimately leaving behind remarkable rock replicas of the long-eroded logs. Eventually, geological upheaval lifted the land where these great logs were buried. Wind and rain began to wear away the overlying sediments, and in time the now-petrified wood was exposed.

The logs became permanent fixtures of the desert, undisturbed for eons, until settlers began shipping the rock back east because of its aesthetic appeal. The forest was pillaged, and Arizonans fretted that all of the petrified wood would soon be gone.

A delicately balanced bridge of petrified logs is one of many astonishing sights to see in the Blue Mesa badlands of Petrified Forest National Park.

President Theodore Roosevelt intervened and designated the Petrified Forest as a national monument in 1906 because he grasped the scientific value in preserving this remarkable fossilized landscape. Congress passed legislation declaring the Petrified Forest a national park in 1962.

Ancient History Revealed

The petrified wood is still the park's star attraction. Giant Logs Trail leads to the park's largest fossil log, a great multicolored trunk with a diameter of nearly 10 feet. Another walking loop, Long Logs Trail, goes to the park's largest concentration of petrified logs. Other trails lead deeper into the park, giving visitors an even firmer grasp of the past.

The Petrified Forest is also renowned for its rich paleontological treasures. The park's fossils, some of which can be seen literally on the ground, include petrified conifers (up to three feet in diameter), fossilized Metoposaurs (a prehistoric amphibian), Aetosaurs (a heavily armored horned herbivore), Phytosaurs (a primeval crocodilelike dinosaur), and Placerias (a rhinoceroslike mammal). The streams of the region once teemed with numerous fish, including freshwater sharks and lungfish. Paleontologists consider the park one of the world's best representations of the Late Triassic paleoecosystems.

The park's most famous fossil is "Gertie," the remains of a Chindesaurus that were unearthed in 1984. Now thought to be one of the continent's first dinosaur species, this velociraptorlike meat eater was about six feet long and hunted in the area 220 million years ago.

The park also showcases more recent, human history in the form of early pit houses and pueblo ruins, which are up to 1,000 years old. The park's museum has numerous artifacts found at the Anasazi, Mogollon, and Sinagua sites. Human occupation of what is now the park dates back about 10,000 years. Offering a glimpse into the lifestyle of this era, the Agate House, accessible via the aforementioned Long Logs Trail, is a partially reconstructed eight-

Besides the prevalent fossilized trees, the park is also home to a noteworthy trove of dinosaur fossils dating back to the Triassic Period.

room pueblo made of colorful bricks of petrified wood and colorful mortar.

Newspaper Rock is the best place in the park to look at petroglyphs left behind by the region's former human inhabitants. Among the dozens of images carved into the rock's surface is Kokopelli, the flute-playing deity of Anasazi mythology. Newspaper Rock is just a mile away from the Puerco Pueblo, occupied as recently as the year 1400. The ruins of the 100-room pueblo are visible from a

Redwood National and State Parks

Sightseers crane their gaze upward at skyscraping treetop after skyscraping treetop, a vast and misty sea of coastal redwood forest that dominates the landscape near the rocky Pacific shore, just south of the California-Oregon border. Visitors to this primeval place get a sense of scale that's like something out of Alice's journey through the looking glass: This is a forest of startlingly immense proportions. Human beings look like miniature toy figures next to these great trees, known to botanists as *Sequoia sempervirens,* that soar 30 stories or more into the sky, higher than any other living things on the planet.

To put their height in perspective, the tallest coast redwoods in the park are taller than the Statue of Liberty, including the torch and the base, topping out over 370 feet. The first branches of these trees begin 100 to 200 feet above the spongy forest floor, forming a delicate green canopy that pushes the blue sky even higher than it usually seems

Northwestern California
Established October 2, 1968
175 square miles

Things to See: *Klamath River Overlook; Coastal Trail; Redwood Creek Trail; Tall Trees Grove; High Bluff Overlook; Lady Bird Johnson Grove; Elk Meadow*

Things to Do: *Hiking; Bird-watching; Horseback riding; Kayaking; Bicycling*

What's Nearby? *Whiskeytown National Recreational Area; Lava Beds National Monument; Lassen Volcanic National Park; Oregon Caves National Monument; Crater Lake National Park*

in the West. California's mighty redwood trees, many now living in their second millennia, are the last large stands of these monumental conifers that flourished all across North America during the lush, humid period before the last Ice Age.

Secrets of the Redwood Ecosystem

Here, near the Pacific Ocean, the climate—gentle, moist, and constant—

Left: *As this historic photo attests, the vast redwood forest that once blanketed the entire region was heavily logged. More than 90 percent of the redwood trees in California and Oregon have been chopped down since 1850.* Opposite: *The often rutted dirt roads that snake their way through these primeval forests make it easy for the parks' visitors to take day trips into remarkably unfamiliar realms.*

sustains them. The mighty trees grow in dense groves in a fog belt along the coast, especially in the canyons and river valleys that open directly to the ocean.

Scientists have only recently begun to understand the complex ecosystem of these ancient redwood forests. The branches that form the canopy at the top of the redwoods eventually fall to earth, where they mix with leaves and branches from hemlock and other species and eventually decay. This process sustains a rich web of life, where many interdependent species of plants and animals are tightly woven into the greater ecosystem.

For example, the red tree vole eats the fir needles in the canopy. The vole rarely descends to the forest floor, but it excretes fungal spores and bacteria with its droppings. The spores grow new fungi that are necessary to carry nutrients and moisture to seedlings and tree roots. And then there are the spotted owls that prey on voles and flying squirrels in the canopy, or the pileated woodpeckers and martens that nest in dead trees.

The wide diversity of animals living in the parks finds habitat in four distinct ecosystems: the redwood forest; the Klamath River, Redwood Creek, and other rivers and streams; the grassy prairies; and the Pacific Ocean. In the forest, there are banana slugs on the floor and chestnut-backed chickadees and northern spotted owls in the canopy. Chinook salmon, steelhead, and river otter are among the denizens of the rivers and streams. Majestic Roosevelt elk roam the prairies, and gray whales and common dolphins swim in the Pacific. Tide pools, beaches, and rocky outcroppings in the ocean provide even more habitat for birds, marine mammals, and assorted sea life. A great many endangered species live in the park, including Coho salmon, bald eagles, and Steller sea lion.

And while the coast redwood deservedly gets marquee attention, the forest itself is comprised of a remarkable range of plant life. The Douglas fir grows alongside the coastal redwood in many areas. Depending on the environmental conditions, the redwood forest is also home to a wide host of enormous ferns,

The undergrowth in Redwood National and State Parks is dominated by evergreen sword ferns, moisture-loving plants that grow up to about four feet in height.

Superheroes of the Plant World: Powers...

Much about the redwood forest is extraordinary. These trees originated more than 20 million years ago, long before the last ice age. When the world froze over, however, most of the species was lost. It's a testament to the adaptability and strength of the species that even three kinds survived in three different areas. Those in Northern California's redwood forest are called the *coastal redwoods,* the tallest trees on earth. Those in Central California are the *giant sequoias,* and they have a national park all their own. They are the widest trees and contain the most physical wood. The third type of redwood lives in China and is called the *dawn redwood.* It's comparatively tiny, rarely growing beyond a height of 140 feet. The dawn, however, is older by far than even the sequoia: The oldest dawn is more than a thousand years older than the General Sherman, which is probably a mature but comparatively youthful 3,000.

Beyond their size and age, there is something captivating about these trees. They have survived natural disasters and flourished. How were they able to do it? They have a naturally occurring substance in their systems that amounts to a plant-world superpower. Most of the earth's trees are susceptible to fungus, insect infestations, rot, and fire. But not the redwood. Its bark contains a chemical called *tannin,* which is a natural astringent, meaning that it has a bitter taste that drives away insects and discourages rot and fungus. It also gives the redwood its red color.

Another naturally occurring superpower of the redwood is its ability to reproduce without seeds. While there are plenty of trees that are able to sprout buds, it is very rare to find one of that sort in the pine family. Early loggers were put out by the ability of the trees to regenerate so quickly; when workers succeeded in chopping down one tree (no mean feat before advanced machinery), they were dismayed to see little redwood shoots popping up all over the stump of the tree. This ability renders the trees almost immune to fire. When even severe blazes manage to penetrate the hardy tree bark, the growth layer comes back in very little time. The tree has healed itself and becomes like new again.

hardy shrubs, and myriad other trees. The coast redwoods don't do well in the salty air immediately adjacent to the ocean; thus, the parks' beaches, dunes, and scrub forests provide a buffer zone that filters the ocean air.

Saving the Redwoods

In the late 19th and early 20th centuries, following the 1849 gold rush, loggers pushed westward across the continent, cutting down mile after mile of the nation's primeval forests. Today, almost all of the old-growth forests are gone. The ancient trees that remain are found along the Pacific, where only about 5 percent of the two million acres of coast redwood trees that once blanketed the region still stand. Unfortunately for these stately giants, the demand for lumber from redwoods has always been great because

A shadowy foot trail offers hikers a route to experience and explore the dramatic redwood forest—and a means to perhaps meet a resident banana slug.

Life at the Timberline

Much of the parkland is above timberline, which is about 11,500 feet high in this section of the Rockies. The park's centerpiece, Trail Ridge Road, is the nation's highest paved highway and leads into the heart of a spectacular alpine world. One stunning ten-mile stretch of the road follows a ridge as it rises to 12,183 feet.

In many ways, the timberline, which is so evident from this dramatic drive, is a biological battle line. Just below the timberline, such hearty trees as subalpine firs, limber pines, and Engelmann spruce struggle upward root by root to find room in which to grow and survive. Above the last trees, an even harsher world challenges the survival of the most robust plants, which cling tenuously to life during a brief growing season and in the face of constant winds. Here are lovely meadows bathed in green grasses and awash with dozens of species of wildflowers that grow low to the ground for protection in this harsh environment.

The park is not just a land of tundra, high rocky places, and ceaseless wind. Below the timberline are lovely hidden places, such as the sublimely beautiful Dream Lake, a rock-rimmed mountain pond nestled in a meadow at the foot of rugged 12,713-foot Hallett Peak.

Left: *Aspen trees are common in Rocky Mountain National Park. Since a stand of trees shares a common root structure, the trees turn colors in the fall nearly simultaneously.* Opposite: *Bighorn sheep are fairly common here. The park supports a population of about 800 of the hardy ungulates, whose horns can weigh as much as 30 pounds apiece.*

Thrilling March of Geology

The majestic scenery of Rocky Mountain National Park came to be after almost two billion years of geologic history. The Rockies have been uplifted and eroded countless times through an eons-long cycle. Glaciation also left its effects, with steep scars, U-shape valleys, lakes, and giant deposits of moraine. The rocks underlying the Rocky Mountains were produced when tectonic plates moved, putting sea sediments under heat and pressure. The result was metamorphic rocks of schist and gneiss about 1.4 billion years old. About 400 million years later, intrusions of hot magma cooled to form crystalline igneous rock, primarily granite. One hundred million years ago, Rocky Mountain National Park was a playground for dinosaurs dwelling on the shoreline of a vast shallow sea.

Then, nearly 70 million years ago, the Rocky Mountain Uplift began with upward thrusts of crystalline rock overlain by sedimentary rock. As the rocks uplifted, streams were already eroding the softer sedimentary rocks, washing new sediment east and west. This erosion left a few isolated protrusions above the slopes, such as what are today known as Trail Ridge and Flattop Mountain. Glacial action also influenced development of the high Rockies. Glaciers eroded V-shape valleys into U-shape valleys and formed lateral moraines, made of debris heaped along the sides of the glaciers, and terminal moraines, found at the ends of the glaciers. Glaciers spread through the high

Enos Mills: Rocky Mountain Champion

Rocky Mountain, Colorado, has a certain presence that is synonymous with the tough, the rugged, and the pure spirit of adventure and environment that turns weaklings to heroes. Because of this, it has become the "spokesmountain" for beer companies, 4×4 trucks, and pure mountain spring water. Though all of this may simply be commercialism at its best (or worst), the advertising echoes the story of the man responsible for the park's creation. The fact is that, without Enos Mills, the park might have been a desolate and deforested place, known as nothing more than a craggy desert. Because of his work, the Rockies are renowned as a place where people can find themselves by getting lost and change themselves for the better.

Mills was born in southeastern Kansas to a businessman and his wife. Though little is known about his parents, Enos Sr. and Ann Mills, historians do know that they spent a good amount of time in the gold mines of Colorado before moving to Kansas to start a family. Living near the wheat fields of the Midwest, Enos Jr. was a sickly child with serious digestive disorders. He was scrawny and weak for the first 14 years of his life, and doctors couldn't determine what was wrong with him. To improve his constitution, they recommended that Mills try a change of location in a different climate. With tales of the Colorado wilderness burning in young Mills's mind, at age 14 he headed up north, by himself.

The voluminous snowfall in the park's high country makes for equally prodigious snowmelt, supplying water to numerous streams, creeks, and waterfalls, such as the pictured Adams Falls.

mountains and receded at least four times, leaving visible evidence of their progress the last two times. Then, glaciers from Forest Canyon, Spruce Canyon, Odessa Gorge, and tributary valleys flowed together and melted in the area now called Moraine Park, depositing distinct lateral moraines along its south and north sides, and a terminal moraine against Eagle Cliff, a small mountain to the east. Similar glacial action carved the areas now called Glacier Basin, Horseshoe Park, and Kawuneeche Valley. Today, the rock is marked by steep semicircular scars that indicate the high points of U-shape glaciated valleys. A cirque on Sundance Mountain can be spotted from Trail Ridge Road, and numerous cirques can be observed from Bear Lake Road, where glacial erosion left some of the rock with striations, grooves, and glacier-polished surfaces.

Parade of People

Human beings have been active in the land encompassed by Rocky Mountain National Park for at least 12,000 years, with Ute, Arapaho, and Apache once living there. The Ute began their residency at least 6,000 years ago, with the Apache (400 years) and Arapaho (since about 1790) the relative newcomers. Anthropologists report that 36 place names in the park come from the Arapaho language. By 1888, all three tribes were gone: The Ute moved to reservations in Utah and Colorado, and

Mills Finds Himself

Enos Mills wound up in Estes Park (in the southeastern corner of today's park) in 1884. It was then a summer resort for tourists. Though Mills's constitution did improve gradually with hiking and the climate, it was the elimination of wheat from his diet that cleared up his digestive disorder—what is now known as Celiac disease.

As a strong and inquisitive youth, Mills worked during the summers as a guide, leading groups up and down Longs Peak. He soon came to know every bit of park terrain, confidently leading the way in every kind of weather. Over the four summers spent wandering the park, Mills logged 297 climbs and had countless adventures, which influenced him, and the rest of the country, for many years to come.

During the winters when the park shut down, Mills made his way to Butte, Montana, where he worked for the Anaconda Copper Company. His quick intelligence and hard work led to his appointment, at 19, as chief mining engineer. Though this early success seemed like a windfall, everything fell apart soon after. A fire ravaged the mines in 1889, forcing them to close and setting Mills to wander once again.

Later that year, he found himself in San Francisco, where one chance encounter with John Muir would change the rest of his life. Muir, who revolutionized the idea of conservation in the Sierra Nevada, encouraged Mills to write down his experiences from Colorado. He told the young man to write about the Rockies so that people who had never even heard of the mountains might feel that they'd been there. This idea lit in Mills's brain a fire that was never extinguished.

Though he spent the next ten years wandering through America and Europe, the Rocky Mountains were never far from his mind. When he returned as an older and wiser man, Mills was sufficiently self-educated and self-motivated to put his ideas into motion. Though they say he was never a man of major writing talent, his passion and dedication to the Rockies made him a success. Over the years, Mills published more than 50 articles in prestigious magazines, including *The Saturday Evening Post*. He also wrote 16 books, 15 of which were published by major houses. In these writings, he talked about everything, from his adventures in the mountains to how to be a guide. He wrote not only to educate people, but also to light within them a fire to see the place he loved and to protect it, calling for the establishment of a national park in the area. He did this not only with his words, but with his photos. His greatest weapon was his camera, which he carried on every hike.

the Arapaho to Oklahoma and Wyoming. But evidence remains; a five-year survey by the University of Northern Colorado recorded some 400 prehistoric and 600 historic archaeological sites in the park.

European and American settlers' exploration of the lands around the park began in 1820, with the Long Expedition, which visited the area but not the mountains. Regardless, Longs Peak now bears the name of the

Saguaro National Park

One of the few national parks in the system that's located on the doorstep of a sizable city, Saguaro National Park calls Tucson, Arizona, neighbor. Established in 1933 and designated a national monument within the past 20 years, Saguaro was designated a park in just 1994. The park preserves an amazing forest of stately giant saguaro cacti, interspersed with other Sonoran Desert flora, such as hedgehog cactus, fishhook barrel cactus, cholla, ocotillo, and prickly pear.

America's Favorite Cactus

But it's clearly the giant saguaro cactus that's on center stage here. Named for the Spanish interpretation of the native Tohono O'odham people's word for the plant, the saguaro is a true icon of the American Southwest. These majestic cacti are long-lived, slowly growing to heights sometimes in excess of 40 feet over the course of their

On the eastern and western outskirts of the city of Tucson, Arizona, Saguaro National Park is home to the largest forests of the stately saguaro cactus in the world.

Southeastern Arizona
Established October 14, 1994
142 square miles

Things to See: *Rincon Creek Trail; Spud Rock; Douglas Spring Trail; Wildhorse Canyon; Cactus Forest Drive; Scenic Bajada Loop Drive; Valley View Overlook*

Things to Do: *Hiking; Desert flora viewing; Bicycling*

What's Nearby? *Casa Grand Ruins National Monument; Tumacácori National Historical Park; Coronado National Memorial; Fort Bowie National Historic Site; Hohokam Pima National Monument; Chiricahua National Monument; Tonto National Monument; Organ Pipe Cactus National Monument*

150 to 200 years. They grow an inch a year during their first years and can take 65 years or more to develop their first side arm; an adult cactus with a triumphant pair or trio of arms reaching skyward is likely 125 years old. Conversely, the saguaro's spines grow very quickly, up to a millimeter per day.

The park boasts one of the largest concentrations of giant saguaro anywhere, with an estimated 1.6 million specimens rooted on park land. While there are populations in Mexico and in a small area of California, this is the place to see the most impressive forests, because the saguaro is perfectly suited to the environment. The Sonoran Desert outside Tucson is dry but has unusually wet monsoon seasons, which provide a perfect climate for these cacti's radial root system and pleated flesh that allows it to absorb large amounts of water to store through a dry season or two. Because of their efficiency in absorbing water, adult plants can

exceed 3,000 or 4,000 pounds at their peak weights.

Saguaro National Park is divided into two distinct districts. The eastern, and, at more than 104 square miles, larger Rincon Mountain District is found in the Rincon Mountains east of Tucson. The roughly 35-square-mile western portion, known as the Tucson Mountain District, includes similar terrain and vegetation and is located on the west side of town.

Wonders of the Desert

Saguaro National Park is the first and only close view of the true Sonoran Desert many people get. It is a superb introduction. The giant saguaro cactus forms the aesthetic and biological centerpiece of the desert and the park. Each giant supports a community

of animals, from ground-dwellers such as rodents to insects such as honey bees and harvester ants to songbirds such as the cactus wren, Gila woodpecker, elf owl, gilded flicker, and Lucy's warblers.

But there is more to this desert wonderland than just its remarkable population of spotlight-grabbing giant saguaro. In fact, 25 different species of cactus grow on park land. There is also a surprising amount of wildlife in both districts. With six distinct ecosystems and peak elevations exceeding 8,000 feet, the Rincon Mountains are especially diverse in terms of habitat, offering a good home to a wide range of bird species as well as black bears, Arizona mountain king snakes, bobcats, mountain lions, and white-tailed deer. The highest point in the

Besides its vast cactus forests, Saguaro National Park is home to numerous rock art sites, some of which researchers believe date as far back as 3000 B.C.

Left: *A rarity in the usually hot and dry Sonoran Desert, a winter snowstorm dusts the mountainsides and tops the resident saguaro cacti in gleaming white caps of snow.* Below: *The vibrant blooms of a saguaro cactus comes in May and June. The flowers open up in the dark of night to attract pollinators such as bees and bats before closing around noon the next day.*

park's portion of the Rincons, 8,666-foot Mica Mountain, is an unexpected departure from the desert: a forest of ponderosa pine, Douglas fir, juniper, and aspen.

The Tucson Mountain District is lower and a bit drier than its Rincon Mountain counterpart. With two desert ecosystems, its wildlife is less diverse and includes coyote, quail, and the long-lived desert tortoise. Of special note are the park's javelinas, the wild pig-like peccaries of the Southwest that feast on the spine-laden prickly pear cactus. The bird-watching in the west unit of Saguaro National Park is also noteworthy: Among the species sighted here are mourning doves, black-throated sparrows, Costa's hummingbirds, and roadrunners. One migratory endangered species, the lesser long-nosed bat, is found in the park in summer. It feeds on the nectar of the giant saguaro blossom and is the plant's prime pollinator.

Both sides of the park offer splendid habitat for a wide range of reptiles, including the infamous Gila monster and six species

of rattlesnakes. Beyond these venomous notables—and the aforementioned desert tortoises, with life spans approaching a century—there are a number of other lizards, nonvenomous snakes, and even two species of turtle that are nicely adapted to the desert heat.

Likewise, a number of nicely evolved amphibian species call Saguaro National Park home. One of the most remarkable is Couch's spadefoot toad, which spends most of its life burrowed several feet underground in a state of suspended animation. Thun-

derclaps rouse it from its slumber, alerting it to water pooling above. The toad climbs to the surface and gorges on termites that also emerge only during storms. A particularly wet storm will allow the toad to look for a mate. Spadefoot eggs hatch in less than a day, and tadpoles develop into toadlets in a little over a week, ready to hunker down underground until the next monsoon season.

World-class Hikes

For humans, the park's outdoor recreation is focused on the trails. Much of the best hiking in Saguaro is in the eastern portion of the park. More than 120 miles of hiking trails are in this region, including the Cactus Forest Trail, which—as its name suggests—takes hikers through a forest of giant saguaro, and the more difficult Douglas Spring Trail. Many backpackers use the latter trail as a jumping-off point for multiday trips into the adjacent Rincon Mountain Wilderness. In the western unit, you'll find a second—albeit shorter—Cactus Forest Trail, as well as more difficult routes, such as the Hugh Norris Trail to the top of 4,687-foot Wasson Peak.

Most desert aficionados agree that the best time to hike in the Sonoran Desert is in late March to early May, before the summer heat takes over, and when the wildflower displays are at their peak. Standouts during the early spring include Mexican poppies, Arizona pestemons, and fairy dusters. Later to arrive at the blooming party are the giant saguaro cacti, which do not blossom until late May or early June. The saguaro's vivid white and yellow blossom, incidentally, is the state flower of Arizona. Evolved to attract the aforementioned lesser long-nosed bats and other pollinators, the blossoms occur in cacti that are more than 35 years old.

These near-iridescent blossoms bloom every night until their red fruit matures in late June. Afterward, the flowers wither as the Sonoran Desert's potent summer sun beats down on the stately giant saguaro, slowly evaporating the hidden moisture reservoir under its thick green skin. The biologically patient plant bides its time until the next deluge falls from the monsoons that come on the heels of the summer heat, and then it greedily refills its barrellike trunk faster than even the hardiest cacti of its hardy desert peers.

Arizona's Creeping Invaders

America is known and celebrated for its diversity. It is proud to be known as a melting pot of cultures, a coming together of people from all over the world. What may surprise many visitors, however, is that, sometimes, immigration and national parks don't mix.

Immigration, in this case, refers to the introduction of new plant species. Nonnative invasive species are a huge problem all over the United States. Invasive plants have been introduced throughout the country for a variety of reasons. Kudzu, the creeping vine that is now synonymous with the South, was introduced from Japan as a means of quickly decorating a mansion's exterior and to help with erosion control. The vine, which grows up to three feet a day, quickly overwhelmed everything in its path. It's nearly impossible to kill, and it sops up the resources of other plants, essentially suffocating them to death.

A similar problem unfolded in Saguaro National Park. The culprit is called bufflegrass. It is native to Asia and Africa but, because of its tolerance for hot, dry conditions, was brought to the Southwestern United States around the 1930s to add food for foraging livestock. When an invasive species is introduced, however, no one can know for sure how it will react to the surrounding landscape and effect native plants and animals. When Bufflegrass spread through the Southwest, it began to leach the available resources from the surrounding vegetation. Now the iconic saguaro cacti face the threat of extinction.

Another threat associated with bufflegrass is fire. In many environments, fire is essential to the life cycle of the ecosystem. There are some plants, for instance, whose seeds cannot germinate without burning, and the plants and animals of those areas are adapted to fire in natural circumstances. Saguaro, Arizona, however, is not one of those places. The area's tortoises and cacti don't need much water, but they are dependent on the little water they get. Fire destroys the natural ecosystem and throws off the balance. Renewed growth doesn't happen easily in this climate, resulting in a loss of overall biodiversity. With a dry grass pervading the park, any little flame catches easily, providing quickly combustible fuel to an area with little natural means of fire control.

Parks rely on ecologists and volunteers to help eradicate invasive species that threaten entire natural ecosystems. Without help, the entire natural desert landscape—which makes Saguaro National Park a national treasure—could be irrevocably damaged.

Sequoia and Kings Canyon National Parks

Whether large or microscopic, the size and scale of the natural wonders of the country's national parks often help visitors put their lives into better perspective. In central California, Sequoia and Kings Canyon National Parks offer perspective on the large end of the spectrum—the *very* large. At these two adjacent California parks, administered jointly since 1943, the sheer immensity of scale is best highlighted by a trio of superlative standouts.

First of all, the parks contain numerous groves of the planet's largest living things, giant sequoia trees that are so huge they far surpass the size of any other species. Sequoia is also the site of Mount Whitney, at 14,505 feet the highest mountain in the lower 48 states. Here, too, is Kings Canyon, the deepest canyon in North America, plunging down steep granite walls more than 8,000 feet from its rim to the Kings River below, making it more than half again as deep as the Grand Canyon.

Established a mere 18 years after Yellowstone, Sequoia is America's second national park. It was established in 1890 as a wilderness sanctuary to protect groves of giant sequoia trees that were being destroyed by logging. Kings Canyon, a steep-walled valley, was mandated as a national park in 1940, absorbing the four-square-mile General Grant National Park, which had been

Eastern central California
Sequoia National Park established September 25, 1890; Kings Canyon National Park established March 4, 1940
1,350 square miles (combined)

Things to See: *Mount Whitney; Kings Canyon; General Sherman sequoia; Giant Forest Museum; Centennial Stump; Kings River; Big Stump Trail; Ash Mountain*

Things to Do: *Hiking; Horseback riding; Skiing; Rock Climbing; Sequoia viewing*

What's Nearby? *Manzanar National Historic Site; Death Valley National Park; Devil's Postpile National Monument; Yosemite National Park; Pinnacles National Monument*

created by Congress almost as an afterthought just three weeks after it approved neighboring Sequoia. Home to the General Grant Tree—the world's third-largest tree, the "Nation's Christmas Tree," and the country's only living war memorial—Grant Grove is the centerpiece of the former stand-alone park and is easily explored via a short nature trail.

Between them, the two parks encompass most of California's High Sierra. Collectively covering more than 1,300 square miles, they contain thousands of acres of sequoias and some of the nation's wildest and loveliest alpine scenery. Here are miles of sweeping mountain vistas, range after range of snow-capped peaks, high meadows, rocky ridges, and green forests of pine and ponderosa.

Left: *The General Sherman Tree in the "Giant Forest" is one of the tallest sequoias left on earth. It is the largest living thing in the world at 2.8 million pounds and 274 feet tall. It is 2,000 years old.* Opposite: *The rugged terrain of Painted Lady, overlooking Lower Rae Lake in Kings Canyon National Park, provides a contrast to the lush and ancient sequoia groves elsewhere.*

The Awe-inspiring Sequoias

The largest trees by weight and volume in the world, the sequoias in this park are the last relics of a species that covered much of the world before the most recent ice age. The glaciers swept over all but a few thousand acres too high in the Sierra Nevada for the ice to reach, destroying all the trees in their path.

Sequoias were formerly considered a subspecies of the coastal redwoods that are found in Redwood National Park and else-where. The scientific term for the redwood tree is *Sequoia sempervirens*. This name came from Sequoyah, the inventor of the Cherokee alphabet, who was much admired by the Austrian botanist who named the redwoods. The same name was, at first, also given to the giant trees of the Sierra Nevada. Today, botanists realize the Sierra Nevada sequoia is a separate species and now call it *Sequoia-dendron gigantea*.

The groves of these huge trees seem to go on forever, but these sequoia forests

Top: Sequoiadendron gigantea, *commonly known as giant sequoias, are the last of their kind. They were stranded in the Sierra Nevada by a climate change thousands of years ago.* Inset: *A popular illustration makes clear the size of these trees.*

can't compare with what existed here just a little more than a century ago. Logging of what was then one of the world's finest and most extensive old-growth forests began in

hiker may not see another person for days at a time. One spot in the park is said to be more distant from a road than any other location in the lower 48 states.

Rough and Rugged

The John Muir Trail, named for the renowned naturalist-writer who founded the Sierra Club, runs through Sequoia National Park. This high-mountain walking route required 40 years to construct. From Yosemite National Park, it leads south for 212 miles across the snow-swept top of the High Sierra all the way to the summit of Mount Whitney. Dozens of supplementary trails connect with the Muir trail, giving hikers good access to the park's stunning alpine world of knife-edge ridges, glaciers, high mountain tarns, and meadows filled with vibrantly hued wildflowers.

Near the southern boundary of Sequoia, Mineral King is another favorite destination for backpackers. Surrounded by peaks of metamorphic rock that resemble the Rockies more than the Sierras, the glacial valley was the site of a silver strike in the early 1870s, luring in miners by the wagonload. They never found a significant lode of ore. They did, however, build Mineral King Road in 1879, opening the valley to summer vacationers and lovers of the great outdoors. The valley and mountains were incorporated into the national park in 1978, nearly a century after the road opened. Numerous hiking trails lead up Sawtooth Pass and to a number of glacial lakes in the area.

The namesake Kings Canyon is without a doubt the most famous of the parks' canyons, and rightly so, a picturesque gorge

Shaded by a dense stand of vegetation, the Kings River churns below the weathered granite cliffs of the Sentinel at the base of Kings Canyon.

carved over the eons by glaciers and today a sheer wonderland that is arguably the deepest canyon on the continent, if only for a short distance. This canyon nearly went the way of Glen Canyon in the 1940s, before the Sierra Club successfully fought hydroelectric dams that would have flooded stretches of the Kings Canyon in the park.

Less accessible than Kings Canyon, but every bit as spectacular, is Kern Canyon, which cuts a 5,000-foot-deep swath in the park's backcountry that runs for more than 30 miles. Many of the rivers running through these dramatic canyons originate in the parks' collective High Sierra. In the park's borders are the alpine headwaters for the Kaweah River, the Kern River, and two forks of the Kings River, as well as tributaries of the San Joaquin and Tule rivers.

The diversity in the Sequoia and Kings Canyon parks is remarkable, as divergent ecosystems coexist in a dynamic partnership.

Spelunker's Delight

With so much attention focused on the above-ground geology, however, it's easy to overlook what's beneath the surface. About 200 impressive caves honeycomb the metamorphic marble rock beneath this artful geological jumble. Lilburn Cave, with at least 17 miles of labyrinthine passages worming through blue- and white-banded marble, is California's largest, and perhaps its most beautiful. Crystal Cave is open to the public, featuring a trail and lights so visitors don't get lost in its dark depths. More adventurous spelunkers take to the ropes that lead to the massive "basement" of Soldier's Cave.

Looming above all of the caves, canyons, and other mountains is the intimidating face of Mount Whitney. The highest mountain of the Sierra Nevada and the lower 48 states, the peak was named for former California State Geologist Josiah Whitney, the man who called John Muir an "ignoramus" for suggesting glaciers carved Yosemite Valley. Strangely enough, Whitney's summit is just 76 miles as the crow flies from Death Valley's Badwater, the lowest point in North America. On days when the air is clear, Badwater, 14,787 feet below the superlative mountaintop, is actually visible from points on the mountain. Unfortunately, those days are increasingly rare.

The mostly granite peaks of the Sierra Nevada continue to grow, just as wind and water continue to erode them. The dynamic landscape is the result of subduction of the Pacific Tectonic Plate under the North American Plate, which causes the earth to buckle upward above the overwhelming heat and pressure. The peaks of the Sierra Nevada are relatively young mountains, about 10 million years in age, over which time four separate ice ages have frozen and thawed all of the High Sierra. The remaining glaciers in the park, which are North America's southernmost, continue to recede, another reminder of the parks' ever-changing landscape.

When compared to the slow-motion natural change that sculpted the Sierra Nevada, the change brought on by humans is lightning fast. Because of pollution that rides warm winds from California's Central Valley and Bay Area, Sequoia and Kings Canyon suffer from some of the worst air quality in the national park system, not only marring the once-phenomenal views but also posing a threat to the health of many interconnected ecosystems. The challenge in improving air quality in these remarkable parks is similarly interconnected to many human factors, near and far, so the solution requires a cooperative, coordinated effort.

On clear days, the views from the parks' mountains still seem to go on forever, luring eyes to focus on an infinite horizon far below. And as it has for countless millennia, the majestic scenery of Sequoia and Kings Canyon National Parks crowns the High Sierra—and the parks continue to wear that crown quite well.

Mule deer are so named because their large ears are reminiscent of that notoriously stubborn offspring of a horse and a donkey. Mule deer nourish themselves through foraging.

Big Stump Basin: Proof for Non-believers

Even today, with television, digital cameras, the Internet, and other means of transmitting visual information, the giant sequoias of Sequoia and King's Canyon National Parks are things that one must see to believe. Without actually standing in the midst of these giant wonders, one cannot actually grasp the majesty of these ancient monarchs. It comes as little surprise, then, that people in 19th-century America discounted the rumors of the giant trees in the West. After all, they reasoned, while the West may be a strange and wondrous place, the rumors that came from across the divide were incredible at best. Wanderers returned with stories of boiling waterfalls that streamed upward and lakes whose waters attracted rocks as a magnet does iron. Eventually, the citizens to the East

wanted proof that trees of such a mythic size actually existed. Three miles south of the famous General Grant in Kings Canyon is a reminder of the tragic nature of this see-to-believe attitude.

In the late 1800s, sawmills and timber companies dominated the western forests. The huge trees were difficult to cut down—not only because of their immense size and the hardness of the wood—but because they were so perfectly straight and symmetrical, getting the trees to topple was a feat in itself. They produced so much wood, however, that one tree was worth the effort—even though it took five workers as many as three weeks to fell it.

When news of Sequoia's giant trees came to the East, the cutters were enlisted to help provide proof. In a field that had already

been logged, they chose a 1,300-year-old tree called the Mark Twain and cut its huge trunk into sections. One section was taken for scientific research; another 9-ton piece was taken to present to disbelievers in New York. The section was so large and cumbersome that it had to be cut into 12 pieces just for handling, to be reassembled after shipping. By that time, logging of the big trees was on its way out of fashion. There still remains, as a monument to the fallen trees, a section of the park called Big Stump Grove. Hikers can tour the area via a one- or two-mile loop around the stumps, which still include hundred-year-old sawdust from the logging operation. Visitors can also see and climb the stump of Mark Twain's tree, the sacrifice for the masses.

Shenandoah National Park

Virginia's Shenandoah National Park pays homage to the rolling hills and mountains of Appalachia as well as to the people who live there. The park has one public road, which travels 105 miles of the ridges of the Blue Ridge Mountains, the eastern rampart of the great Appalachian Range, then connects with the Blue Ridge Parkway and the Great Smoky Mountains National Park in North Carolina.

Shenandoah National Park spans 199,100 acres and rises to 4,051 feet at Hawksbill Mountain, one of two peaks more than 4,000 feet high. It boasts 500 miles of hiking and climbing trails, including 101 miles of the Appalachian Trail. The park is uplifted over the Virginia Piedmont on the east and the Shenandoah Valley on its west.

One of the densest populations of black bears in the United States takes refuge here, as do numerous rare animal and plant species. Some of the most satisfying hikes in America are here, as well. The largest protected area in the mid-Appalachian region, Shenandoah National Park is also a continuing source of controversy.

The Question of Relocation

This controversy goes back to the park's origins. In 1934 assistant forester R. B.

Northern Virginia
Established December 26, 1935
310 square miles

Things to See: *Lewis Mountain; Big Meadows; Skyline Drive; Loft Mountain*

Things to Do: *Hiking; Camping; Birdwatching; Wildlife viewing; Fishing; Bicycling*

What's Nearby? *Manassas National Battlefield Park; Appalachian National Scenic Trail; Fredericksburg & Spotsylvania National Military Park; Thomas Stone National Historic Site; Richmond National Battlefield Park; George Washington Birthplace National Monument; Antietam National Battlefield; Oxon Cove Park and Oxon Hill Farm; Piscataway Park*

Shenandoah National Park is world-renowned for its waterfalls, which run with particular vigor in the spring months when the snow melts and the first drenching rains come. Pictured here crashing down the cliffs is Lewis Spring Falls.

Moore mapped the forest, finding that about 85 percent of its lands were forests and the rest was open land either farmed or used as pasturage. Moore also identified 11 watersheds that had forest communities and no signs of logging, with monikers that echo the region's culture and origins, such as Hogwallow Flats, Hogback, Hangman Run, and Devils Ditch. As Moore pieced together a picture of the park-to-be's forests and pastures, watercourses and wilderness, the park was assembled from more than 3,000 individual pieces of land that had been either purchased or condemned by Virginia and given to the U.S. government.

Congress authorized Shenandoah National Park in 1926, after the Southern Appalachian National Park Committee, a group of scientists and park planners, had scoured the Appalachian and Blue Ridge mountains for the most suitable site. In the end, they decided that there was no choice but to evict the families remaining in the park. Five hundred or so families, about 2,500 people in all, were uprooted in the process, leaving behind a number of abandoned settlements.

"I ain't so crazy about leavin' these hills but I never believed in bein' ag'in the government," explained 85-year-old resident Hezekiah Lam. "I signed everythin' they asked me." Much land was condemned by the commonwealth of Virginia for $1.69 per acre, while productive land drew as much as $50 per acre. Most people left quietly. A few of those who resisted eviction were permitted to stay. The park's last resident was Annie Lee Bradley Shenk, who died in 1979 at age 92.

The park's next goal was to restore the landscape to its natural state, so the Civilian Conservation Corps destroyed and planted over what remained of the settlements. One major exception was granted: Nicholson Hollow, where 14 ruined buildings remained. Today, Nicholson Hollow is a popular day hike, following the Hughes River to Corbin Hollow's Corbin Cabin, built in 1910 by George Corbin and his friends. (Ruined dwellings also remain in Corbin and Weakley Hollows, where a mid-1990s survey noted 88 home sites, many of them destroyed in forest fires in the year 2000.)

The rock outcrops along the Blue Ridge Mountains, such as Little Stony Man pictured here, contain some of the oldest rock in the eastern United States.

A Short History of the Appalachian Trail

In the early 1900s Americans began to call for national parks in the East. Most people lived on the East Coast, and travel at the time was still not easy. Citizens not only wanted the national park experience without traveling hundreds upon hundreds of miles to get there, they also wanted to honor the natural beauty in their own backyards.

When the government began looking for sites to turn into national parks, two major contenders stood out: Shenandoah and the Great Smoky Mountains. Although the Smokies won the honor of becoming the first park in the East, Shenandoah was not far behind—and with it came much larger dreams. Original park speculators had imagined national parks all throughout the eastern United States, hoping that weekend getaway travelers and extended-stay adventurers alike would be able to park-hop all the way down the eastern seaboard from Maine to Georgia. They hoped for a park every 200 miles, allowing drivers the road trip of a lifetime. It was partially from this hope that the idea of a "Super Trail" began.

Benton MacKaye was the original advocate for the Appalachian Trail, as we know it today, along with the Appalachian Trail Conservancy, which was formed in 1925. MacKaye petitioned for the creation of not just a recreational trail up and down the eastern peaks but for trail shelter camps, food stops, and farms for hungry, weary hikers. In 1927, the Potomac Appalachian Trail Club was founded to begin the formation of segments of the trail in the mid-Atlantic region.

Shenandoah was strongly promoted as a means of preserving nearly wilderness land throughout a large stretch of the trail. Unfortunately, park founders differed in their ideal, hoping to make Shenandoah accessible to cars and vacationers via the Skyline Drive, creating bitter controversy between the park and the trail. Because of this, plans for the trail were moved farther down the mountain, prompting a furious Benton MacKaye to leave the Appalachian Trail Conservancy and establish the Wilderness Society.

In the 1930s, workers with the Civilian Conservation Corps, as they did for so many other parks, swept through and took up their tools. They built the trail and created the shelters that still stand today. Rangers and volunteers maintain 101 miles of trail that wander through the park. The trail is one of the best loved in the world, attracting thousands of hikers each year and generating myriad thrilling stories.

Still, the human history of Shenandoah National Park left its mark. The land had been forested, largely in the search for bark with the tannic acid required to tan leather. Due to its supplies of iron ore, limestone, and charcoal, the Shenandoah Valley was also an iron-production center in the 19th century.

Reforestation has been a theme of the park since its founding, and the park's dense forests have benefited from protection. In 1940 the park was 85 percent forest. By 1990, forests covered 95 percent of the area, with yellow poplar stands increasing from nothing to 16 percent of the park's forests, and hardwoods rising from 6 percent of the forest to 15 percent. These increases mirrored the displacement of scrub tree and brush and the improvement of the park's soils.

Tapestry of Wildlife

Today, more than half the flowers in the park are wildflowers. Beginning in late March, hepatica and bloodroot begin to bloom. Then purple and yellow violets flower, as do wild geraniums, pink lady's slippers, and large-flowered trillium. As the weather warms, blooms called Quaker ladies appear; so do pink azaleas, mountain laurel, and,

The view from Hawksbill Mountain is a reward for hikers. A number of trails lead to the summit of Hawksbill, where the National Park Service has built a stone observation platform.

come summer, columbine, ox eye daisy, and Turk's cap lily. As autumn begins, asters, goldenrods, and wild sunflowers greet the season. Park veterans recommend wildflower viewing from Skyline Drive and from Big Meadows, a popular camping site.

More than 200 species of birds dwell in, or at least travel through, Shenandoah National Park. Roughly 30 live in the park all year, including wild turkeys, barred owls, red-tailed hawks, and Carolina chickadees. The peregrine falcon was successfully reintroduced to the park in the 1990s.

More than 50 species of mammal inhabit Shenandoah, from the big brown bat to striped and spotted skunks, and from tiny moles, voles, and shrews to bobcats, bears, coyotes, and cougars.

Most famed of the park's animals are its American black bears. By the early 20th century, the bears had almost vanished from what became the parklands. In 1937, two bears were spotted. By 1944 the park's bear population had increased to ten. By the 1950s an estimated 75 bears lived there. "The mosaic of agricultural lands, woodlots and stream corridors surrounding the park created nearly ideal conditions for the bear population to expand and disperse," the park service says. Estimates today are that the bear population measures in the hundreds, perhaps close to 1,000 in some years.

Waterfalls and Lava
The park is also the source of the headwaters of three river drainages: the Shenandoah River to the west and the Rappahannock and James rivers to the east, which spill out into more than 90 smaller streams that form

a myriad of cascades, rapids, and waterfalls that range up to 90 feet high, including 93-foot Overall Run, the park's tallest waterfall; 86-foot-high Whiteoak Canyon Falls, which climaxes a series of six waterfalls; 34-foot Cedar Run; Rose River, 67 feet high; and 70-foot Dark Hollow Falls, the closest waterfall to Skyline Drive and the park's most popular falls.

Like many mountain parks, Shenandoah offers geological fascinations, too. Three hundred million years back, the Blue Ridge and Appalachian mountains stood as high as the Himalayas. Igneous and metamorphic rocks form the mountains' foundation, and they make their scenic contribution to the boulder-strewn summits of Old Rag Mountain, Hogback Mountain, and Mary's Rock.

Perhaps the most dramatic geological leftovers are the park's ancient lava flow sites, 570 million years old. Today, lava forms the jagged cliffs of Stony Man, Hawksbill, and other park mountains. Lava flows,

Top: *Shenandoah National Park rises to 4,051 feet on Hawksbill Mountain, one of two peaks more than 4,000 feet high. The park hosts 500 miles of hiking trails.* Bottom: *More than 50 mammal species inhabit the park, including white-tailed deer* (pictured), *ranging in size from tiny moles, voles, and shrews to bobcats, bears, coyotes, and cougars.*

one atop the other, make for topography of sheer cliffs and flat benches that resembles gigantic gray and dark green stair steps. The ancient lava is a key basis for the park's gorgeous waterfalls.

Theodore Roosevelt National Park

Theodore Roosevelt National Park is part of a forbidding land. "This broken country.... has been called always, by Indian, French voyager and American trappers alike, the Bad Lands," wrote Roosevelt.

Yet Roosevelt also said, "I would never have been President if it had not been for my experiences in North Dakota," namely the North Dakota Badlands area now memorialized as his namesake national park.

Roosevelt first visited the Badlands in 1883 to hunt buffalo. The next year his wife and mother died on the same day. Roosevelt very deliberately headed to North Dakota to both salve his grief and salvage his health, which suffered from asthma. He bought a small cattle herd to run on Maltese Cross Ranch. The next year he bought the rights to a ranch 30 miles away; he called the place "Elkhorn." Roosevelt's ranch prospered in

Table rocks are a striking feature of the badlands incorporated into Theodore Roosevelt National Park, sculpted over the millennia by wind and rain.

1885 and 1886 but then foundered during the hard winter of 1887, when the ranch lost about 60 percent of its herd.

The park still rewards Roosevelt-like energy. Hikes and horseback rides can go on for days out of sight of civilization. Or

Western North Dakota
Established November 10, 1978
110 square miles

Things to See: *Elkhorn Ranch; Maltese Cross Cabin; Little Missouri River Badlands*

Things to Do: *Hiking; Camping; Horseback riding; Bicycling; Canoeing and kayaking; Cross-country skiing; Fishing; Snowshoeing; Wildlife viewing*

What's Nearby? *Fort Union National Historic Site; Knife River Indian Villages National Historic Site; Lewis & Clark National Historic Trail; North Country National Scenic Trail*

visitors can choose leisurely drives, tours of the restored cow town Medora, or the half-mile hike up Wind Canyon Trail to a view of the strangely beautiful Badlands and the Little Missouri River.

Theodore Roosevelt National Park comprises more than 70,000 acres including almost 30,000 wilderness acres. The park is made up of three "units," 218-acre Elkhorn Ranch and the much larger North and South units, about 70 miles apart. Park headquarters is in the town of Medora in the South Unit. The Marquis de Mores, a figure of French nobility and an officer, built the 27-room chateau that dominates

the view of the town. It was de Mores who named the town Medora, after his American wife, the daughter of a New York banker.

But the heart of the park is Roosevelt's Maltese Cross Ranch cabin, where the future president lived in 1884 and 1885. The cabin originally was located about seven miles south of Medora, at the Little Missouri River. Roosevelt asked ranch managers Sylvane Ferris and Bill Merrifield to build a one and a half story cabin of ponderosa pine logs with wooden floors and a kitchen, living room, a bedroom, and an upstairs sleeping loft for the ranch hands.

Roosevelt was a prolific writer, and he toiled at the living room desk while preparing his memoirs and reminiscences of life in the Badlands. He wrote *Hunting Trips of a Ranchman* at the Maltese Cross cabin. A hutch in the cabin's living room served as a library and foldout writing table. The living room's rocking chair was Roosevelt's favorite piece of furniture.

Roosevelt's second ranch, the Elkhorn, was located about 35 miles north of Medora; he maintained ranching interests in the area until 1898.

Theodore Roosevelt National Park's Oxbow Overlook offers visitors a breathtaking view of the Badlands and the Little Missouri River.

A New Life for Teddy

While at the Badlands, Roosevelt found the proverbial "new lease on life." The president-to-be arrived there a sickly New York rich boy. As he subsequently cowboyed around the countryside on horseback, he transformed his asthma-wracked physique. The influence the Badlands had on the young Roosevelt later translated into historic change. Roosevelt saw the destruction of the bison with his own eyes, which caused him to become a conservationist who was responsible for creating 150 national forests, 51 wildlife refuges, 18 national monuments, and five national parks.

"I do not believe there ever was any life more attractive to a vigorous young fellow than life on a cattle ranch in those days," Roosevelt said. "It was a fine, healthy life, too; it taught a man self-reliance, hardihood, and the value of instant decision. . . . I enjoyed the life to the full."

Perhaps the unbridled spirit of the young Roosevelt is best embodied by the Badlands' wild horses, which have lived in the Dakota Badlands since at least the middle of the 1800s. Roosevelt wrote, "In a great many—indeed, in most—localities there are wild horses to be found, which, although invariably of domestic descent, being either themselves runaways from some ranch or Indian outfit, or else claiming such for their sires and dams, yet are quite as wild as the antelope on whose domain they have intruded."

Some of the national park's horses seem to have descended directly from their 19th-century

Left: *Theodore Roosevelt poses in buckskin for this 1885 portrait. At this time, he had moved to the Dakota Territory to try his hand at ranching.* Above: *The park service has preserved the modest Maltese Cross Cabin in which Roosevelt lived while working on his ranch.*

forebears, which were notable for their short backs and large heads with faces that often were "bald" (white). Blue and red roans were common. Horses with these characteristics are frequently seen in the pastoral paintings of C. M. Russell and Frederic Remington.

The history of North Dakota's badlands and prairie goes back at least 65 million years, after the Rocky Mountains arose over the Great Plains and just after the dinosaurs became extinct. For 50 million years streams and winds eroded the mountains, carrying their sediment across the plains. Then, between five million and ten million years ago, the Great Plains uplifted, and the Little Missouri River began to scour the Badlands and create the towering cliffs, twisted gullies, domelike hills, and rugged pinnacles like needles, all daubed with colored striations that run on for miles. It is, as Roosevelt said, "a chaos of peaks, plateaus, and ridges."

Bison and Much More

The Badlands famous inhospitality to humankind masks the area's great variety of flora and fauna. The park is home to more than 180 species of birds, prominently songbirds. Mule deer and white-tailed deer are plentiful, the mule deer in the uplands, the white-taileds in the river woods. Prairie dogs crowd their grassland towns, providing food for numerous predators. Bison and elk once were near extinction in the park. Bison were reintroduced in 1956, elk in 1985, each successfully.

Animal- and bird-watching are popular park pastimes. Bison roam throughout the park—and should receive a wide berth if met along the trail. Mule deer most often are to be seen between dusk and dawn, and in daytime in open areas in the shade of dense juniper groves. White-tailed deer seek thick woods and river bottom lands. Elk and feral

Few sights at Theodore Roosevelt National Park are as inspiring as that of bison, here wandering through the Badlands portion of the park.

Left: *The Badlands of North Dakota offer a rich source of evocative eroded rock formations, many of which are featured at the park.* Below: *Cannonball concretions such as these can be found in the North Unit of Theodore Roosevelt National Park. They are a result of a separation within the mineral-rich groundwater.*

horses can be seen in the South Unit only. Pronghorns favor the South Unit as well. Golden eagles can be glimpsed soaring along the North Unit's River Bend Overlook.

Theodore Roosevelt National Park is a less-well-known source of fossils and fossil lore than its cousin, South Dakota–based Badlands National Park, but a recent pale-ontological inventory revealed more than 200 fossil sites in the rock layers known as the Sentinel Butte and Bullion Creek forma-tions. Champsosaur was a semiaquatic reptile, an aggressive predator up to ten feet long with powerful back legs. Park exca-

The Conservationist President

During his time up north, Teddy Roosevelt fell in love with ranching and the lands that surrounded him. Though he had never been much for the outdoors previously in his life (he makes fun of himself repeatedly for this in his autobiography), his time in the Dakotas colored everything he did as president. When he came into office, he immediately began to change the way people saw land use. He hired Gifford Pinchot, a leading American conservationist, as a national forester and encouraged logging companies to selectively remove some trees and replant others.

Furthering his conservationist agenda, Roosevelt was responsible for the creation of five national parks: Crater Lake in Oregon; Wind Cave in South Dakota; Sully's Hill in North Dakota, which was later redesignated a national game preserve; Mesa Verde in Colorado; and Platt, Oklahoma, which is now a part of the Chickasaw National Recreation Area. In June 1908, Roosevelt created the Federal Antiquities Act, which gave the president the ability to name places of cultural or natural significance as federal monuments. In total, he named 18 federal monuments, including Petrified Forest in Arizona and Devil's Tower in Wyoming.

Had Teddy Roosevelt done nothing else with his life, however, his contribution to the national park system and conservation would define him as one who was compassionate toward the needs not only of people, but nature. He was known for his deeds in service to America—its lands and its way of life, which he preserved through his parks and his service to his country.

vations have yielded three partial Champsosaur skeletons, plus freshwater mollusk remains, snapping and soft-shelled turtles, and partial crocodile and alligator fossils.

Plant fossil finds have been numerous, too, particularly petrified wood that includes cypress and sequoia stumps seven feet to eight feet in diameter. The South Unit's petrified forest came from ancient date and palm trees, dawn ginkgo, cypress, redwood, and magnolia trees from subtropical forests 70 million years past. The petrified wood was made by groundwater moving through silica-rich volcanic ash and other sediments that dissolve silica (quartz). When silica-laden water soaked into the trees, the wood dissolved to be replaced by tiny quartz crystals.

Visitors take special pleasure from the Elkhorn Ranch Unit, the location of Roosevelt's home ranch, 35 miles north of the South Unit Visitor Center. The North Unit Visitor Center at the park entrance has an

information desk, a film about the park, and exhibits. It connects with the 14-mile Scenic Drive that leads from the entrance station to the Oxbow Overlook. Painted Canyon Visitor Center, about seven miles east of Medora, provides frequent sights of wild horses and elk from its overlook, while bison often roam the visitor center grounds.

In 1961, John Steinbeck captured the beauty of the park in *Travels with Charley*: "And then the late afternoon changed everything. As the sun angled, the buttes and coulees, the cliffs and sculptured hills and ravines lost their burned and dreadful look

To viewers looking out from the Badlands Overlook in the South Unit, the panorama of Theodore Roosevelt National Park is truly breathtaking.

and glowed with yellow and rich browns and a hundred variations of red and silver gray, all picked out by streaks of coal black. It was so beautiful that I stopped near a thicket of dwarfed and wind-warped cedars and junipers, and once stopped I was caught, trapped in color and dazzled by the clarity of the light.... I can easily see how people are driven back to the Bad Lands."

Virgin Islands National Park

Trunk Bay, on the northern side of St. John, offers one of the loveliest panoramas in the entire Caribbean Sea, a tropical region known for its exceptionally lovely views of lush isles, white beaches, towering mountains, and old pirate strongholds. The superlative view from the bay is a series of beautiful, palm-ringed beaches glistening in the sun.

Sailboats dance in the sparkling blue water alongside kayaks and windsurfers. Off in the distance, Whistling Cay, a small speck of land floating in an azure sea, seems to change color on the whim of the sky. During the 19th century, customs officers used the tiny island as a lookout for smugglers sailing between St. John and the nearby British Virgin Islands.

Away from the Mainland

Within the borders of Virgin Islands National Park are some 9,000 acres of spectacular Caribbean beaches, forests, and mountains, as well as 5,650 undersea acres and several stunning underwater nature trails. Located west of Puerto Rico near the confluence of the Caribbean and the Atlantic Ocean, the park encompasses approximately 60 percent of St. John, the third largest of the U.S. Virgin Islands, as well as a few parcels on St. Thomas, to the west of St. John. Here visitors will find an incredible diversity of

Virgin Islands National Park contains a panoply of western tropical Atlantic ecosystems ranging from dry subtropical to moist forest, salt ponds, beaches, mangroves, seagrass beds, coral reefs, and algal plains.

plant life, owing to a huge amount of annual rainfall, as well as the island's exposure to seed-bearing winds.

Wandering through high-elevation subtropical forests in the park's interior, one can see more than 800 plant species. At lower elevations, there are dry, desertlike areas, as well as mangrove swamps rich with mango trees, palms, soursops, peeling red "tourist trees" that smell like turpentine,

U.S. Virgin Islands
Established August 2, 1956
23 square miles

Things to See: *Trunk Bay; Hawksnest Bay; Annaberg Sugar Mill; Cinnamon Bay; Reef Bay; Catherineberg Sugar Mill*

Things to Do: *Snorkeling; Swimming; Sailing; Hiking; Kayaking; Scuba diving; Windsurfing; Camping; Bird-watching*

What's Nearby? *Virgin Island Coral Reef National Monument; Buck Island Reef National Monument; Salt River Bay National Historic Park and Ecological Preserve; Christiansted National Historic Site*

vibrantly blooming flamboyant trees, and century plants.

Underneath this lush carpet of flora, the park's undulating topography is quite dramatic: The average slope here on St. John is about 30 degrees. And the highest peak on St. John, Bordeaux Mountain at 1,277 feet, plunges into the sea over a distance of just three-quarters of a mile.

The Virgin Islands owe their natural beauty to the work of volcanoes. Geologists believe eruptions first occurred some 100 million years ago on the floor of the ocean. Over the eons, molten rock flowed from volcanic vents and formed the foundation of the island now known as St. John. About 30 million years after this igneous island-building began, the sea floor itself began to rise, lifted up by cataclysmic geologic forces. A series of violent eruptions above the sea then created a large island of solidified lava covered by sedimentary rocks, primarily limestone formed from the remains and secretions of marine plants and animals.

Wildlife Above and Below the Surface of the Sea

The park contains a stunning marine preserve where visitors can explore the complexity of life beneath the sea: coral reefs, broad expanses of underwater grassland, and white sands moving slowly in the water. One of the park's nature trails lies beneath the sea in lovely Trunk Bay. As visitors swim along the 10-foot-deep, 225-yard-long trail, signs explain how the reef was formed and indicate the kinds of underwater life the visitors are likely to see. Fifty different coral species populate the park's waters. In addition to coral, snorkelers can observe brilliantly colored conchs, sea urchins, starfish, sea turtles, and other creatures. However, much of the coral has been blemished by the trail's overuse. Marine mammals, dolphins and whales, are sometimes seen in the park's waters.

As for the island of St. John itself, bats are the only native land mammals—one species eats fish—but there are also nonnative (albeit wild) populations of mongoose, donkeys, and goats. About 150 species of birds can be seen in the island's varied habitats, as well as a number of reptiles and amphibians.

St. John is one of about 100 jewellike islands that dot the blue waters of the northern Caribbean. While native North American populations lived here beginning about 1,000 years ago, the islands were visited by Columbus in 1493. Imagining the array of islands to be more extensive than it is, he named them for the 11,000 virgins who accompanied St. Ursula on her ill-fated

Many of the interesting views at Virgin Islands National Park can be found off the coast under the surface of the waves. Snorkeling and scuba diving are among the most popular park activities.

Voyageurs National Park

When the snow masses in the woods,/I march through it up to my knees,/I take my snowshoe and I drive out/The moose and the caribou/But when the shade of the evening arrives,/I have a good bed of fir tree,/Sleeping near the jumping flames,/I sleep, I dream until the morning. —from the "Song of the Voyageurs"

Voyageurs National Park is the rare road-less national park and the only park where a canoe can be a travel necessity. The park pays historic tribute to the Voyageurs, fur trappers and traders required to work 14 or more hours per day, portage—carry over land—26-foot canoes with 180 pounds or more worth of goods, and sometimes paddle at a rate of almost one stroke per second. Today, the park's nearly 220,000 acres are accessible only by waterway; nonetheless about a quarter-million visitors come yearly. Voyageurs National Park lies in Minnesota close to International Falls. Fifty-five miles of the park run along the border with Ontario, Canada.

The Icy Past

Voyageurs National Park flows from the southern edge of the great Canadian Shield, some of the world's oldest exposed rock formations. Also known as the Laurentian Plateau, the shield comprises an enormous stretch of North America including most of

> **Northern Minnesota**
> **Established January 8, 1971**
> **340 square miles**
>
> **Things to See:** *Kabetogama Lake; Boundary Waters Canoe Area; Oberholtzer Trail; Rainy Lake; Little American Island; Kettle Falls*
>
> **Things to Do:** *Camping; Canoeing; Hiking; Fishing; Cross-country skiing, Wildlife viewing; Snowshoeing; Ice fishing*
>
> **What's Nearby?** *Boundary Waters Canoe Area Wilderness; Grand Portage National Monument; Apostle Islands National Lakeshore; Isle Royale National Park*

Canada and parts of Michigan, Minnesota, and Wisconsin. The Canadian Shield's bedrock has been sculpted by four ice ages, which have left in their wake the varied topography seen today and a surface skin of topsoil sufficient to grow the North Woods. More than 35 percent of the park's surface is covered by water, most of it contained in four large lakes. The lakes—Rainy, Kabetogama, Namakan, and Sand Point—are intertwined through streams and narrow channels. The Canadian Shield consists of tundra in the north; to the south lie enormous pine and hardwoods forests, bogs, swamps, and beaver dams. The 75,000-acre Kabetogama peninsula, the park's most popular wooded site, is a vast agglomeration of hills, forests, swamps, and small lakes.

Ten millennia ago, the glacial lake covering what is now Voyageurs National Park vanished, and hunters and gatherers began to arrive. Today, the park hosts more than

Cranberry Creek feeds in Locater Lake in the northwestern area of Voyageurs National Park. Locater Lake is part of the Chain of Lakes Scenic Trail.

220 archaeological sites. The first people on modern-day park land arrived perhaps 10,000 years ago as glacial Lake Agassiz— an ancient body of water that once covered 110,000 square miles—receded. These paleo-natives hunted, fished, and gathered crops. The next period of Native American settlement was characterized by the increased cultivation of wild rice and the development of ceramics and arrowheads. At the time Europeans first arrived in the region, the dominant tribes were the Monsoni, Cree,

and Assiniboin. By the middle 1700s, however, they had largely abandoned the area, and their place was taken by the Ojibwe.

Exploiting the Resources

When the Europeans came, the place became a paradise for trappers, and the Ojibwe were important to them as guides. The area's first European explorer is believed to have been Jacques de Noyon of France, in 1688. De Noyon noted the area's rich populations of beaver. With beaver sup-

The northwoods atmosphere is unmistakable at Rainy Lake, which sits on either side of the U.S.-Canada border.

plies diminishing in the East, large numbers of fur trappers and traders were drawn here, trapping and canoeing goods to Montreal and Canada's Northwest.

The voyageurs themselves were iron men, colorful characters who attracted favorable attention even from their contemporaries. The voyageurs' standard routes included 120 portages, the toughest of which, called Grand Portage, demanded an arduous nine-mile hike. In 1819, Daniel Harmon, a Vermonter who became a partner in the North West Company, wrote: "The Canadian Voyageurs possess lively and fickle dispositions; and they are rarely subject to depression of spirits of long continuance, even when in circumstances the most adverse.... When necessity compels them to it, they submit to great privation and hardship, not only without complaining, but even with cheerfulness and gaiety.... Trifling provocations will often throw them into a rage, but they are easily appeased when in anger, and they never harbour a revengeful purpose against those by whom they conceive that they have been injured." By the 1850s, however, demand for beaver hats had slumped, dealing a death blow to the fur trade.

The Voyage for the Beaver

What is now Voyageurs National Park was an important spot contributing to westward expansion, thanks largely to the beaver. These creatures are the world's second-largest rodent and are found throughout North America and some places in Europe. With the supply in Europe dwindling in the 1700s, trendsetters became aware of the seemingly endless natural abundance of the animal in the new American colonies. As the fashion of the day was beaver-felt top hats, suddenly all eyes were on the colonies to supplement the growing demand for fur fashions.

The beaver's durable waterproof rain-slicking hides were perfect for the rainy weather in Britain and the eastern North American colonies. As fur in the East became scarce, companies contracted voyageurs to trap and trade beaver skins. These adventurers hiked through dangerous, uncharted territories, boarding canoes and braving frigid weather to collect beaver pelts near today's Canadian border.

Voyageurs National Park is the perfect habitat for beavers, with its many inlets and outlets, as well as plentiful trees and bushes. Trees are both food and shelter for the rodents, and the inlets provide waterways for beaver families building dams and lodges. Keeping house in the middle of water helps keep out natural predators, such as wolves, lynxes, bears, wolverines, and otters. One other way beavers keep predators at bay is to work at night, bringing down trees for shelter while all others sleep.

The one enemy beavers could not keep at bay, however, was people. By 1900, beavers were all but extinct in the northern United States and southern Canada. It wasn't until then that they became a protected species.

Beaver populations have returned today—not to their original strength, but in large enough quantities that they are not only off the endangered list but are now once again hunted legally. Through careful regulation of seasons, licensing, and numbers killed, beaver pelts once again grace haberdashers and fur retailers worldwide.

Then, in 1893, gold was found on Little American Island in Rainy Lake, giving life to a boom town called Rainy Lake City and seven gold mines. By 1894, Rainy Lake City was an incorporated municipality; by summer it boasted hotels, a bank, a schoolhouse, a general store, restaurants, a newspaper, and, of course, several saloons. By 1901, however, the mines had played out and the gold miners departed.

The next major change came with the arrival of loggers looking for pine, fir, and spruce trees. This didn't last long, either. By 1920, logging had cut away the Voyageurs area's last virgin forests.

Commercial fishing, followed by sport fishing, led to the establishment of an increasing number of resorts. Voyageurs was named a national park in 1971 but didn't open until 1975. By that time, more than 120 private recreational properties, 12 resorts, and 97 leased cabin sites existed inside the park lands, with another 60 resorts around it. Many property owners sold their land to the U.S. government, while others remained in the park either through lifetime tenancy or a 25-year use and occupancy reservation. The National Park Service plans to destroy most of these properties as time goes by, but it also intends to preserve 20 properties with more than 50 structures notable for their historic significance.

Northern Recreational Paradise

Today, about 250,000 visitors annually enjoy more than 45 miles of hiking, skiing, and snowshoe trails, plus a seven-mile ice road from Rainy Lake Visitor Center in winter and

110 miles of snowmobile trails. Sport fishing continues to be a popular pastime, with walleye, northern pike, smallmouth and largemouth bass, crappie, lake trout, bluegill, and yellow perch in abundance.

Boat excursions are another popular, low-key way to see the park. One trip, from Kabetogama to Kettle Falls, takes six hours to sail 28 miles, following the paths of the Native Americans, voyageurs, lumberjacks, and gold miners. Today's voyagers can get to Kabetogama peninsula and the rest of the dry portions of the park by watercraft in warm weather or by skis, snowshoes, or snowmobiles in winter.

Speaking of winter, how cold does it get in Voyageurs National Park? Cold enough so that nearby International Falls sometimes is called "The Icebox of the Nation," a place where manufacturers such as General Motors have taken products to test their performance in cold weather. Yet visitors don't have to be made of iron themselves to enjoy Voyageurs. Unlike Boundary Waters Wilderness Canoe Area next door, the national park permits motorized watercraft. A tour boat cruises Lake Kabetogama, a glorious vantage point from which to see the park's cormorants, great kingfishers, loons and blue herons, ospreys and eagles, wolves and coyotes. Visitors also can cruise to the historic Kettle Falls Hotel, a spot on the National Register of Historic Places that can be explored only by boat or seaplane. The hotel, located near Kettle Falls between Lake Namakan and Rainy Lake, was built in 1910 and is still operated as a hotel and resort. Kettle Falls, by the way, is one of the rare spots in the lower 48 states where visitors can see Canada—to the south.

Top: *The harsh rocky shoreline is not a deterrent to canoers intending to explore the waters.* Left: *Following the path of an ancient glacier, Voyageurs National Park's 25,000-acre Kabetogama Lake is one of the park's four major lakes. Its islands contain 42 mammal species, including this velvet-antlered white-tailed deer.*

Wrangell–St. Elias National Park and Preserve

Three great mountain ranges converge in Wrangell–St. Elias National Park and Preserve, creating a reckless jumble of ragged peaks, lovely river valleys, and enormous glaciers. The St. Elias Mountains, the world's tallest coastal range, shove their way up from the Yukon Territory in the southeast, where they join the Chugach Range in a torrent of glaciers and ice fields. The mighty Wrangell Range, coming down from the north, is the backbone of the park.

Near the point where the three ranges come together, in the southeast corner of the park, spectacular Mount St. Elias rises 18,008 feet. It is the second tallest mountain in the United States (Denali, otherwise known as Mount McKinley, is the tallest). Only 30 miles from the rugged, glacier-scoured coast of the Gulf of Alaska, Mount St. Elias rises so dramatically and precipitously that it dominates its surroundings like few other mountains. As people fly over the park, the mountains come at them in waves of ranges that change color with the weather.

Dominating the National Park System

In much the same way, Wrangell–St. Elias National Park and Preserve comes

Southeastern Alaska
Established December 2, 1980
20,587 square miles

Things to See: *Mount St. Elias; Mount Wrangell; Nabesna Glacier; Copper River; Malaspina Glacier; Hubbard Glacier; Bagley Icefield; Liberty Falls Trail; Kennecott Mines National Historic Landmark*

Things to Do: *Hiking; Mountain biking; Fishing; Hunting; Backpacking; Sea kayaking; Mountaineering*

What's Nearby? *Klondike Gold Rush National Historic Park; Glacier Bay National Park and Preserve; Kenai Fjords National Park; Yukon–Charley Rivers National Preserve; Denali National Park and Preserve; Sitka National Historical Park*

at the visitor in waves of superlatives. Wrangell–St. Elias is the largest national park: 20,587 square miles or more than 13 million acres. The park is six times the size of Yellowstone and larger than Switzerland. It has nine of the sixteen highest U.S. mountains—four of them are above 16,000 feet. With Glacier Bay National Park and Canada's Kluane National Park and Tatshenshini-Alsek Park, Wrangell–St. Elias

Left: *These vibrant colors seem to come alive in the autumn at Alaska's Wrangell–St. Elias National Park.* Opposite: *Mount Wrangell, standing more than 14,000 feet, is seen in the distance from a spot overlooking Copper River.*

The deep blue of this glacial pool is a striking contrast to the whites and grays of the ice and mountains around it.

mountains where people probably have never set foot, and countless peaks remain unnamed and unscaled. The park is so vast that it contains more unexplored terrain than the Himalayas, largely as a result of the short summers and long winters that come with its proximity to the Arctic.

Getting Around

The park's size is overwhelming, but it is not inaccessible. Road access to the north and west boundaries of the park is provided by the Alaska and Richardson highways. Glenn Highway provides access from Anchorage. Then, two rough roads lead into the heart of the park. One, the McCarthy Road,

is crown of the biggest part of the largest internationally protected area in the world (24 million acres). It has been recognized as a World Heritage Site. Wrangell–St. Elias received 65,693 visitors in 2007, an astonishing number for such a faraway park.

Wrangell–St. Elias contains the nation's largest glacial system, more than 150 gla-

ciers; glaciers cover more than one-quarter of the park. One of them, the Malaspina Glacier, is North America's largest nonpolar piedmont glacier (which is a glacier formed not in a valley but at the base of a mountain), blanketing an area larger than Rhode Island. The Nabesna Glacier is 75 miles long, and the Hubbard Glacier advances 80 feet per year.

This rugged region has been called the Himalayas of North America. In fact, the rugged terrain of the park may actually be wilder than the great Asian mountains. There are still valleys in these mighty Alaskan

leads visitors back in time to the Alaska gold rush days at the turn of the century. It starts from the ranger station at Chitina on the east side of the park and follows an old Copper River and Northwest Railroad bed 62 miles into the park's southern preserve. There, a hand-pulled cable tram takes you across the Kennicott River to the tiny community of McCarthy—now almost deserted, once a town that thousands of miners, hustlers, and cardsharps passed through—and the Kennecott mine and town. The second road, the northern preserve's 46-mile-long Nabesna

Road, runs to the village of Nabesna. Access to more remote areas is available by small plane, pack train, or foot.

Before the miners, Native Americans lived in what today is the park area. We have some details of their lives through 115 documented Athabaskan sites that include winter villages, hunting and fishing camps, trails, house sites, food caches, caribou fences, cemeteries, and other historic sites. The coastal Tlingit were the most numerous of Native Americans, living from the Alsek River northwest to Yakataga, including

Yakutat Bay and Icy Bay. The Copper River begins on Mount Wrangell at the terminus of the Copper Glacier and flows about 280 miles to its mouth at the Copper River Delta near Cordova. Tlingit and other groups traded copper implements—found along the coast by explorers in 1741—on the Copper River, south-central Alaska's only water route across the Chugach Mountains.

The river area remained lightly explored until 1885, when Lieutenant Henry Allen investigated the upper Copper River and drew the first published map of the Copper

River basin. Next came the 1898 Yukon Gold Rush, which sent prospectors into the area and led to 1899's Abercrombie expedition. Then, just a year later in 1900, prospectors Clarence Warner and "Tarantula Jack" Smith were exploring the east edge of the Kennicott Glacier when they discovered the green copper cliffs they called the "Bonanza Mine Outcrop." The mine was played out by 1938, although it had already yielded $200 million worth of copper.

Today, the historic mining town of Kennecott (named after the Kennicott Glacier,

Dora Keen Climbs Mount Blackburn

Mount Blackburn, the fifth highest point in the United States, towers 16,390 feet at its peak and is virtually always covered in ice and snow. In 1911, Dora Keen came to Alaska seeking adventure. Having grown up in Philadelphia and graduated from Bryn Mawr College, she thirsted for excitement after a short-lived career in the world of insurance.

From 1908 to 1910, the intrepid Keen climbed prominent summits in the Alps as training for her Alaska expedition. When she arrived in Alaska in 1911, her goal was to be the first to climb the uncharted Mount Blackburn. She hired prominent climbers and explorers who knew the area well to guide her through its unexpected chasms and frequent avalanches. Chief among these was John Barrett.

Even with the best planning and helpers, the edge along Blackburn's eastern slope is treacherous, even for experienced climbers. Not only that, but the weather is terrible more often than not, with high winds and

raw temperatures. Keen's first attempt was unsuccessful due to all of these factors. After climbing 8,700 grueling feet, the climbers were prepared to summit the mountain in spite of avalanches and icy, slushy snow. Suddenly, however, a great snowstorm blew up, and the climbers, short on rations, knew it was going to be a long one. They abandoned the mission.

Keen spent the winter in Alaska planning her next bid, this time plotting it out herself. With the exception of John Barrett, none of her former crew joined her for the 1912 expedition. Instead of expert climbers and guides, she engaged local prospectors. As spring began to set in, she and her party set out from Kennecott on April 22 while the snow was still solid.

This time, they attacked the mountain in a different way. Instead of relaying food in stages, as was the general method of climbing, they anticipated the changeable weather and packed light, taking the food to a higher

camp and preparing for a big run in the last stages. When they reached 12,000 feet, well above their highest camp, another sudden storm swept in, and they were trapped for three days with nearly no food, fuel, or bedding, in ice caves they dug for themselves. Keen returned to the high camp, where five of the men lost their nerve and retreated down the mountain. Those who were left had to wait two weeks while a new storm rolled in before attempting another climb. In the end, Dora Keen, Bill Lang, and George W. Handy reached the summit. Triumphant telegrams arrived at all the major newspapers, proclaiming, "After thirteen days' snowstorm spent in caves, made the summit on May 19. DORA KEEN."

Keen went on very soon afterward to be the first white woman to ever cross Alaska's Skolai Pass. She spent her days as an adventurer, and even well beyond her 90th birthday she was still writing articles and lecturing on her experiences.

The Bremmer River cuts through this valley displaying the fullness of its autumn colors. Unexpectedly, green leaves coexist beside yellow and brown.

which was then misspelled) remains an impressive sight. At one time the mine was owned by the Alaska Syndicate, a group that included the Morgans and the Guggenheims. The Alaska Syndicate became the Kennecott Copper Corporation in 1915. At the height of its operations, the Kennecott mines employed about 600 people—300 in the mines, 300 in the mills—plus another 300 on the railroad. Kennecott became a company town with its own school, hospital, recreation hall—even a tennis court and a skating rink. Hiking the area is fascinating but can be hazardous. Kennecott's buildings are collapsing, and debris is widely scattered. Tours are available and advisable.

There's Still Room for Wildlife

Among its many other superlatives, Wrangell–St. Elias also boasts the world's highest concentration of Dall sheep, about 13,000 of them. Look for them along rocky ridges and mountainsides. In fact, floating on a raft down one of the park's many rivers, visitors can see Dall sheep on the tundra and mountain goats on the rocky crags of mountain slopes. But there are so many huge glaciers in this park that there is not very much habitable terrain.

Moose are often seen near willow bogs and lakes. In autumn, bears and other animals may be sighted near salmon spawning streams. Other notable mammals include: caribou, transplanted bison, lynx, wolverines, beavers, marten, porcupines, foxes, wolves, marmots, and river otters. If you're looking for grizzlies, a hike to Goodlata Peak pass is advised. Looking for moose and Dall sheep? Try the Orange Hill and Bond Creek area. The Dixie Pass Trail, a rare road-accessible hike, is a three-day to four-day adventure to a 5,150-foot alpine pass in the Wrangell Mountains that is considered a

wildlife corridor. The view from the pass to the south takes in the lower slopes of the Wrangell Mountains and the craggy Chugach Mountains to the north.

Unlike some of the other Alaska national parks, Wrangell–St. Elias has a wide choice of hiking and biking trails. Some of these qualify as easy and picturesque, such as the half-mile Boreal Forest Trail, by the Wrangell–St. Elias Visitor Center. With views

of Mount Drum (12,010 feet) in the foreground, the massive dome shape of Mount Wrangell (14,163 feet) to the right, and the park's highest volcano, Mount Blackburn (16,390 feet), to the south, the half-mile walk is short but breathtaking. As for the more challenging rambles, Hidden Creek Valley might be considered representative: A strenuous four- or five-day hike, accessible only by air-taxi flight from McCarthy to the Hidden Creek Strip west of the lake, the hike follows the western edge of the Kennicott Glacier past icebergs in Hidden Lake, waterfalls, pristine alpine meadows, and abundant wildlife.

Top: *Wrangell–St. Elias National Park's Kennecott Copper Mine, located by the Kennicott Glacier, offers a stunning view of Mount Blackburn. The National Park Service has preserved and rehabilited these buildings as a monument to the area's past.* Left: *The Bagley Icefield, which is 127 miles long, six miles wide, and as much as 3,000 feet thick in places, is North America's largest subpolar icefield.*

Yellowstone National Park

Truman Everts was the first man to get lost in what is today Yellowstone National Park. In September 1870, he got separated from his party, better known today as the Washburn Expedition, and spent 37 days alone in the wilderness, eating thistles, sleeping near thermal vents that spouted steam, and barely making it out alive. Then 54 years old, the Vermont-born Everts was not experienced in outdoor survival. He had little in the way of food, gear, and clothing.

Today, rangers recommend you bring all of these things while exploring the trails in the park—not to mention a map. But visitors to 21st-century Yellowstone National Park will see many of the same sights and experience many of the same wonders that Everts did more than a century earlier: the geysers and hot springs, the bears and mountain lions, and an artful tapestry of alpine wilderness.

Out of Sight

One thing that Everts did not see, at least not with his naked eye, were the microorganisms that call Yellowstone's thermal features home. Called *thermophiles*—heat lovers, literally—these often colorful life forms were only fairly recently found in the scalding waters that trickle to Yellowstone's surface as hot as 170 degrees Fahrenheit— or explode through it in the form of geysers.

Nearly a century after Everts's unfortunate ramblings, Dr. Thomas Brock discovered the first such microorganism,

Northwestern Wyoming, southern Montana, and eastern Idaho
Established March 1, 1872
3,468 square miles

Things to See: *Old Faithful; Roosevelt Arch; Mammoth Hot Springs; Yellowstone Lake; Bridge Bay; Fountain Paint Pot; Morning Glory Pool; Continental Divide*

Things to Do: *Hiking; Camping; Horseback riding and llama packing; Boating; Fishing; Bicycling; Cross-country skiing; Wildlife viewing*

What's Nearby? *Grand Teton National Park; John D. Rockefeller, Jr. Memorial Parkway; Bighorn Canyon National Recreation Area; Craters of the Moon National Monument and Preserve; City of Rocks National Preserve; Big Hole National Battlefield*

Thermus aquaticus, here in 1966. But it wasn't until researchers synthesized from that hardy species an enzyme that proved especially useful in DNA fingerprinting that the research world rushed to Yellowstone's hot springs for a closer look at the life in their extreme depths. Researchers even compared the fossil record of Yellowstone's thermophiles to rocks from Mars in their usefulness for peering into how life may have begun on planets other than Earth.

But here on Earth, Yellowstone is as close to another planet as it gets. This alien landscape is home to more than half of the

Measuring 308 feet in height, the Lower Falls in the Grand Canyon of the Yellowstone River are twice as tall as Niagara Falls in Ontario, Canada.

world's thermal features, an amazing variety of magma-powered plumbing that includes the archetypal thermal features of ferocious and majestic geysers, along with brilliantly

After its number dwindled to almost zero in the early 20th century, Yellowstone's bison population was fostered back to sustainability on the park's Lamar Buffalo Ranch. There are now about 3,000 of these magnificent creatures in Yellowstone.

hued hot pools, steaming fumaroles, and lethargically belching mud pots—about 10,000 in all, including more than 300 geysers.

With all of the thermal activity going on below ground, the otherworldly geology that's above the surface in Yellowstone sometimes gets short shrift. The ruggedly picturesque landscape, carved by many millennia of wind and water, varies from the hoodoos near Mammoth Hot Springs to the gnarled lava flow of the Pitchstone

Plateau, frozen and preserved in time like a bug in amber. Looking down from the alpine tundra atop Mount Washburn, the panorama includes a series of superlative sights: the golden chasm that is the Grand Canyon of the Yellowstone; the vast and glassy blue surface of Yellowstone Lake; and the unmistakable mountaintops of Electric Peak to the north and Mount Sheridan to the south, and even farther toward the horizon, on a clear day, the jagged comb of the Tetons.

Two years after Truman Everts got lost in the wilderness here, the U.S. government designated Yellowstone the world's first official national park. That 1872 act has since inspired the creation of hundreds of national parks around the world. Located in the extreme northwestern corner of Wyoming and spilling over a bit into both Idaho and Montana, Yellowstone remains a true wildlife paradise and geological wonderland.

Despite the peaceful appearance of the landscape today, the high country in Yellowstone has undergone extremely violent periods over the past million years. About 600,000 years ago, the Yellowstone Caldera erupted with the force of thousands of volcanoes to completely reshape the landscape. This incendiary past has resulted in the thousands of springs, pools, mud pots, and geysers that can be found scattered throughout the Yellowstone Plateau today. And there is reason to believe the future will be just as incendiary: The Yellowstone Caldera may be overdue for its next big blowout, since it has erupted with cataclysmic force, almost like clockwork, every 600,000 years for the last 1.8 million years.

Fortunately, Yellowstone's timepiece is set to geological time. That means the next big bang here could be thousands of years away. In other words, there is no time like the present to pack a tent and backpack and go on the classic Yellowstone adventure, a vacation that's as American as apple pie.

The vividly hued terraces at Mammoth Hot Springs in the northern reaches of Yellowstone National Park are the result of mineral-rich water bubbling to the surface for millions of years.

the wildlife. Visitors to the north entrance of the park are often greeted by the spectacle of bull elk jousting a few feet from the steps to the park library or of an old bull bison pensively ruminating near the picnic tables by the visitor center. A few miles away, grizzly bears are often seen in the Lamar Valley in the spring, on the prowl for newborn elk and bison calves. In the vicinity of the Lower Falls of Yellowstone, osprey and golden eagles dive for native cutthroat trout. Moose are partial to the meadows near the Yellowstone River, and the rare trumpeter swan is also often seen. Hayden Valley is one of the best spots for wildlife viewing in the park.

Casual Exploration

But outsiders can truly explore this living landscape: Yellowstone is a hiker's paradise. For those wishing to walk near the road, a day's hike up Mount Washburn, covering about three miles and reaching more than 10,000 feet in elevation, provides that wonderful panorama of the park, from Antelope Creek at the foot of the mountain to the distant snow-covered peaks of the Absaroka Range to the north.

One of the best medium-distance hikes leads from Lewis Lake to the Heart Lake Geyser Basin, which sits at the base of Mount Sheridan

in the southeastern corner of the park. The geyser basin, about 1,000 acres in size, offers hikers a region of brilliant blue pools, boiling hot streams, and bright orange algae terraces. Heart Lake also provides some of the best fishing in the park and is a great camping spot. Longer trips generally concentrate on either the southwestern corner of the park, near Idaho, or the southeastern corner, in the wild Thorofare Country.

It is hard to hike in Yellowstone without seeing the impact of the 1988 fires, which charred more than a million acres of the

Left: *This illustration from the 1880s shows guests enjoying Mammoth Hot Springs during the park's early years.* Below: *The Yellowstone wolf population was hunted out of existence by the 1930s, but in the '90s the park instituted policies to restore its numbers. At the end of 2008, at least 124 wolves in 12 packs were reported in the park.*

a truly American experience. Old Faithful attracts a crowd when it spurts hot water a hundred feet into the air. The most predictably punctual geyser in the park, Old Faithful erupts once every 90 minutes, give or take. But Old Faithful is just one of many geysers in the Upper Geyser Basin—many "geyser gazers" say neighboring geysers Riverside and Grand are even more spectacular. And the Upper Geyser Basin is just one of nine major geyser basins in the park.

As spectacular as these eruptions can be, the thermal features have a hard time living up to another big attraction in Yellowstone:

park's forest. Many areas bounced back nicely, but some will forever remind people of the awesome power of nature.

Another good spot for witnessing this power in action is the shores of Yellowstone Lake. With a surface area of 132 square miles—making it the largest lake at a high elevation in North America—these cold and stormy waters cover more geysers and hot springs, as well as a canyon that's nearly 400 feet deep.

West Thumb, located on the southwestern shores of Yellowstone Lake, is one of the park's smaller geyser basins but also among its most dramatic. While West Thumb is home to a myriad of steaming pools and springs, the trademark thermal feature here is undoubtedly Fishing Cone, a lakeside vent anglers once used to boil their catch—that is, until tests revealed that the hot water contains natural traces of arsenic.

Another noteworthy body of water in the park is the Yellowstone River, the longest undammed river in the lower 48 states and a favorite of anglers. The Yellowstone cuts an impressive swath from the lake through the Grand Canyon of the Yellowstone (and over two spectacular waterfalls) before leaving the park by its northern border.

The Frigid Season

Increasingly, visitors are coming to Yellowstone during the winter months when snow covers the roads and trails and travel is restricted to those with cross-country skis, snowshoes, or snowmobiles. Snow-cats, hardy vehicles with tanklike treads, are also available for tours and transportation. The short days pass pretty quickly between the

An Abundance of Elk

Yellowstone has more elk than it has any other large animal. Although there is evidence that the elk has lived in the area for at least a thousand years, there is also controversy about quite how many are natural to this region. The argument has been made that, due to the high elevations and inhospitable winters, elk may have been fairly scarce. It is also possible that elk lived here during the summer months but followed a migratory pattern that took them to warmer climates for the winter. Elk were highly desired by hunters during the 19th century, and by the 1870s, they were nearly hunted to extinction within the whole of the United States.

In order to save them, elk and bison were to be protected within the Yellowstone area. Initially, however, the lack of antipoaching laws didn't allow them to be safe even there, and the hunting continued. Finally, in 1894, the government passed laws for protection. Rangers stamped out poachers in the park grounds and erected fences to prevent the escape of the animals.

Soon, however, animal populations exploded and started causing new problems for the park. One likely reason elk did not remain in the park during the winter months is that the bitterly cold weather blocked much of their food sources. Kept in the park, they overgrazed on anything they could find, and soon the overabundant elk competed with other animals for food, depleting an area that had once been rich in nutrients. The white-tailed deer, once common to the park area, began to disappear.

Ultimately, a plan to thin the herd was put into place. A portion of the elk population was killed, and measures were put into place to keep overall numbers down. Some of the species of other animals that had been lost, such as the gray wolf, have been reintroduced to the area. Yellowstone remains an experiment in ecosystem and natural habitat management.

Wintertime visitors to Yellowstone experience a nearly polar opposite environment from the one that emerges after snowmelt, featuring the same classic landscapes painted with a new snowy brush.

bundling up, adventuring, and unbundling. The cozy lobby at the Old Faithful Snow Lodge is the perfect place to kick back and warm up after a hard day of play.

But make no mistake: Winter is the most extreme season in this extreme land.

Yellowstone's all-time low temperature of −66 degrees Fahrenheit was recorded in 1933. And with annual snowfall of 150 inches, a deep white blanket covers the Yellowstone landscape, at once familiar and completely unknown.

But none of this fazes the bison, who doggedly plow the snow away with their noggins in search of grass to graze. During wintertime, large numbers of bison, as well as elk, deer, and bighorn sheep, graze in the river valleys, especially the Lamar Valley. The geysers and thermal pools are especially lovely, with their steam clouds rising thickly into the frozen air. Otters often look for holes that thermal features melt through the ice and snow to dive in and fish. Wily coyotes often look for these very same holes in hopes of stealing away an otter's catch.

Come spring, this winter wonderland melts away. The grizzlies come out of their dens, the bison and elk give birth to their calves, and the warm-weather tourists start to trickle back into the park. Likewise, an even more ancient springtime tradition continues: The water trickles from the mountains, refills the plumbing below the thousands of thermal features in the park, and again and again drains from view then percolates to the surface with a rush of steam. And just like that, the geothermal clockwork continues to tick forward toward a future unknown.

Not even winter can slow the rapids of a rushing Yellowstone river. The snow in the trees on the shore will only add to the rush come spring, as it melts and joins the race downstream.

Yosemite National Park

Legendary naturalist and writer John Muir might have contributed more to the preservation of Yosemite National Park and its bounty of natural wonders than any other human being. It was love at first sight for Muir when he first glimpsed Yosemite's remarkable landscape in the heart of the Sierra Nevada Mountains in central California. After walking 1,000 miles from Indiana to Florida, he set off for San Francisco, just months before his 30th birthday. But the moment the train arrived in the City by the Bay, Muir immediately left it for a place about which he only had read, Yosemite Valley. One quick glimpse of the scenery there hooked him for life. After working that winter as a sheepherder in the nearby San Joaquin Valley, with the coming of summer, Muir took his flock up Mono Trail and ventured into the verdant scene of Tuolumne Meadows, a half-mile above Yosemite Valley.

Muir had a way with words. In his 1868 description of being at the brink of Yosemite Falls, he lovingly depicted the panorama he saw from the meadows, perched above the tallest waterfall in North America. "The noble walls—sculptured into endless variety of domes and gables, spires and battlements and plain mural precipices—all a-tremble with the thunder tones of the falling water," he wrote. "The level bottom seemed to be dressed like a garden—sunny meadows here and there, and groves of pine or oak; the river of Mercy sweeping in majesty through the midst of them and flashing back the sunbeams. The great Tissiack, or Half

Central California
Established October 1, 1890
1,200 square miles

Things to See: *Half Dome; El Capitan; Mariposa Grove of giant sequoias; Yosemite Falls; Glacier Point; Badger Pass; Yosemite Valley; Vernal Falls; Wawona*

Things to Do: *Hiking; Rock climbing; Fishing; Horseback riding; Backpacking; Rafting; Downhill skiing and snowboarding; Biking; Bird-watching; Ice skating*

What's Nearby? *Devils Postpile National Monument; Sequoia and Kings Canyon National Parks; Manzanar National Historic Site; Death Valley National Park; Pinnacles National Monument*

Dome, rising at the upper end of the valley to a height of nearly a mile, is nobly proportioned and life-like, the most impressive of all the rocks, holding the eye in devout admiration, calling it back again and again from falls or meadows, or even the mountains beyond."

Muir's eloquent writing continues to ring true. Visitors today find themselves equally moved by this profoundly lovely gorge, cut by the Merced River, with its sides gouged out by glaciers into enormous monoliths. Granite cliffs rise 3,000 feet above a forested floor, a tranquil and solemn river flows grandly through its proud channel,

Right: *Yosemite National Park may be as famous for its waterfalls as for its many other features. The abundance of water is directly acknowledged in the green field below. Opposite: The unmistakable granite mass of El Capitan, carved by a mantle of glacial ice as much as a mile thick, overlooks the Merced River.*

and waterfalls tumble from the heights. The famed Yosemite Falls is 2,425 feet high.

Overwhelming Beauty

Just as it did during Muir's days here, the grandeur of Yosemite tugs at the soul. A park ranger was once asked what he would do if he had only one day to visit Yosemite Valley. The ranger replied, "I'd weep." Whether apocryphal or not, the anecdote contains much truth about this grassy, tree-filled defile cut deep into the heart of the Sierra Nevada.

Although it contains less than one half of one percent of the total area of the park, this valley is undoubtedly what most people think of when they think of Yosemite. Here is where you'll find most of Yosemite's lodgings, restaurants, campgrounds, and—last but not least—automobiles.

This gorge is guarded by two famous sentinel rocks; their massive shapes are well known around the globe. The park's most famous landmark, the previously mentioned Half Dome, with its great sheared-off face,

rises 4,800 feet above the eastern end of the valley. El Capitan, a monolith that rises 3,600 feet above the evergreens along the Merced River, stands at the western entrance. One of the most precipitous cliffs in the world, El Capitan, which translates in Spanish to "The Chief," is made of granite so hard and free of cracks and blemishes that the powerful forces of erosion have scarcely seemed to affect it over the eons.

An easily traversed and self-contained area, the floor of the valley is the perfect

Right: *Rocks are balanced in order to form cairns as landmarks or memorials. The National Park Service discourages backpackers or rock climbers from erecting stacks such as this in its effort to "leave no trace."* Opposite: *A storm clears out of Yosemite Valley, as the sun's warmth begins to dry everything out again.*

vantage point for taking in the superlative views of El Capitan and Half Dome, tubing in the Merced River, and riding on the paved bike routes. But it's the trails that radiate out—and up—from the valley floor that allow one to make the jump from an observer of this stunning landscape to a participant *in* this stunning landscape. A good pair of hiking boots and a well-stocked day pack can take guests places no paved roads will ever go.

Of the routes that are tailor-made for serious hikers, the serpentine trail to Upper Yosemite Fall is one of the park's steepest, but it's also one of the most rewarding. It begins with a strenuous set of switchbacks

Young John Muir

John Muir was born in 1838 in Dunbar, Scotland. His father, Daniel Muir, has been described as a religious fanatic and was involved with the Campbellite (or Restorationist) Movement, a group that believed in a return to the basic, "unspoiled" beginnings of Christianity. The Campbellites wanted to go back to what they called the bare facts of the Bible, restoring Old Testament beliefs and rejecting the idea of denominations, arguing that they were Christians and nothing more. Daniel Muir moved his family with a Campbellite group to Wisconsin in 1849, where they worked in a series of farms.

As a religious zealot, Daniel Muir often forced his son to work long hours while beating him and delivering fire-and-brimstone sermons. His mother was kind and loving, and John did not agree with his father's hard take on religion. In the early 1860s, John Muir parted from his parents, wanting to search out his own ideas of God through nature and wilderness. Though he didn't know it, many of his father's absolute preservationist beliefs of the Bible would manifest themselves in Muir's absolute preservationist beliefs of nature.

Muir did quite a bit before he found his place in the world—in nature. After leaving the

farm, he pursued a degree in natural sciences at the University of Wisconsin but dropped out before graduating. Afterward, he worked in a steam-powered Indiana factory called Osgood, Smith & Company. His talents from the farm and his intelligence led to his quick promotion in the company, though his career came crashing down within seconds. While repairing a belt on a circular saw in 1868, a file flew into Muir's face, blinding him temporarily. Even after he recovered his sight and his health, Muir refused to return to the factory. Instead, he began the 40-year hike that would change all of America.

that climb 1,000 feet in just a mile to Columbia Rock, a perfect spot for a water break and a breather. The next stretch is not as steep, but the final approach to the brink of the upper waterfall—where Muir surveyed the valley more than a century ago—is a real lung-burner. The view is worth the effort, however, not to mention the cool mist from the half-mile ribbon of water that is Yosemite Falls.

Not every trail that originates in Yosemite Valley, however, is quite so demanding. The three-mile loop to Mirror Lake gains only 60 feet. The Mist Trail to Vernal Fall gains 400 feet en route to the perfect spot to soak away a hot summer afternoon. On the extreme end of the spectrum, hardcore climbers can take to Half Dome for a 17-mile round trip that gains a total of 4,900 feet. On the last 600 feet of this momentous gain,

hikers are aided by cables attached to Half Dome's granite skin.

The Range of Nature

Beyond this justifiably famous valley, Yosemite National Park is a showcase for the wonders of nature. This vast and varied domain includes giant sequoias, alpine meadows, peaks soaring above 13,000 feet, lovely alpine lakes, sparkling trout streams,

Muir's Travels

When John Muir first set out to explore the natural world, his wanderings led him south. Walking from Indiana to Florida, he kept detailed journals and drawings of his journeys, the first of more than 70 notebooks he kept throughout his life. As he reached the Florida Keys, Muir's intention was to keep going farther south—perhaps to the Amazon, to find exotic plants. The tides turned, however, when Florida's own exotic animal, the mosquito, struck. Muir contracted malaria, and his plans changed. When he recovered, instead of going to the southern continent, he caught a boat to San Francisco and hiked more than 200 miles to Yosemite.

On this first visit he did not stay for long. "A strong butterfly full of sunshine," he wrote, "settles not long at any place. It goes by crooked unanticipated paths from flower to flower." Be that as it may, after he left, the valley remained in his mind. He knew that this was a place to which he would return time and again.

Whether viewed from the banks of the Merced River on the floor of Yosemite Valley (above), or seen only in part (right), Yosemite Falls, measuring 2,425 feet in height, is the tallest waterfall in North America, and one of the tallest in the world. It is truly an iconic symbol of this park.

John Muir, urged that Yosemite also be established as a national park.

Yosemite National Park was finally mandated in 1890, but it was administered as two separate state parks for 16 more years. Two years after the mandate, Muir founded the Sierra Club. In 1903, he accompanied President Teddy Roosevelt on what turned out to be a trip to Yosemite that helped shape the future of the entire national park system. En route to the park, Muir convinced Roosevelt that the federal government needed to dedicate more resources to Yosemite.

After arriving in Yosemite Valley, the pair set off on a camping trip in the backcountry. As the story goes, Muir and Roosevelt talked late into the night by the flicker of a campfire and slept under the stars at Glacier Point, waking the next morning to an inch of virgin white snow. The outing made an indelible impression on the president and catalyzed his implementation of Muir's vision of an entire system of national parks. Roosevelt not only expanded Yosemite, he also doubled the number of national parks during his tenure as chief executive from five to ten and dedicated more federal resources to the growing inventory of parks.

Despite Roosevelt's intentions, national park protection quickly proved to be far from absolute. In Yosemite, Muir steadfastly fought the plan to flood Hetch Hetchy Valley into a reservoir to slake San Francisco's growing thirst for water, comparing the lesser-known valley's beauty to that of Yosemite Valley. The fight to keep Hetch Hetchy dry, however, was a battle Muir ultimately lost. Congress voted to authorize the construction of Hetch Hetchy Dam on the west side of the park in 1913. The resulting dam remains controversial to this day; many environmental groups believe it should be removed and the valley restored to its natural condition.

Muir passed away in 1914, after the vote but before crews built the dam he so desperately fought. Some say he died of a broken heart. He remains an icon in Yosemite and California (at one time he graced the state's quarter) and his vision of conservation and preservation remains in the park as we see it today.

But certainly John Muir would not approve of summer afternoon traffic jams in Yosemite Valley and some of the other modern problems of the 21st-century High Sierra. However, he would enthusiastically approve the untouched wilderness that still dominates the park: About 94 percent of Yosemite's 1,169 square miles is designated wilderness, roughly the same land area as the state of Rhode Island.

In this vast and varied mountain landscape, it is easy, almost too easy, to get far away from it all, make camp, and sleep under the brilliant night sky, just as Muir liked to do more than 100 years ago. As he wrote, "The clearest way to the Universe is through a forest wilderness." Indeed, Yosemite is just the forest wilderness to go looking for it.

Right: *Yosemite's Mariposa Grove is home to numerous giant sequoia trees that are more than 300 feet tall and 1,000 years old, bearing names such as The Bachelor and Grizzly Giant.* Opposite: *Yosemite National Park is home to countless waterfalls, including some of the country's tallest. Peak runoff is usually in May; some falls dry to a trickle by August.*

Muir's Writings

In the early 1870s, John Muir took a break from his wilderness life and stayed with friends in Oakland, California. He began to write several eloquent articles about the wonders of Yosemite. For him, this was the beginning of the new era. Muir's first article, published in the *New York Tribune* in 1871, began the slow revitalization of nature in the eyes of America. One writer said that Muir's articles "awakened a new enthusiasm for the preservation of natural wonders for their own sake."

Muir's work was welcomed by magazines and newspapers alike, fanning the ideals of people all over the country. While flourishing as a writer and activist, however, Muir chafed under the pressures of "civilized" life, longing to return to those lands of which he so often wrote. In 1874 he trekked back to Yosemite. While wandering the canopies and waterfalls of that place he so dearly loved, he came to the conclusion that he would be the one to protect them. Though Yosemite had been declared a national preservation area in 1864 by President Lincoln, Muir maintained the philosophy that "wilderness freedom, like political freedom, was perennially in danger and could be maintained only by eternal vigilance."

Over the ensuing years, he published many works, such as *The Mountains of California, Our National Parks, My First Summer in the Sierra, Steep Trails,* and *Stickeen.* As the founder and first president of the Sierra Club, Muir was responsible for incalculable strides in the conservation movement. His devotion to the beauty and sanctity of America's wonderlands led to an entire generation—if not an entire century—of people dedicated to following in his footsteps.

eight fish and 44 reptile and amphibian species. Among the most commonly seen mammals are mule deer, bats, and coyotes; rarer species include back bear and bobcats. The amazing variety of bird species in Zion runs the gamut from loons, cranes, and pelicans to vultures, bald eagles, and wild turkeys.

Among the rare and endangered species that make their home here are Mexican spotted owls, desert tortoises, endemic Zion snails, and peregrine falcons. The superstars of the park's many invertebrate species are antlions (aka doodlebugs) and tarantulas. Also notable are the wasps that prey on the latter; these insects, aptly named tarantula hawks, inject a paralytic poison into the spiders before dragging their victims' prone bodies away for their larvae to eat alive.

Fallen petrified trees are a common sight in the Petrified Wood Forest in Zion's Southwest Desert, as are the signature panoramas of vibrantly striped sandstone cliffs.

Settlements of the Mormon Pioneers

When people think about Utah, several things automatically spring to mind: skiing, amazing rock formations, and Mormons. Over the years, many different cultures and religions have flourished throughout the area, from the early Pueblo Anasazi tribes to the Paiute, all playing their part in the formation of the state and region. One of the major religions that formed Utah as it is currently known was that of the Church of Jesus Christ of Latter-day Saints, or the Mormons.

Mormons don't drink or dance, but they *are* known for their former practice of marriage to multiple spouses—and they are often belittled for all of these reasons. What many people don't know is that this intrepid and enterprising group of people settled most of the Utah area.

The Mormons had not been accepted throughout much of the United States when Brigham Young was the first to lead a group of settlers to the territory, founding a community near Salt Lake in 1847. After settling, the Mormons organized a provisional state they called Deseret and sought to join the Union. In the early 1850s, Utah was organized as a U.S. territory with Brigham Young as governor, but the quest for statehood continued. So did the trouble. A few years later, the Utah Expedition, a dustup between the U.S. militia and the Mormons, commenced when the American government tried to displace Brigham Young as governor. As a part of this conflict, Young ordered a great "Move South," abandoning the northern settlements should the U.S. military arrive with hostile intent.

It wasn't until 1863, however, that Issac Behunin built the first log cabin in Zion Canyon. From there, the settlement continued to spread, encompassing many parts of the Virgin River valley. Life in the area, however, was not easy. The soil was poor, which made farming difficult. Worse, however, was the flooding that destroyed much of the progress that was made over the first 50 years. It was only persistence and the idealism so characteristic to the Mormon faith that saw many through the harshest times in the region.

Many settlers eventually left the area due to the inhospitable conditions, though their names and ideas remained. They had been awed by the staggering natural beauty of the area and called it Zion—where, in the Old Testament, God was sometimes said to dwell.

People Make History

Zion has a human story that is just as rich as its natural and geological history. More than 10,000 years ago, indigenous people hunted mammoth, camels, and giant sloth in what is now southern Utah. This era ended abruptly about 8,000 years ago as the climate changed, rendering (in tandem with over-hunting) these animals extinct, and the people started to adapt to the new realities of the region. Around 1,100 years ago, this Ancestral Puebloan culture evolved into what is known today as the Virgin Anasazi, a community of people who farmed the land that is now Zion National Park, as the Virgin River and its tributaries represented the only reliable water sources in this arid land. The Virgin Anasazi were the artists responsible for galleries of ornate rock art, leaving behind cliffs adorned with colorful painted pictographs as well as enigmatic carved petroglyphs and other archaeological sites of note.

Drought ended the era of the Virgin Anasazi by about A.D. 1200, and they were followed by the Paiute in subsequent centuries. Mormon pioneers established towns on the Virgin River in the vicinity of the modern park in the 1860s, and John Wesley Powell explored the canyons of Zion on his famous expedition in the next decade. Cabins sprang up in Zion Canyon proper, but their resident pioneers were plagued by floods and other hardships.

In 1909, President William Howard Taft designated Zion Canyon part of Mukuntuweap National Monument in honor of the canyon's Paiute name. Lodgings were developed, and tourists began arriving on combination bus and railroad trips

that lasted ten days. In response to local Mormons, the name was changed to Zion National Monument in 1918. Congress established the monument as Zion National Park in 1919, but Kolob Canyon was later established as another Zion National Monument in the 1930s. It was merged with the rest of the park to establish the modern 229-square-mile area in 1956.

Besides its status as the first national park in the state, Zion is also Utah's most-visited national park, with more than 2 million visitors annually. The historic Zion Lodge, built in 1925, is booked solid for much of the year. One of the key factors in opening up Zion to more visitors was the construction of the Zion–Mt. Carmel highway into Zion Canyon, including a 5,613-foot tunnel strung through the sandstone cliffs—no small feat of engineering in 1930.

All of this means it can get a bit hectic out here during the peak seasons. In recent years, cars have been banned from certain roads in favor of a free shuttle. To avoid the crowds, one of the best times to visit Zion is in late October and early November, when the autumn leaf displays are spectacular beyond words. This is particularly the case in the vicinity of the east entrance to the park—with the red-crowned groves of oak and maple—and in Zion Canyon, with the cottonwood groves that turn brilliant hues of yellow. Hard to believe that just a few miles to the west is the Mojave Desert, where it is still quite hot at that time of year, and that higher in the peaks of the nearby Henry Mountains, the first snows have long since fallen. In fact, Zion might just be the perfect medium between these two extremes—in more ways than one.

The trail up to Angels Landing is the most popular trail in Zion National Park. The strenuous, two-mile hike is well worth the effort for the superlative view of Zion Canyon from the summit.